Islam and Politics in Kenya

ISLAM AND POLITICS IN KENYA

Arye Oded

LYNNE
RIENNER
PUBLISHERS

BOULDER
LONDON

Published in the United States of America in 2000 by
Lynne Rienner Publishers, Inc.
1800 30th Street, Boulder, Colorado 80301
www.rienner.com

and in the United Kingdom by
Lynne Rienner Publishers, Inc.
3 Henrietta Street, Covent Garden, London WC2E 8LU

© 2000 by Lynne Rienner Publishers, Inc. All rights reserved

Library of Congress Cataloging-in-Publication Data
Oded, Arye.
  Islam and politics in Kenya / Arye Oded.
  Includes bibliographical references and index.
  ISBN 1-55587-929-2 (alk. paper)
  1. Islam—Kenya. 2. Islam and state—Kenya. 3. Islam and politics—
Kenya. 4. Kenya—Politics and government. I. Title.
BP64.K42 2000
                                                                                                                      00-031094

British Cataloguing in Publication Data
A Cataloguing in Publication record for this book
is available from the British Library.

Printed and bound in the United States of America

∞ The paper used in this publication meets the requirements
of the American National Standard for Permanence of
Paper for Printed Library Materials Z39.48-1984.

5 4 3 2 1

To Professor David Ayalon

Contents

Acknowledgments	ix
Map of Kenya	xi
Introduction	1
1 A Profile of the Muslim Community in Kenya	11
2 Muslim Organizations	21
3 Muslims in the Establishment	29
4 The Political Importance of the Muslims	33
5 Religious Leadership and Muslim Solidarity	41
6 Religious, Political, and Personal Divisions	47
7 Muslims and the State	73
8 Muslims and the Law	89
9 Muslims and Education	95
10 Muslim-Christian Relations	101
11 Arab-Islamic Activities	111
12 The Islamic Factor in Kenya and the Middle East Conflict	125
13 The Islamic Party of Kenya	135
14 Islamic Extremism: The Rise and Fall of Shaikh Khalid Balala	149
15 Similarities and Differences in the Political Status of Muslims in Kenya, Uganda, and Tanzania	163
16 Conclusion	173

Appendix 1	Declaration by a Person Being Converted to Islam (in English and Kiswahili)	179
Appendix 2	An Open Letter from the Islamic Party of Kenya to the Attorney General	181
Appendix 3	Objectives of the United Muslims of Africa	185
Appendix 4	"Principles of Democratic Leadership"	187
Appendix 5	Excerpts from "Imam Khomeini and Other Scholars on Muslim Unity"	195
Appendix 6	A Letter from Muslim Lecturers at the University of Nairobi	197

Notes 201
Bibliography 219
Index 225
About the Book 236

Acknowledgments

I wish to thank the Harry S Truman Research Institute for the Advancement of Peace, the Hebrew University of Jerusalem, for its assistance in the writing of this book and in the preparation of the manuscript for publication. My special thanks go to Lisa Perlman, publications coordinator of the Truman Institute, for her help and advice in all matters pertaining to the publication of the book. I would like also to express my gratitude to David Hornik, who patiently edited the final version of the manuscript, and to my research assistant, Bridget Levitt, for her useful and knowledgeable remarks, which went beyond the typing of the manuscript.

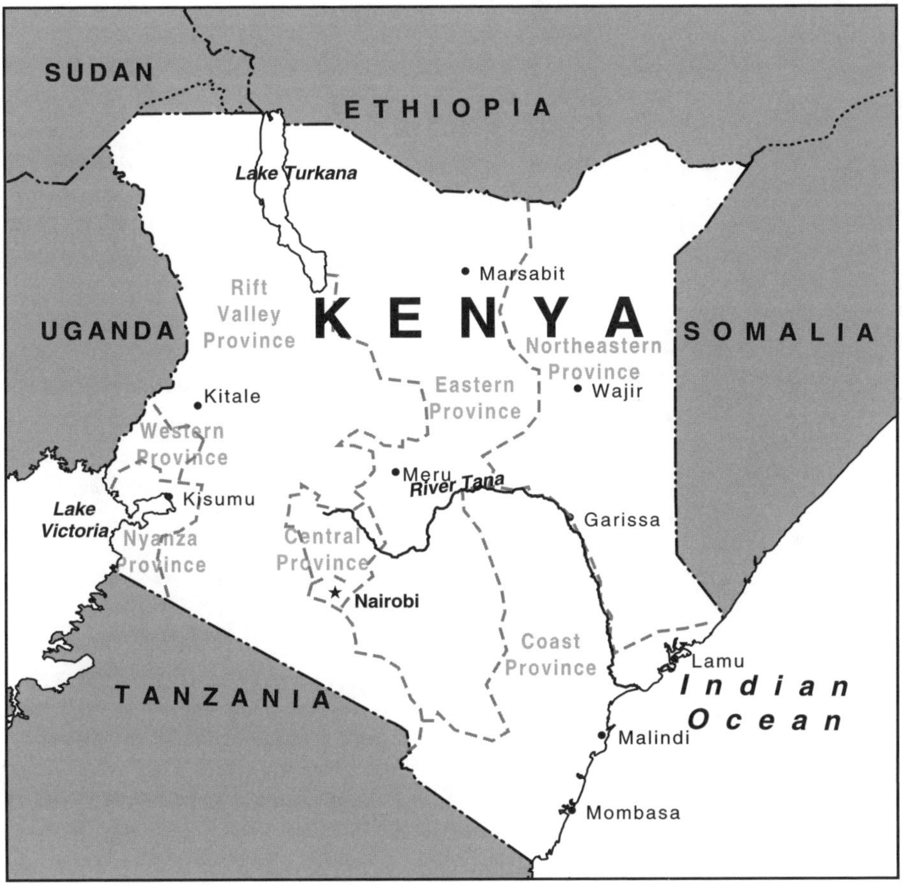
SUDAN
ETHIOPIA
Lake Turkana
Marsabit
Rift
Valley
Province
KENYA
UGANDA
SOMALIA
Northeastern
Province
Eastern
Province
Wajir
Kitale
Western
Province
Meru
River Tana
Kisumu
Lake
Victoria
Garissa
Nyanza
Province
Central
Province
Nairobi
Coast
Province
Lamu
Indian
Ocean
TANZANIA
Malindi
Mombasa

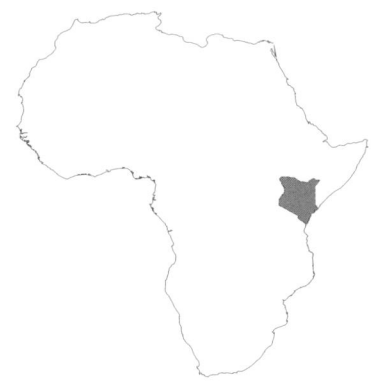

Introduction

Muslims in Kenya form a minority, but a significant minority. Their number is estimated at 5 million (1998), which represents 20 percent of the population. This large figure, together with the fact that the Muslims are concentrated in areas that are economically and strategically important, gives them at least potential political weight, especially in periods of municipal, parliamentary, and presidential elections.

During the colonial period and since independence, however, Muslim community leaders have repeatedly complained of discrimination. They have pointed out, among other things, that before colonialism Muslims were the most advanced in culture and development and were the rulers of Kenya's coastal region, whereas today Muslims are less advanced than the country's majority Christian population and lag behind them in education. Widespread feelings of discrimination among Muslims were exploited by extremists, leading to serious outbreaks of violence in 1992–1994. This study probes the political standing of Islam in Kenya, especially since independence (1963), and identifies the factors that, respectively, strengthen and weaken Islam's position.

Historical Background

The nucleus of the Arab community on the coast of East Africa, from Somalia to Mozambique, came into being even before the advent of Islam. Written evidence to this effect from the second century A.D. indicates that Arab traders would sail from the Arabian Peninsula to the coast of East Africa to trade with local inhabitants. When some of them remained and intermarried with women from local Bantu tribes, the Swahili community was formed. This community adopted

Islam during the first centuries of its existence, and Swahili culture absorbed significant Arab influences. About 30 percent of the vocabulary of the Swahili language, Kiswahili, derives from Arabic, whereas the structure and grammar of Kiswahili are based on Bantu languages.

During the thirteenth through fifteenth centuries, the Muslim cities that were established along the coast—such as Mombasa, Kilwa, Lamu, Malindi, and Pate—and the islands of Zanzibar (Unguja) and Pemba flourished, reaching the peak of their economic and religious development. The Portuguese occupation of the coast in the sixteenth and seventeenth centuries put an end to this prosperity and caused destruction and misery all along the coast as a result of frequent conflicts between the Christian Portuguese and the Muslim populations. The Omani occupation of the eighteenth and nineteenth centuries brought the coast, from Somalia to the Rovuma River (north of Mozambique), under Muslim rule again. Of special importance was the reign of Sultan Sayid Sa'id ibn Sultan (1832–1856), who moved his capital from Muscat in Oman to Zanzibar in 1840. Zanzibar became an important trade center for ivory and slaves, from which large numbers of trade caravans were dispatched to the interior of East Africa, with the encouragement and protection of the sultan, who himself owned some of these caravans. Arab commercial centers and large trade depots were established along the trade routes, which penetrated even deeper inland.

These trade routes became the main channels by which Islam was disseminated. The trade centers in the interior eventually became the foci of Islamic expansion. The most important trade centers that were established by Arab and Swahili merchants, such as Bagamoio, Tabora, and Ujiji (the latter on the shores of Lake Tanganyika), were located along the trade routes in Tanganyika—this is one of the reasons Islam is more widespread in Tanzania than in Kenya or Uganda. In Tanzania today, Muslims constitute around 35–40 percent of the population; in Uganda they are 10 percent and in Kenya, as noted, 20 percent.

During Sayid Sa'id's rule, the Arabs penetrated deep into the interior of East Africa, reaching the great lakes of Victoria and Tanganyika and establishing important trade centers; but their main interest remained ivory and slaves, not religion, and they rarely made any effort to convert the native tribes to Islam. As of the mid-nineteenth century, Muslim influence on the Bantu peoples was weak. The Omani Arabs, who belonged mainly to the Ibadiya sect, did not try to disseminate their religion among the natives. In contrast, the Arabs from Hadramaut of southern Arabia, who followed in the footsteps of the Arab traders, included religious teachers who preached the Sunni-Shafi'i school of Islam. Among these were Sunni teachers who introduced the Islamic Sufi orders or brotherhoods (in Arabic the *tariqa,* which means "a way," i.e., a way to God). From the late nineteenth century Sufism played a major role in disseminating Islam in East Africa. However, most of these teachers arrived in inner East Africa only at the beginning of the twentieth century, after the development of transportation in the region. This late start seems to have hindered the expansion of Islam in the interior of East Africa, especially when compared to West Africa.

Among the groups that contributed to the diffusion of Islam throughout East Africa were Muslim craftsmen who found employment in trade centers and in African settlements. They included metalworkers, builders, carpenters, leather tanners, and goldsmiths. In West Africa their influence was felt in places such as Togo, Dahomey (today Benin), and Kumasi (a city in Ghana); in the Horn of Africa they were influential in Mogadishu and Harar and in East Africa in the coastal towns, in the interior trade centers, and in the bustling areas around the railway stations that began to sprout in the early twentieth century. Some of the Muslim missionaries in East Africa were dependent on Swahili craftsmen (*fundi*) and would take them along to the mission stations in the interior. The missionaries often found that the Swahili craftsmen had been more active in spreading Islam than the Muslim traders had been. Once aware of this role, the missionaries began to provide the indigenous people training in crafts. For example, King Mutesa of Buganda (1856–1884) used Muslim craftsmen's services, and they exerted great influence in his court.

Muslim traditional healers and writers of amulets also spread Islam in East as well as West Africa. Kings and chiefs, as well as ordinary people, respected them and believed in their power to invoke blessings or curses. To this day there are considerable numbers of Muslims among the "medicine men" of East Africa.

Nomadic tribes, such as the Berbers of the Sahara, and the Beja and Somali tribes in the Horn of Africa, also contributed to the expansion of Islam. A large part of Kenya's Muslim population in the northeast originated in Somali nomadic tribes who came from the north.

Islam's ability to adapt to local customs, sometimes by imbuing them with Islamic meaning (such as ancestor worship), was an important factor in the Islamization of tribes such as the Baganda of Uganda and the Yao of central Africa. The prestige that accompanied acceptance of the relatively advanced civilization and technology of the Muslims also contributed to the diffusion of Islam, the spread of spoken and written Arabic, and the adoption of certain

Arab and Swahili customs. Because of their literacy, some Arabs and Swahilis had already been integrated in the precolonial era into the ruling hierarchy of tribes such as the Ha in Ujiji, Tanganyika, and the Ganda in Uganda.

Interestingly, there were important developments in Islam in precolonial Buganda, even though it was relatively distant from the coast. The first Muslims arrived in Buganda in the mid-nineteenth century through the trade routes that crossed Tanganyika, and they established their center in the *kabaka's* (king's) capital. On the coast of Kenya and Tanganyika, the arrival of Islam preceded Christianity by hundreds of years, and by the time the Christian missionaries arrived, Islam was already well established. In Uganda, on the other hand, the Christian missionaries arrived shortly after the Muslim traders and before Islam could become deeply rooted. In Uganda, therefore, the clash between the two monotheistic religions was much fiercer. This violent struggle between Muslims and Christians was intensified by certain distinctive features of the kingdom of Buganda and by the political and economic interests of Kabaka Mutesa I, who sought to exploit the two religions for his personal benefit and to consolidate his position in his kingdom and in the Lakes Region in general.[1] Mutesa, an intelligent and experienced king and a cunning diplomat, knew well how to maneuver between the two religions. During part of his reign he even declared himself a Muslim and imposed Islam on all of his subjects. But immediately following his death, when his young and inexperienced son who succeeded him proved unable to deal with the complicated religious situation, a bloody struggle broke out between Christians and Muslims. For a short period the Muslims had the upper hand and installed a Muslim king, Kabaka Kalema (1889–1890), but finally, with outside help from Christians, the Muslims were routed. Their defeat and subsequent marginalization during the Christian colonial period afforded the Christians the power they still wield today. Christians constitute about 80 percent of Uganda's population and Muslims only 10 percent.

In Kenya, Islam lost the preeminence it had enjoyed on the coast when the coastal strip was annexed to the protectorate of Kenya by the British colonial authorities. Nairobi, in the interior, became the center of government. The struggle of the coastal Muslims to retain their superiority by joining the sultanate of Zanzibar or by receiving wider autonomy from the protectorate did not succeed. Instead, it created deep suspicion among the Christian leadership, the ramifications of which are still felt today, as we shall see. To this struggle should be added the lengthy and violent campaign that independent

Kenya launched against the Muslim Somali tribes in the Northeastern Province, which wanted to secede from Kenya and join Somalia.

The significant number of Muslims in Kenya, and their concentration in important regions of the coast, in the Northeastern Province, and in the large towns, are factors that should give them strength and political influence. On the other hand, historical developments in this area fostered distrust toward them by the Kenyan government, and this weakens their position.

The Book in the Context of Related Scholarly Works

The general issue of religion and politics has occupied many scholars and been widely researched. Some attribute to religion a decisive role in politics. "Religion appears as a source of enormous creative political energies," asserts Daniel H. Levine, who has reviewed ten books dealing with religion and politics in Europe, Asia, Latin America, and, in one case, South Africa.[2] Most of these works, however, deal with these issues in general and theoretical terms. Terence Ranger, in his illuminating article "Religious Movements and Politics in Sub-Saharan Africa,"[3] focuses mainly on traditional and Christian religious movements and gives a long and impressive list of books and articles on this subject.

Likewise, there exists a voluminous literature on Islam in Africa. J. Spencer Trimingham has written several works on Islam in various regions of Africa. His *Islam in East Africa,* published in 1964, focuses particularly on "the traditional type and forms of East African Islam."[4] In a pamphlet published in 1962, Trimingham notes that he was encouraged to write his books on Islam in Africa by the Church Missionary Society because "misconceptions exist in Christian circles in East Africa concerning Islam and, without deeper knowledge of the actualities, it is impossible for them to develop any clear attitude to Islam and shape their policy."[5]

A more recent book is *Religion and Politics in East Africa,*[6] edited by Holger Bernt Hansen and Michael Twaddle, a compilation of papers presented in 1990 at the international conference in Denmark on the subject of religiopolitical conflict in East Africa, including Sudan. The papers deal with specific topics connected with Islam or Christianity.

Islam in Kenya, edited by Mohamed Bakari and Yahya Saad, is a compilation of the proceedings of a seminar on this subject held in Mombasa in 1994. According to the editors, the book's main purpose is to correct "the perception of Muslims as a group, as foreign tissue in the national body politic" and also to correct "the misconception of Muslims by their compatriots." The chief concern of the seminar participants was to show that Islam had played a significant role in the development of Kenyan society "so that politicians, administrators, policy-makers and ordinary Kenyans are furnished with some information about Islam and Muslims as an integral part of Kenyan multi-ethnic, multi-cultural society."[7] The essays reflect the attitudes of Muslim intellectuals and have great value as a reference source.

The contribution of the present study is that it focuses on Islam as a political factor in Kenya, systematically taking into consideration all the elements that contribute to its strength and its weakness in this role. In addition to analyzing the Muslims' point of view, the book examines the attitudes toward Muslims of the government and of the Christian churches. I believe that an adequate understanding of religiopolitical dynamics in Africa can be achieved only by in-depth and locally focused investigations in different countries. Only then can one draw systematic comparisons between countries and reach well-founded conclusions. As Michael Gilseman points out, the interaction of Islam and politics is not the same everywhere and at all times, and it is necessary to specify the "specific conditions" of each relevant location.[8] Victor C. Ferkiss likewise asserts that "before any generalizations [about Africa] can be raised from the level of hypotheses to developed theories," studies must provide reliable information on "the social, ethnic and national backgrounds of the religious leadership in each country," as well as the correlation of religious affiliation with other politically relevant factors within each nation.[9] That is what the present study on Kenya attempts to achieve, in the hope that it will be one link in a chain of studies on other African countries that will enable us to understand better the impact of religion on politics in Africa and the relationship between the two. Ferkiss concludes that only when other data are available in all areas will it

> be possible to discuss the interrelationship of religion and politics in Africa with greater authority. Greater knowledge of religiopolitical interaction in Africa will fill an important gap in our knowledge of Africa, help us understand how and to what extent African politics do, in fact, differ from politics elsewhere, and contribute significantly to the development of a universal theory of the relationship of religion and politics in the contemporary world, thus extending the study of comparative politics.[10]

This study also deals with relevant contemporary issues not discussed in previous studies, such as Arab-Muslim activities in Kenya, their influence on the political and social standing of local Muslims, and the attitude of the government and the Christian churches toward these activities. Christian fears of Arab-Muslim activity are shown to derive from mutual distrust, stemming from historical events. The study pays special attention to Iranian operations in Kenya in the religiopolitical field, including the Iranians' main goals and the methods they use to promote their influence. Chapter 12 also looks at Kenyan Muslims' attitudes toward the Middle East conflict. The chapter considers whether the Kenyan Muslim position has affected government policy on this issue.

Another topic discussed—one that occupies the attention of the world at large—is the rise of Islamic extremism. Chapters 13 and 14 analyze the emergence of radical Muslim groups in Kenya and the methods used by the government to contain them. The main exponent of Islamic extremism in Kenya during this period, Shaikh Khalid Balala, demanded the legalization of the Islamic Party of Kenya, which was banned by the government in the context of a prohibition on political parties based on religion. Balala stressed that in Islam there is no separation of religion and state, and he also challenged the legitimacy of President Moi's regime. This development fits in with Levine's observation that "much of the struggle around religion and politics centers in some way around legitimization."[11] In Kenya, Shaikh Balala called for an alternative structure of power and authority that, according to him, would be more democratic, considerate of Muslim interests, and based on *shari'a* (Islamic law). However, unlike the churches, which tried to strengthen their position and achieve democracy and human rights by peaceful, unified actions, Balala preached violence, which was one of the reasons for the government's harsh reaction leading to his fall. Balala also, however, acted out of a deep religious conviction that enabled him to struggle for a considerable time, with unprecedented vigor and audacity, against overwhelming odds and against the government security forces. His courageous stand against the government attracted mainly poor and unemployed youth and marginalized groups. Initially Balala enjoyed wide Muslim support, and here one can observe similar developments in other countries experiencing Islamic extremism. As Gilseman puts it: "A rhetoric of liberty and independence breaks on the barren shores of food scarcity or low-paid and dead-end government jobs. . . . Out of instability, unease and immobility comes the call for a transformation of society through the application of the Qur'an and the Holy Law to the whole of social life."[12]

This study analyzes the religiopolitical situation in Kenya from a strictly objective viewpoint. It is empirically grounded rather than theoretically oriented. Although the book concentrates on Kenya, Chapter 15 compares the relationship between Islam and politics in Kenya and in the two neighboring countries, Uganda and Tanzania; all three countries were under British colonial rule. This comparison reveals that several similar factors underlie the increased activism of the Muslims in the three countries:

- The democratization process and the introduction of a multi-party system in Kenya and Tanzania allowed greater freedom of expression, including criticism of the government. This emboldened the Muslims to publicly express their frustrations and to try and establish Islamic parties, charging that the other parties were led by Christians who neglected Muslim interests. In Uganda, too, there has been greater freedom of expression under President Museveni's unique no-party system of government.
- The Iranian Islamic revolution has spread its ideology by means of the growing number of Iranian embassies and cultural centers in Africa as well as through Iran's radio broadcasts in major African languages. Iran emphasizes that the main purpose of the revolution is to unite all Muslims, Shiites, and Sunnis alike and to restore Islam to its former glory and dignity in the face of the defamatory propaganda of "imperialism and Zionism" (see Appendix 5). As explained in Chapter 11, Kenya is one of the Iranians' major centers in East Africa.
- The Arab oil boom of the 1970s, and the resulting increased Arab-Islamic activity in sub-Saharan Africa, intensified the politicization of Islam.

The awakening of the Muslims in recent years has brought the emergence of militant Muslim groups in all three countries, especially among the young. This study also analyzes the local causes of Islamic extremism, its conflict with the regimes in question, and its demand for the redistribution of authority.

Ferkiss suggests that the influence of what he calls African nationalism "can be expected to be thrown against any tendencies for religious cleavages to be reflected in politics."[13] He points out that Africans are especially conscious of the need for unity in nation building and especially prone to see in any kind of subnational division a device of neocolonialism. He refers to the resolution passed at the All-African People's Conference of December 1958 that condemned religious separatism as a tool of imperialism. Forty years later, however, it seems that the efforts to create unity and national consciousness in most African countries have not yet succeeded and that ethnic and religious factors still play an important role in African politics. This is certainly the situation in Kenya, Uganda, and (to a lesser extent) Tanzania.

Kenya is a case where the separation of religion and state has created potential religiopolitical conflicts not only between Muslims and the mainly Christian government but also between the government and the Christian churches, as discussed in Chapter 7. Moreover, in view of the fact that neither Kenya, Uganda, nor Tanzania is predominantly Muslim, it seems that the conflict between Islam and the state derives not only from Islam's identification of religion and state but also from the special association of Christianity and Christian institutions with colonialism in the preindependence period. In Kenya, the close association of the postindependence regime with Christianity, especially during Moi's presidency (despite the ongoing controversy between Moi and the Christian churches concerning democratization and human rights), enhanced the tension between Muslims and the government.

Concerning the role Muslims in Kenya have actually played in the recent social and political changes, Muslims' own opinion, as expressed in *Islam in Kenya,* has already been mentioned. The Muslim minority in Kenya, because of its numerical significance, constitutes a political factor that the government must take into account, especially during elections, and some of whose demands it must accede to, as shown in Chapter 4. Nevertheless, the Muslim impact on all aspects of the democratization process, including the introduction of the multiparty system, was, as a whole, marginal compared to that of the Christian churches.

In addition to the suspicion toward Muslims felt by the mainly Christian regime, Muslim marginality in these areas also reflected the lack of any significant cooperation between Muslim and Christian opposition groups. Attempts at joint political action, such as that on the eve of the 1997 general elections, were rare and unavailing because of the long-standing mistrust between the two sides. Moreover, ethnic, religious, political, and personal rivalries within the Muslim community (analyzed in Chapter 6) have weakened its ability to contribute significantly to political and social changes.

Finally, the concluding chapter assesses the possible future impact of Islam as a political factor, based on historical and current trends in Kenya, including Islam-state relations and the development of Islamic extremism. The chapter also discusses the possible involvement of local extremist elements in the bombing of the American embassies in Kenya and Tanzania in August 1998.

I collected most of the sources for this study while living in Kenya during 1977–1981 and 1990–1994. I was able to interview leading Muslims and to gain firsthand impressions of events and developments, some of which I had the opportunity to witness myself. In 1960–1968 I lived in Uganda, part of the time as a research fellow at the University of Makerere, in Kampala. During this time I also carried out fieldwork for my Ph.D. thesis on Islam in Uganda, which was eventually published as a book. While in East Africa, I visited Tanzania, including Zanzibar, several times in the 1960s and 1990s, allowing me to compare the position of Muslims in the three countries.

1

A Profile of the Muslim Community in Kenya

It is difficult to state exactly the number of Muslims in Kenya, but they clearly constitute a significant minority. The accepted estimate, as of 1998, is that Muslims form about 20 percent of the population of 25 million. Censuses taken in the colonial period tended to underestimate their numbers. According to a census taken on the eve of independence in 1962, Muslims accounted for 8 percent of the population. Since 1963, the government of independent Kenya has also reported a low estimate of 8–10 percent.[1] The most recent census, taken in 1989, does not categorize according to religion. The Muslims themselves contend that their percentage of the population is much higher than 20 percent. For example, Sharif Nassir, a minister and chairman of the Mombasa branch of the ruling party, the Kenya African National Union (Kanu), puts the number of Muslims today at about 8 million. Hassan Mwakimako, a lecturer at the University of Nairobi, claims that the number is as high as 10 million.[2] Shaikh Khalid Balala, one of the leaders of the Islamic Party, has stated that Muslims form 40 percent of the population; another Muslim leader, Ahmad Khalif, asserts that they constitute 45 percent.[3] As for the number of Christians, the accepted estimate is 60 percent of the population—35 percent Protestant and 25 percent Catholic. The rest of the population follows traditional religion.[4]

Most Muslims are concentrated in specific areas of Kenya, which gives them considerable political weight in those areas. On the coastal strip and in the towns there, such as Mombasa, Malindi, and Lamu, Muslims account for more than 50 percent of the population. On this strip live the Swahilis, all of whom are Muslims, and the Digo, one of the coastal African tribes that embraced Islam in great numbers.[5] In all of the Coast Province, which covers a large area and includes different African ethnic groups, Muslims form about 30 percent. In the north of Kenya, most of the residents are Somalis, who are almost all Muslim. There are also considerable numbers of Muslims in the large towns, including Nairobi, Kisumu, Nakuru, and Eldoret. In Kenya's west, there are concentrations of Muslims in the areas of Mumias and Homa Bay.

Among Kenya's Muslims there are various groups and denominations. Because Islamic penetration into the area came primarily from Hadramaut to the south of the Arabian Peninsula and was spread by Sunni Shafi'i shaikhs, the great majority of Kenya's Muslims are Sunni of the Shafi'i school. The following are the main groupings.

The Swahilis

The Swahilis are a unique and important community[6] that began to form before the arrival of Islam, as a result of intermarriage between Arab traders who came to the coast and women from local ethnic groups. (There is evidence that traders from the Arabian Peninsula visited the east coast of Africa as early as the second century A.D.; during the Islamic period, the earliest archeological evidence of Muslims on the coast dates from the eighth century.) Most of the Swahilis are Sunni-Shafi'i. It is estimated today that about 2 million Swahilis live on the coast of Kenya and in Tanzania.[7] (The origin of the word *Swahili* is the Arabic *sahil*, meaning coast.)

Not all those who speak Kiswahili are considered Swahilis, and there are different definitions as to who is a Swahili, even among the Swahilis themselves. It is therefore difficult to state exactly the number of Swahilis.[8] One accepted definition of a Swahili is someone who was born on the coast or whose parents were born on the coast, who is a Muslim, and whose first language is Kiswahili.

The Swahilis are not a homogeneous group; they are divided into various subgroups.[9] Hyder Kindy, a Swahili leader, categorizes them into four main subgroups:

1. Those living on the Tanganyika coast (Mrima) and speaking a local Kiswahili dialect (Kimrima)
2. Those living on the islands of Zanzibar (Wahadimu, Watumbatu) and Pemba (Wapemba)
3. Inhabitants of Mombasa and its surroundings
4. Those living north of Mombasa up to the Somali coast (Bajun)

The Swahilis in the Mombasa area are organized into a loose confederation of twelve groups (Miji Kumi Na Miwili or Miji Ithna'ashara).

The twelve groups are further subdivided into two sections: one section is composed of nine groups living in north Mombasa (Miji Tisa); the other is composed of three groups living in south Mombasa (Miji Mitatu). Each group is headed by a leader whose title is *tamim* and who is assisted by a council of elders (Wazee).[10]

Among the Swahilis there are some minor religious differences. One, which dates to the beginning of the century, concerns the question of Friday prayers. The dispute is over whether only the special Friday prayer, the *jum'a*, should be chanted or whether the daily afternoon prayers (the *zuhr*) should also be chanted on Fridays. This dispute also exists among other Muslims in East Africa and is especially bitter in Uganda.[11] There are also differences of opinion as to how to determine the start and finish of the Ramadan fast—namely, whether to set it according to the sighting of the moon (*hilal*) or according to the calendar. Most determine it according to the moon, but on this issue as well there are disagreements among Muslims, especially in East Africa (see Chapter 6).

Islamic mysticism, or Sufism, is widespread among the East African Swahilis, especially in Tanzania. The order of the Qadiriya is particularly widespread, but in Kilwa (in Tanzania) and in Uganda, the Shadiliya order is prevalent. In Kenya there are other orders as well, with rivalries among them based on differing beliefs, practices, personality conflict, and competition for leadership.

During the colonial period, the British authorities considered the Swahilis black Africans as far as their position and rights were concerned. Since those who were defined as Arabs had more rights, some Swahilis wanted to be thought of as Arab and not as African. Because, the Swahili people were formed by intermarriage between Arabs and African ethnic groups, the Swahilis saw themselves as racially distinct from the Africans.[12] At Kenya's independence there were Swahilis who supported those groups that demanded autonomy for the coastal strip, and this brought about a confrontation with African nationalists (see Chapter 6).

The Arabs

The number of Arabs in Kenya is estimated at about 60,000.[13] Some of them are descendants of the Omanis, who drove the Portuguese from the coast of Kenya and Tanganyika in the late seventeenth century and ruled the region. Even after they married local Africans, their descendants continued to identify themselves as Arabs. Some of them belong to the Ibadiya sect of Islam; others, over time, became Sunnis.[14] Among those who define themselves as Arabs are descendants of those who came from Hadramaut—some at the beginning of Islam, some at the time of Islam's renaissance on the coast (thirteenth through fifteenth centuries). Other Arabs came after the Omani conquest, in the nineteenth and early twentieth centuries. The Sayyids and Sharifs, who consider themselves related to the family of the Prophet, were a part of this community, and it is they, as noted above, who disseminated Sunni-Shafi'i Islam.

In the early twentieth century, with improvements in transportation and the building of the railway from Mombasa to Uganda, the Hadramaut Arabs came as traders and teachers from the coast into the interior of Kenya and to towns such as Kisumu and Mumia, to the Rift Valley, and to the area of Nyanza in the west. Everywhere they came, they spread Islam and the Islamic system of education based on *chuo* (primary school in Kiswahili, like the *kutab* in Arab countries) and religious high schools (*madrasa*). With the arrival of the Hadramaut and Swahili traders, the railway stations gradually became trade centers, and Muslims congregating there came into contact with the local tribespeople, some of whom converted to Islam. Among the Hadramaut immigrants were religious teachers (*'ulamaa*), who influenced the character of Islam in Kenya by introducing religious festivals, the worship of holy men, and the Sufi orders. They also developed Swahili literature and poetry and created a core of 'ulamaa for the whole of East Africa.

Among the important 'ulamaa who strongly influenced the diffusion of Islam in Kenya in the latter half of the nineteenth century was Habib Salih Jamal al-Lail, who set up the famous Al-Riyadha madrasa (known as Riyadha Mosque College) in Lamu, based on the model of a madrasa in Tarim, Hadramaut. The Riyadha Mosque College produced many religious teachers, *qadis* and *imams,* including several chief qadis of Kenya. It offered special courses on *da'wah,* the propagation of Islam. The "pure" Arabs took a superior attitude toward the Swahilis, and this, as we shall see, intensified the disputes between them.[15]

The Somalis

An important group of Muslims in Kenya are the Somalis, who live in the Northeastern Province. Their number is estimated at about 600,000.[16] The Somalis are Sunni-Shafi'is and the Sufi orders are very prevalent among them, especially the Qadiriya. Their language is Somali and most of them are camel or cow herders. When Kenya received its independence in 1963, most of them wanted to break away and join Somalia, to which they felt closer because of a common cultural, linguistic, tribal, and religious identity. In the first years after independence they caused Kenya serious security problems, including brutal clashes between groups of armed Somalis known as Shifta and Kenyan security forces. The Somalis insisted on upholding the results of the 1959 referendum, in which the Northeastern Province had voted to secede from Kenya and join neighboring Somalia. Although the secessionist movement disintegrated, the people of the province are still victimized by acts of banditry and lack of security.

Today most of the inhabitants of the Northeastern Province affirm their support and loyalty to the president and the government, and several of them have achieved high positions in the establishment, such as Mahmud Mohamed, a former chief of staff, his brother Hussein Maalim Mohamed, a cabinet minister, and several members of parliament and assistant ministers. Some Somalis are active in Islamic organizations; one is Ahmad Khalif, who has for some years been secretary-general of the Muslim umbrella organization known as the Supreme Council of Kenya Muslims (Supkem). There is a considerable concentration of Somalis in the Eastleigh quarter of Nairobi, and at election time they carry some political significance; candidates for mayor and for the town council visit the quarter and promise benefits, such as the building of schools and mosques.[17]

African Muslims

The overwhelming majority of Kenya's Muslims are members of different African ethnic groups scattered throughout the country, mostly in the large towns of Mombasa, Nairobi, Kisumu, and Nakuru. Most are Sunni-Shafi'is, the main subject of this study.

Asians

In 1962, on the eve of independence, there were about 176,000 Asians in Kenya, most of them Indians and Pakistanis, of a total population of 8.6 million.[18] Most of Kenya's Asians are Sunnis, among whom the Hanafi school of Islamic law is widespread. Many of the imams in the country's mosques are of Indian or Pakistani origin.

Enjoying a superior economic position, the Asians have contributed funds to the building of mosques and were an important factor in the spread of Islam in Kenya. They play a significant part in running Nairobi's central mosque, the Jamia Mosque (see Chapter 6). The Asians, however, both Sunni and Shiite, are careful not to get involved in politics and keep a low profile; because they are better off than the black African community, they are sometimes resented or attacked.

Shiite Muslims

A significant number of Asian Muslims are Shiites of different sects; on the whole they are better organized than the Sunnis.[19]

The Ismailis

The most important group among the Shiites are the Ismailis (or Sab'iya—the Seveners), followers of the Aga Khan, who originally came from India. There are about 10,000 of them in Kenya.[20] According to the Aga Khan's directives, Ismailis are supposed to adapt to whatever country they live in. The Ismailis in Kenya profess loyalty to the regime and stay away from political and party matters. They include successful traders and bankers and are involved in social services; as early as the 1930s they set up the East African Muslim Welfare Society (EAMWS), whose aim was to distribute assistance and charity throughout East Africa.

When the Aga Khan visited Kenya in 1971 and received a splendid welcome by the government, he promised to urge members of his community to increase their contributions to development projects for the good of Kenya. He also called for the "integration of the Ismailis as citizens of the state." The Kenyan foreign minister, Njoroge Mungai, promised that the government would treat the Ismailis as citizens with equal rights and guaranteed the security of the community and its institutions.[21] The Aga Khan Hospital and the Aga Khan Secondary School, both in Nairobi, are considered among the best institutions of their kind in Kenya and accept members of all religious groups. With the help of the Aga Khan Foundation and wealthy members of the community, the Ismailis have established mosques and schools, not only for their own community but also for African Muslims of different persuasions. In 1993, for example, a wealthy Ismaili family, the Gilani family, contributed 100,000 shillings to set up the Muslim Nursing Maternity Hospital in Nakuru, through the Nakuru Muslim Association headed by the patriarch of the family, Hassan Gilani.[22] From time to time, similar contributions to Muslim charities are publicized in the press. The community leaders make a point of demonstrating their loyalty to the state and their positive contributions by means of events and receptions that they organize in honor of the country's leaders, and at which they collect money for charity. In October 1977, for example, the leader of the Ismaili community in East Africa, Sir Eboo Pirbhai, organized a lavish reception in honor of President Jomo Kenyatta and his wife.[23]

The Ithna'ashriya

The Ithna'ashriya (the Twelvers) in Kenya number about 3,000–4,000. Most of them live in the large towns of Mombasa, Nairobi, and Nakuru, and they engage in trade and shipping. They receive their instructions on religious matters from their religious leaders in Iran and Iraq. Unlike the Ismailis, the Ithna'ashriya carry out active missionary work not only among non-Muslims but also among the Sunnis, seeking to convert them to Shi'a. This conversion work intensified after Khomeini's Islamic Republic of Iran was established. The Ithna'ashriya set up the Bilal Muslim Mission, which runs a network of bookshops that emphasize books on Shi'a. The community runs a number of schools that are open to members of all religions. An important educational institution is the Al-Rassoul madrasa in the Karen neighborhood near Nairobi, which is run by Lebanese Shiite Arabs. Because the madrasa includes accommodation and classes are free, it also attracts members of ethnic groups such as the Kikuyu and the Luo. Among the well-known Kenyan intellectuals who have converted from Sunni to Shi'a is Shaikh Abdillahi Nassir, who today is principal of the Shi'a Theological Seminary near Mombasa. From this institution students are sent to study in Iran.[24] A politically active member of the Ithna'ashriya is the Mombasa businessman Rashid Sajad, who is close to President Moi, is active in Kanu, and was appointed by the president as a member of parliament and chairman of the Kenya Port Authority, a post he held until 1996. In recent years he has been deeply involved in the inter-Islamic conflicts in Mombasa (see Chapter 13). In the last parliament, dissolved in 1997, Shiites were represented for the first time by two members, one of whom was a Bohra.

The Bohra

The Bohra, a breakaway group from the Ismailis, number about 7,000–8,000 in Kenya and are divided into different subgroups. They engage primarily in trade and in crafts.[25] They contribute to different Muslim organizations and have set up a number of primary and secondary schools. Their world leader, who visited Kenya in 1980, contributed 52,000 shillings to Supkem.[26] Like the Ismailis, they set up a foundation, the Burhani Foundation, in 1980; its patron is President Moi. Some 5.2 million shillings of this fund were earmarked for the establishment of schools, clinics, and various charities.[27] One of their most important leaders was A. M. Jeevanjee, who came to Kenya from Gujarat in India late in the nineteenth century and founded a business empire, dealing primarily in metal and glass—the chief business interests of the Bohra to this day. Jeevanjee was the first Asian to be appointed to the constitutional council in the colonial period. In the previous parliament the Bohra were represented by Abdulkarim, who was active in the ruling Kanu Party and served as deputy minister of labor. The Bohra usually vote as a block for Kanu. Another major and respected personality among the Bohra was the high court judge Fidahussein Abdullah, who, until his death in 1996, served as an important link between his community and the government.

On the whole, within the framework of Iran's Islamic activities in Kenya, only circumspect efforts are made to propagate Shi'a among the Muslims, and for the time being only a few Kenyans are known to have converted from Sunni to Shi'a (see Chapter 11).

Other Muslim Sects

The Ahmadiya

The Ahmadiya in Kenya number only a few thousand. Unlike the Ismailis, who do not seek to propagate their religion among the Sunni Muslims or among the Africans in general, the Ahmadiya, like the Ithna'ashriya, carry out missionary work among the population. Ahmadiya missionaries who came from Pakistan operate throughout all of East Africa, and they have built their own mosques in the main towns and disseminate their propaganda in pamphlets and newspapers, such as *Mapenzi Ya Mungu* (Love of God in Kiswahili) and the *East African Times*, which are published in Kenya and distributed all over East Africa. Part of their propaganda is directed against the Bahais, who, like them, work among the Africans. The Sunnis try to counter the Ahmadiya, whom they regard as infidels and agitators. The Sunnis are especially angry that the Ahmadiya have translated the Qur'an into Kiswahili, claiming that many sections of the Holy Book were distorted to fit the Ahmadiya's beliefs. From time to time letters and articles by Sunnis about the danger posed by the Ahmadiya appear in the press, such as that by Salim Awadhan, who attacked the Ahmadiya leader in East Africa, Shaikh M. Munawar, for publishing several articles on Islamic issues, including one on the meaning of the *jihad* (holy war). Awadhan warned the Muslims not to be tempted to think that the Ahmadiya were Muslims, stressing that they were actually infidels.[28]

The Ibadiya

The Ibadiya are a small Muslim sect named after its founder Ibn Ibad. Most of the sect's religious leaders are Omanis living in Zanzibar and Kenya. They interpret the Qur'an literally, are puritanical, and oppose the worship of holy men and the Sufi orders. Although the Omanis ruled East Africa for many years, and many of the great traders who penetrated into the continent were Ibadiya, they—unlike the Sunnis—did not try to propagate their religion. One of the reasons seems to have been that they considered themselves superior to the black Africans.[29]

2

Muslim Organizations

The Kenyan government, like the governments of Uganda, Tanzania, and other African countries, prohibits the formation of political parties based on religion. Religious leaders, Muslim and Christian alike, therefore set up "religious" or "social" organizations through which they can express their views. Since independence, many Muslim organizations of this type have come and gone. Some of them were regional or sectional, others nationwide. They were supposed to deal with educational, religious, and social matters only and to avoid getting directly involved in political matters. Nevertheless, these organizations have frequently attacked non-Muslim or even Muslim political rivals.

The authorities in Kenya, like those in Uganda and Tanzania, themselves established Muslim umbrella organizations and worked through them to obtain Muslim support and to supervise and influence their activities. Many of the key positions in these organizations are occupied by Muslims who support the government, among them ministers and senior government or ruling-party officials. The following are some of the main Muslim organizations.

The National Union of Kenya Muslims

The National Union of Kenya Muslims (Nukem) was established in 1968. It was headed by two Muslim assistant ministers, Mohamed Jehazi and Shaikh Mohamed Salim Balala. Its stated main goal was to unify all Muslims in Kenya, especially those who lived in the Coast Province, against the ambitions of Roland Ngala, a Christian from the Giryama ethnic group and one of the leaders of the ruling Kanu Party. Nukem claimed that Ngala wanted to control the party in the

Coast Province and be the recognized political leader in the region. Some of his Muslim rivals tried to play the Muslim card against him.

Another factor that prompted the formation of Nukem was the concern that the government of independent Kenya would accede to the demands of some parliamentarians and public figures and repeal all customary and religious laws, imposing one modern secular law on all citizens. The Muslims feared that the Islamic laws dealing with personal matters such as inheritance and marriage would be abrogated, and they objected to the proposed reforms. It was because of these Muslim objections that the proposal to draft the unified law was postponed (see Chapter 8). Another aim of Nukem was to check what was perceived as the danger of Christian missionary activities among the Muslims and anti-Muslim activities in general. In January 1993, for example, Amin al-Hinawi, Nukem's chairman in the Coast Province, sharply criticized a statement by the Catholic archbishop Otunga warning against the expansion of Islam in Africa (see Chapter 10).

As Nukem evolved, its primary purposes were to represent Muslim interests to the government, to fight discrimination against Muslims, to promote education among Muslims, and to introduce reforms to modernize Muslim society.[1]

The organization had several branches in the country, and it continued to function even after the establishment of Supkem. Nukem leaders had close connections with some Arab countries, especially Saudi Arabia, which donated funds through it for building schools and mosques. Thus, in May 1994, Nukem chairman Ali Shaikh Amin announced that, after his meeting with the Saudi ambassador in Nairobi, the Saudis had promised to assist financially in the building of an Islamic university in Kenya.[2] In the 1980s, Nukem maintained close relations with Libya. In August 1980, Nukem's secretary-general, Mohamed Yusuf, accompanied a group of nineteen Muslim preachers and teachers who traveled to Libya for studies.

The Supreme Council of Kenya Muslims

Supkem was established in 1973. In an article published in 1977, Farouk Muslim, then Supkem's secretary-general, pointed out that since World War II many Muslim organizations had been set up in Kenya to deal with religion, education, and social matters. To avoid duplication and inefficiency, it had been decided to consolidate these efforts to promote Muslim interests under one roof.[3] In actual fact, as Farouk Muslim noted, Supkem's aims were the same as

Nukem's; but apparently there was closer government involvement in Supkem. Among Supkem's senior officials were cabinet ministers such as Kassim Mwamazandi, who served as assistant minister of energy in the 1980s and was at the same time Supkem's chairman; Mohamed Shaikh Aden, who was assistant minister holding different portfolios (such as industry and energy) and at the same time Supkem's director of education; and Ahmad Abdallah, who was deputy governor of the Central Bank of Kenya and served as Supkem's director-general. Usually the same people were reelected to key posts in the organization.

During their conferences, and indeed at every opportunity, Supkem's leaders emphasize that Muslims should declare their absolute loyalty to the president, his government, and the Kanu Party, pointing out that Islam demands loyalty to the authorities.[4] They repeatedly call for keeping religious issues separate from matters of state.[5]

In his article, Farouk Muslim notes that in Supkem's early years there was very little contact between the organization's leaders and its members. They usually met at annual general meetings, which lasted a day or two, and there was no real opportunity to hold intensive discussions on problems that arose during the year. At the annual general meeting of 1975, therefore, it was decided to ask legal advisers to prepare a detailed constitution for Supkem; this was done and confirmed a year later.

As stipulated by the new constitution, district councils were set up all over the country and their functions, duties, and authority were delineated. Each district council was entitled to send three representatives to the annual general meetings. A new department for women's affairs was set up to advance the position of women in the Muslim community and give them equal opportunity to receive education and training. According to reports circulated by Supkem in the media, the organization's activities were varied and impressive. It represented Muslim requests before the authorities and arranged occasional meetings between Muslim leaders and the president. In December 1978, for example, immediately after President Moi was elected, Supkem organized a large delegation of 3,000 people representing all the Muslim communities in the country. The delegation met with the president, expressed their loyalty, and raised problems and requests.[6] Supkem was also active in obtaining scholarships from Arab-Muslim countries such as Egypt, Kuwait, Libya, Saudi Arabia, and Sudan, as well as from Islamic organizations such as the Islamic Development Bank, the Arab League, and the Organization of the Islamic Conference (OIC).[7] Supkem recruited Muslim teachers from Egypt and other Muslim countries, organized seminars on Islamic and educational subjects, and called public gatherings (*harambe*) at which donations were made for setting up Muslim institutions. Supkem also reorganized the pilgrimage to Mecca (the *hajj*). In the area of public relations and information, in the late 1970s and early 1980s Supkem published an English monthly magazine called *Nurul-Islam* that dealt with Islamic issues in the Muslim community. In 1979, the government officially recognized Supkem as the only organization that was entitled to represent all the Muslims in the country and to maintain links with Islamic organizations outside of Kenya. This helped Supkem to expand its international activities.

In 1979, Supkem purchased a four-story building in Nairobi to serve as its headquarters. Occasionally it published information about plans to build more schools and cultural institutions. Thus, the organization announced that it had received land from the Nairobi municipality for building a secondary school for 800 pupils costing tens of millions of shillings, which it had helped to raise.[8] By the end of 1999 nothing was known about the execution of this plan.

According to the organizations's long-serving secretary-general, Ahmad Khalif, who has also been assistant minister in several governments, in 1996 Supkem had fifty district branches and 150 registered Muslim associations and organizations affiliated with it.[9] However, not all organizations joined Supkem. Several Shiite groups and Muslim organizations that opposed the government did not join, among them the Islamic Party of Kenya (IPK), which is discussed in Chapter 13.

Occasionally Supkem was criticized, sometimes very sharply, for its policies and activities. One of the main criticisms was that its leaders were corrupt and disorderly in financial matters, especially concerning donations by individuals and organizations from Kenya and abroad. There was much disparagement of Supkem's officials, who were accused of seeking only their personal benefit. There were other accusations, sometimes by Supkem's own members, of inefficiency and negligence.[10] These resulted in a decline in contributions to the organization, which led to financial problems and the canceling of planned events.

Supkem's rivals among the Muslims, and specifically those in the opposition parties, criticized Supkem's pro-Kanu activities and its close relationship with the government, demanding that the organization be truly neutral. In the course of the 1994 conference of the Muslim Education Welfare Association, a lecturer from Nairobi University criticized Supkem as a "government agent" and charged that this was why it opposed the registration of the IPK. Shaikh Ali Shee, imam of the great Jamia Mosque in Nairobi, maintained that Supkem did not in fact represent the Muslims and their leaders and had not received a mandate from them. This was disputed by Ahmad Khalif, who stressed that Supkem's officials were reelected every three years. Many Muslims, however, claimed that these elections were not free and fair.[11]

One of the most persuasive arguments against Supkem is that it is unable to carry out its main task—that of uniting Kenya's Muslims and significantly improving their position. An illustration of this is the disturbances that broke out in Mombasa in 1992–1994, particularly the violent conflict between the opposition IPK and the pro-government United Muslims of Africa (UMA). In fact, Supkem, though it was accused of being unable to prevent this clash, opposed both these organizations, fearing that they might take over the leadership of Mombasa's Muslims. The UMA's leaders actually asserted that they had been compelled to organize themselves and to take action against the IPK only because they had seen that Supkem had been incompetent since its inception and had done nothing to promote Muslim interests or to fight against extremist elements in the community (see Chapter 13).

Supkem's ongoing efforts to mellow the Muslims' attitude toward the government was also reflected in connection with the "Wajir Massacre" in the Northeastern Province in October 1998. This event led to sharp criticism of the government for neglecting security arrangements in the province. Secretary-General Ahmad Khalif issued a press release on behalf of Supkem in which he joined the criticism against the government but also called for restraint and dialogue with the relevant authorities in order to find a solution to the problem.[12]

Even Supkem's own officials frequently expressed their disappointment with the organization's performance, especially its lack of achievements. Fatma Hyder, director of women's affairs, accused Supkem of neglecting Muslim women and doing nothing to improve their position in society. She also expressed reservations about the chief *qadi's* influence within Supkem and supported demands that he be elected by members of the Muslim community instead of being appointed by the government. She asserted that Supkem showed little interest in Muslim education or in projecting a positive image of Islam among the public at large and demanded the inclusion of Islamic studies as a recognized subject in Kenya's universities. Supkem, Hyder complained, was not doing enough.[13]

Supkem's influence on religion, society, and politics seems to be much smaller than its announcements and publications would lead one to believe. It is interesting to note the similar weakness of the Muslim organizations that were established and influenced by the governments of Uganda and Tanzania: in Uganda, the National Association of African Muslims (NAAM), set up by President Milton Obote to support his policies; in Tanzania, the Supreme Council of Muslims in Tanzania (Bakwata), founded by President Julius Nyerere. Idi Amin, for his part, seeking to strengthen his control over the Muslims, in 1972 banned all existing Muslim organizations and established the Uganda Muslim Supreme Council (UMSC). In theory, these government-supported organizations were set up to promote Muslim interests in legislation, education, and religious affairs; in practice, they were ineffective and disappointing because of excessive bureaucracy, rivalry between members, and struggles for leadership. Moreover, their leaders exploited these organizations for their personal advancement. For the governments, on the other hand, these bodies were an important tool for controlling Muslim activities and for recruiting Muslim support when they needed it, such as during elections.

Other Muslim Organizations

The Association for Reforms in Islam (Islahil Islamiya) was established in Mombasa in the 1960s with the aim of promoting and defending Islam. Among its activities is the circulation of a series of pamphlets in English called "In Defence of Islam." The association has organized conferences on Islam and demanded an improvement in the position of the chief qadi, as well as reforms in Muslim education and in Islamic law as it is practiced in the shari'a courts. Shaikh Mohamed Amana, the chairman, has frequently published appeals for Muslim unity.[14] The association also organizes groups of pilgrims to Mecca every year.[15] Supkem regards the association as a rival and objects to its activities.[16]

The Muslim Students Association of the University of Nairobi was established primarily to promote higher education among Muslims; contributions from Arab countries help support the association's activities. Its journal, *Minaret*, supports the Palestinians and the anti-Israeli policies of Arab countries. The government has accused the association of involvement in politics and has banned its activities (see Chapter 11).

The Islamic Foundation, an international organization based in Saudi Arabia, has opened a branch in Kenya. It publishes brochures on Islam in English and Kiswahili and builds and reconstructs mosques. In Isiolo, a town in northeast Kenya, it has built a Muslim school.[17]

The Muslim Education Welfare Association (MEWA), headed by Awadh Jezan, organizes seminars and conferences on Islam and the position of the Muslims in Kenya, with the participation of Muslim academics and public figures. It held an important conference on Islam in 1994, the deliberations of which were published in a book edited by M. Bakari and Y. Saad (see Bibliography).

Jumuia-til-Baladia was established in Nairobi in 1937 with the aim of spreading Islam among the rural population and of constructing mosques and madrasas in Muslim areas. Its founders were Maalim Hamise Ngige, Abdullah Tairara, and Omar Said. Among its activities was the establishment of the Institute of Islamic Teaching in Nyeri, a Kikuyu area. This organization, which functioned until the late 1950s, played an important role in disseminating Islam in the Central Province of Kenya and in the Rift Valley.

In all, Kenya has dozens of Muslim organizations, both local and regional; these include women's organizations, youth and student associations, and several Muslim nongovernment organizations (NGOs). As we shall see later, some of the Muslim NGOs were shut down by the government after the bombing of the U.S. embassy in Nairobi in August 1998. Those Muslim political organizations that appeared after the ban on political parties was lifted (such as the IPK and the UMA) are discussed in Chapters 13 and 14.

3

Muslims in the Establishment

Since independence, the authorities have seen to it that Muslims are represented in the government, in the ruling party, and in public institutions. Muslims have generally been represented in government by two or three assistant ministers who are loyal to the regime, out of a total of forty to fifty ministers and assistant ministers.[1] The Muslim assistant ministers usually come from a very small circle. Some of them serve in the same position in successive governments or are reappointed as assistant ministers in other ministries.

The following are assistant ministers who served for a long period during President Kenyatta's tenure:

- Mohamed Jehazi, of Arab descent, was assistant minister of health in the 1970s and was known for his efforts to promote Arab countries' influence in Kenya.
- Shaikh Mohamed Salim Balala, also of Arab descent, from Hadramaut, served in a range of ministries, among them financial and economic planning; he was also director of education of the Muslim umbrella organization, Supkem.
- Ahmad Khalif was assistant minister of housing in the early 1970s and for many years secretary-general of Supkem.
- J. M. Ngala served as assistant minister of information in the late 1960s and early 1970s.
- Osman Aruru, of Somali descent, served as assistant minister in the president's office during Kenyatta's tenure.
- Jan Mohamed, an Ismaili, was assistant minister of tourism.
- Kassim B. Mwamazandi served as assistant minister of foreign affairs in the 1970s (and was also chairman of Supkem).

By appointing Muslim assistant ministers from different areas and sects, President Kenyatta wanted to demonstrate that every segment of the population was represented in his government.

During the tenure of President Daniel arap Moi, Muslims have been more widely represented in the government. One of the most eminent long-serving assistant ministers is Sharif Nassir, member of parliament from the Mombasa-Central constituency and chairman of the Kanu Party's Mombasa branch. He has served as assistant minister in different ministries, such as trade and industry, information, and public works. Nassir's position in Moi's government is particularly strong because he was one of the first to vigorously support Moi's candidacy for the presidency immediately after Kenyatta's death in 1978, and he worked hard to garner support for Moi among the coastal Muslims. He is still one of the most devoted supporters of Moi and his Nyayo ideology (*nyayo* means footsteps in Kiswahili, and Moi promised to follow in Kenyatta's footsteps, or political path). Nevertheless, Nassir's pomposity and a bitter ongoing struggle against his rivals for Muslim leadership in Mombasa and on the coast have led to many disputes and splits in the Muslim community (see Chapter 6). He is also one of the Muslims who receive financial help from Arab countries, and he supports them in their activities against Israel. Following the last elections, on 29 December 1997, Nassir was again appointed assistant minister, this time of transport and communications, and in 1998 he was promoted to become the second Muslim minister in Moi's government, holding the portfolio for home affairs and national heritage, culture, and social services. Early in 1999, he again demonstrated his loyalty to Moi by suggesting that the president should remain in office even after the termination of his second five-year term in 2002.[2]

During Moi's tenure, the first Muslim minister was appointed: Hussein Maalim Mohamed, a Somali, and a member of parliament. In the 1980s, he was minister of state in the president's office and in the 1990s was minister of culture and social services, minister of energy, and minister of research and technical training. In 1997, before the last elections, three Muslims were serving in Moi's government—one minister, Hussein Maalim Mohamed, and two assistant ministers, Sharif Nassir and Ali Mohamed.

After the failed coup attempt against Moi in August 1982, the brother of Hussein Maalim Mohamed, Mahmud Mohamed from Garissa (who as an army officer had played a key role in foiling the coup), was appointed chief of staff. In 1996, Mahmud Mohamed ended his term of office and retired.

In Moi's government of 1998, the number of Muslim assistant ministers increased to six out of thirty-seven assistant ministers. The number of Muslim ministers increased from one to two. They were Hussein Maalim Mohamed and Sharif Nassir, who was promoted from assistant minister to a cabinet minister.

It should be noted that on 6 September 1999, when President Moi, under pressure from the World Bank and the International Monetary Fund, reshuffled his cabinet and reduced the number of government ministries from twenty-seven to fifteen, he retained the two Muslim ministers. Hussein Maalim Mohamed became minister of rural development, and Sharif Nassir became a minister of state in the office of the president.

As for Muslims in parliament, after the December 1992 parliamentary elections there were twenty-four Muslim members of parliament (MPs) out of 200 (12 percent). After the 1997 elections, there were thirty Muslim MPs out of 210. Of the twelve additional members nominated by the president, four were Muslims. Most of the Muslim MPs belonged to Kanu.

The Muslim MPs were organized in a Muslim Parliamentary Group (MPG). In the 1970s, the MPG was headed by Shaikh Mohamed Salim Balala, who was assistant minister in the Finance Ministry.[3]

The mayor of Mombasa is always a Muslim. The majority of council members are also Muslims.

In addition to Sharif Nassir, until 1997 Boy Juma Boy played a key role in the Kanu Party as parliamentary chief whip. His father, Juma Boy, played a very important role in the 1970s as secretary-general of the Kenya Confederation of Trade Unions (COTU).

As of 1998, there were four Muslim ambassadors, two of them to Muslim countries:

- Said Hamed served until 1996 as Kenya's ambassador to Saudi Arabia. He was appointed to this post in 1993 after he failed to win one of the Mombasa seats in the 1992 elections. On his return to Kenya in 1996, he tried to seize the Muslim leadership of Mombasa and was a rival of Sharif Nassir (see Chapter 6). His successor is also a Muslim.
- Salim Ibrahim Juma was appointed ambassador to Iran in 1995.
- Professor Ahmad Idha Salim, a descendant of a Swahili family from the coast, has been Kenya's ambassador to Sweden since 1993. Formerly a lecturer in the Department of History at the

University of Nairobi, he is the author of *Swahili-Speaking People of Kenya's Coast*.
- Habib Jilani was ambassador to China until 1994 and was then appointed ambassador to Tanzania.

The following are other Muslims who have held senior positions:

- Ahmad Abdallah served for many years (until 1997) as deputy governor of the Central Bank; he is highly respected for his ability and integrity. In the 1970s, he was chairman of the parastatal economic companies, ICDC (Industrial and Commercial Development Corporation). He is active in Muslim affairs and in the 1970s served as director-general of Supkem, of which he is still an active member.
- Yossuf Haji was for many years the provincial commissioner in various provinces.
- Fidahussein Abdullah, a Shiite, served as chief magistrate until his death in 1996.

Several Muslims hold senior academic positions (see Chapter 9), and there are several Muslim broadcasters in television and radio.

Although the authorities give the Muslims representation in the government and in public institutions, Muslims complain that this representation is too small and does not constitute real equality. Even the Muslim minister, Hussein Maalim Mohamed, issued a statement in February 1993 criticizing the government for discriminating against Muslims. As it happened, this was not the only time the minister publicly spoke out against the government, especially concerning the difficult situation in the Northeastern Province, including the Wajir Massacre of October 1998, which is discussed later.

4

The Political Importance of the Muslims

The political importance of the Muslims is especially noticeable just before party, parliamentary, or presidential elections. Their importance grew after the introduction of a multiparty system, particularly when the need arose to combat the extremist Muslim opposition, the IPK, and when Muslim complaints about discrimination increased. The leaders of independent Kenya did not completely ignore the Muslims' complaints and tried to conciliate them and to demonstrate that the government was not discriminating against them.

Even during Kenyatta's time, the president made efforts to obtain Muslim support during elections, despite his basic suspicions of them. Kenyatta would spend several weeks a year on Kenya's coast, usually in August, the coolest time in that region, not only to enjoy the weather and the beautiful Indian Ocean coastline, but also to maintain contact with the leaders of the Muslim minority in an area that had both political and economic importance. During this time the government in Nairobi was semiparalyzed, as the ministers would rush to the coast to consult with the president on various matters. Foreign ambassadors too would go down to Mombasa to meet with the president or his ministers. Kenyatta not only visited Muslim leaders during his stays in Mombasa, but also participated in Muslim religious festivals such as the Maulidi (the Prophet's birthday) and delivered speeches in Kiswahili.

The Muslim leadership, for its part, would exploit this opportunity to meet the president and to request economic and religious benefits or concessions for the Muslim community. For example, during the president's visit to the coast just before elections to the ruling Kanu Party in 1971, he met with political and religious leaders, including the chief qadi, Shaikh Abdallah Saleh al-Farsy, who was the highest Muslim religious authority in Kenya and resided in Mombasa.

He also met with the mayor of Mombasa, Abdallah Mwidau, as well as Muslim members of parliament. They presented him with a memorandum requesting that the government recognize 'Id al-Fitr (the end of the Ramadan fast) and 'Id al-Hajj (also known as 'Id al-Adha—the day when pilgrims to Mecca make sacrifices) as national holidays like Christmas. At the same time, they pledged their loyalty to the president, the government, and the Kanu Party. Kenyatta asked them which of the two festivals was more important, pointing out that there were already many national holidays and it was impossible to close down the whole country for two additional days. It was agreed that 'Id al-Fitr would be a national holiday, and 'Id al-Hajj would be a holiday only for those Muslims working in government and public offices and in schools.[1] Immediately afterward, Kenyatta made a celebratory public statement before Muslim leaders, declaring that 'Id al-Fitr would be a national public holiday in Kenya, on which all government offices and public institutions would be closed. This declaration was published in the official gazette.[2] The media throughout Kenya, especially the newspapers, reported this event extensively, and Muslim leaders around the country heaped praise on the president for his relationship with the Muslims and announced special prayers for his welfare.[3]

Even in colonial times, Muslims had complained that they were forced to work on important religious festivals, and students had complained that they had to take examinations on these days. During the colonial period, the authorities had agreed that 'Id al-Fitr would be a public holiday for Muslims on the coastal strip and in the area of Mombasa only.[4] But the first president of independent Kenya acceded to the Muslims' request to turn 'Id al-Fitr into a national public holiday.

President Daniel arap Moi, like his predecessor, visits the Muslims in Mombasa and the coastal area from time to time. Sharif Nassir, Moi's main contact in the area, organizes mass receptions for him. There are other Muslims who work for Kanu among the Muslim community, such as Rashid Sajad, an Asian Shiite businessman living in Mombasa, who was appointed by Moi as an MP; the mayor of Mombasa; and wealthy individuals such as Mohamed Bawazir, a businessman originally from Aden.

To show consideration and support for the Muslim community, the president and his ministers send hearty greetings to the Muslims on the occasion of their festivals. For their part, too, Muslim leaders and organizations that support the government take this opportunity to send greetings to the president and his administration, thanking them for providing religious freedom and good government. These mutual greetings are widely publicized in the media. In 1978, when it turned out that the date set for elections to Kanu fell on 'Id al-Fitr, President Moi announced a postponement out of consideration for the Muslims; Muslim leaders quickly hailed him for this.[5] On the occasion of 'Id al-Hajj in 1979, Moi dispatched the following telegram to the Muslim community: "On the occasion of 'Id al-Hajj which is celebrated today in Kenya, I am sending warmest greetings to all Muslims in Kenya in the Nyayo spirit of peace, love and unity. I am united with you on this important day for Islam and I wish you a very happy holiday."[6] In another such telegram from Moi in 1980, he declared that "Kenya's Muslims have always been loyal to the state, and therefore I wish you happiness, wealth and success."[7] Similar telegrams are sent every year, and Muslim leaders reply to them by repeatedly stressing their gratitude and loyalty.

There are other ways in which the government tries to show its consideration for the Muslim community. During official ceremonies, such as the opening of parliament or the main Independence Day festivities, the chief qadi is invited to make a speech along with church leaders, and his address is in Arabic or Kiswahili, or a combination of the two.

Harambe (meaning "pull together") assemblies, which are fundraising assemblies and are also organized for the purpose of building Muslim schools or mosques, give the government an opportunity to show its concern for the Muslim community. In Kenyatta's time, government ministers would sometimes participate in these events and would make personal contributions in addition to the contribution that was always made by the president. At the harambe held to mark the laying of the cornerstone of the mosque in the town of Eldema Ravine, the vice-president participated and made a sizable contribution in Kenyatta's name.[8] President Moi has continued this practice. In 1979, he participated in the opening of the Multi-Purpose Islamic Centre in Mombasa and contributed 20,000 shillings; the Muslims responded by making him a "Traditional Elder."[9] At a fundraiser for the building of a mosque in Kibera in 1983, in which the vice-president and government ministers participated, 600,000 shillings were collected, 150,000 of which were donated by the president; the president also granted a title deed on land to the local Muslim community.[10]

Programs on Islam have been introduced on radio and television, such as *Forum on Islam* on Friday evenings at seven o'clock, which is prime-time viewing. The program consists of a half-hour discussion between learned Muslims on topics in Islam. Several days a week, radio and television stations conclude their broadcasts with the prayer and sermon of a shaikh. The Kiswahili radio broadcasts offer more programs on Islam than does television, and each morning the opening ten minutes are devoted to the reading of the Qur'an as are another five minutes at night at the close of the broadcasts. In the month of Ramadan there are additional special programs, such as the broadcast of the ceremonies and sermons from the central mosque in Nairobi.

Muslim values and practices are also taken into account in areas such as animal slaughter, autopsies, attire, and identity cards. Since Muslims do not eat the meat of animals slaughtered by non-Muslims, animal slaughter for public consumption has been entrusted to Muslims. At the abattoir Halal Meat Products Ltd., Muslim shaikhs supervise the slaughter to ensure that it is performed according to Islamic law.[11] This is also the case in Uganda.

In 1983, President Moi acceded to Muslim requests and issued an edict declaring that Muslims who died a natural death or were killed in road accidents could be buried without a postmortem being performed on them. The president made this announcement while participating in a harambe to raise money for the building of a mosque.[12]

As a gesture to the Muslims, President Kenyatta would don Muslim attire whenever he took part in events in Muslim centers. He did this, for example, when he laid the cornerstone for the Kanu headquarters in Isiolo, which is in the northeast where Somali Muslims live.[13] Some Christian MPs and mayors have also followed this custom, especially at election time. For example, Mayor Andrew Ngumba of Nairobi wore traditional Muslim dress when he organized a harambe in the Pumwani neighborhood of Nairobi, and the Muslims gave him the honorary title of shaikh.[14] As we shall see, President Moi also followed this practice, especially before the 1992 elections and during his struggle with the Muslim opposition.

In 1978, when the government proclaimed the requirement of carrying an identity card with a photograph, some Muslim leaders in the Garissa district opposed the requirement that Muslim women remove their veils in order to be photographed, claiming that this contravened Islamic law. The Garissa authorities agreed to exempt married Muslim women from being photographed.[15]

In the sphere of education as well, some concessions were made to Muslims. With no connection to the problem of Muslim education (see Chapter 9), Kenyatta's government, immediately after independence in 1963, decided to introduce reforms into the educational system as a whole. That year the government nationalized all schools, a large number of which had been run by the churches. In 1964, the Education Committee of Kenya was set up to make recommendations regarding religious education. It asserted that public schools should not be used as vehicles for religious propaganda and proselytizing and should be open to pupils of all religious persuasions.[16] This was a move to conciliate the Muslims. But the rules were not always observed, especially since most schools continued to be the responsibility of the churches and to be run by Christians.

In several cases when Muslims complained about infringement of their religious rights, the government ruled in their favor. For example, Muslims complained that girl students had been expelled from several schools for wearing the veil (*hijab*), particularly in the coastal area. Two of the schools were girls' secondary schools in Mombasa run by the Catholic Church, and one was a primary school in Nairobi run by Sikhs. When the matter was brought to court, the court ruled in favor of the Muslims.[17] The question of the veil became a religious-political issue when Muslim MPs took this opportunity to jump on the bandwagon and proclaim that Muslim female students were harassed because they observed the laws of the Qur'an. The president himself intervened in this dispute and ruled that female Muslim students should not be forced to act against their beliefs.[18] A similar incident occurred in the Meru area in a girls' secondary school that has a Christian majority and is run by Catholics. Seven Muslim girls were expelled because they did not turn up for school in the evening but went to the mosque to pray at the end of the Ramadan fast, despite the fact that the school's rules expressly forbade both Muslims and Christians from fasting. This incident also became a religious-political issue and caused tension between Muslims and Christians. The Muslims demanded that the girls be reinstated and allowed to fast during Ramadan. The matter was brought to court, which ruled in favor of reinstating the girls and allowing them to fast in accordance with their religion.[19]

On the eve of the first multiparty elections in 1992, when there was an intense struggle between Kanu and the opposition parties, the authorities made a special effort to obtain the votes of the Muslims in the coastal region. In February of that year, President Moi organized a rigorous weeklong tour of the coast and visited the important Muslim centers of Mombasa, Malindi, and Lamu. Sharif Nassir succeeded in bringing out into the streets and to the gatherings tens of thousands of Muslims who applauded the president. In popular assemblies and in meetings with Muslim leaders, Moi, in Muslim attire, emphasized the freedom of religion that existed in the country and his own efforts on behalf of the Muslims.

In April of that year, when the Muslims were celebrating 'Id al-Fitr, Moi and his ministers sent warm greetings to them. Several government ministers were present at the festivities, and Muslim members of

Kanu exploited the events to attack the opposition parties, especially the largest of them, Ford-Kenya, arguing that this party ignored the concerns of Muslims. They contended, for example, that Ford-Kenya had declared a general strike in the month of Ramadan without taking into account the difficulties this would cause Muslims.

Kanu leaders were also very active at this time in Lamu. Cyrus Jirongo, a Kanu activist and leader of the party's youth wing, YK92, visited Lamu and recruited shaikhs to work for Kanu, including Shaikh Ali Faruki, who was appointed chairman of the YK92 branch in Lamu and tried to register new members.[20]

In large towns, such as Nairobi, Nakuru, and Kisumu, where there are large concentrations of Muslims, candidates are extremely active politically before municipal or parliamentary elections. In the parliamentary elections of 1979, for example, there were two rival candidates from Kanu seeking Muslim votes in the constituency of Mathare Valley in Nairobi, which includes a populous Somali-Muslim community. The two were both Christians—the mayor, Andrew Ngumba, and the foreign minister, Munyua Waiyaki. They organized a host of rallies at which each promised assistance for poor neighborhoods. Ngumba even built a bridge over the valley to ease the movement of the residents.[21] Waiyaki, for his part, took part in a harambe to raise money to build a mosque and contributed 28,200 shillings himself.[22] In subsequent elections, especially the multiparty elections of 1992, there were vigorous contests to win Muslim hearts with promises of assistance.

These different efforts to propitiate Muslims partially helped to moderate Muslim criticism of the government for a long time, and there were even open displays of support for the government, especially by Muslims who received public or government posts or benefited from concessions.

In 1976, a serious crisis in relations broke out between Idi Amin, the Muslim president of Uganda, and Kenyatta. Amin demanded the release of three Palestinians who had been captured by the Kenyan security forces at Nairobi's airport and been accused of trying to shoot down an Israeli El Al plane with surface-to-air missiles that were found in their possession. Kenya handed the three over to Israel, and this angered Amin, who at the time had close links with the Palestine Liberation Organization (PLO) and had allowed it to establish a base on Ugandan territory. Amin even threatened to bomb Nairobi with his MiG jets if Kenya did not commit itself to return those areas of eastern Uganda that were annexed to Kenya in 1902 by the British colonial administration.

Kenya's Muslim organizations, headed by Supkem, came out in support of Kenyatta and severely condemned Amin. On 22 July 1976, Supkem published an announcement with which Muslim MPs who were ex officio members of Supkem associated themselves; it included the statement that "it is Uganda and not Kenya that has caused the deterioration in relations between the two countries." The announcement condemned Uganda's military regime, which had massacred large numbers of Kenyan and Ugandan citizens alike; it also mentioned Amin's boast that he had a direct link with God—"a man like that is neither reliable nor a true Muslim." It stressed that any attack on Kenya was an attack on Islam. The Muslims in Kenya, the announcement continued, dissented from the support that several Muslim countries had given Amin. Sharif Nassir published another declaration in the name of twenty-two MPs in which he requested Muslim countries to cease all military and financial aid to Amin. Moreover, a warning was issued to Ugandan Muslims that Amin was leading them to disaster, and this announcement also stressed that "Amin is not a true Muslim because Islam condemns the killing of innocent people."[23] Other Muslim leaders also rejected Amin's call for a jihad against Kenya. Kenya's most popular newspaper, the *Daily Nation,* praised Supkem for its declaration in an editorial of 30 July 1976, noting that this action proved the Muslims' loyalty to the state. In another editorial the newspaper condemned those Arab countries that supported Amin out of Muslim religious solidarity, among whom it mentioned in particular Libya and Kuwait, and asserted that "whoever supports our enemy—is our enemy."[24]

Especially stirring was the support of a number of Muslim leaders for Moi immediately after Kenyatta's death in August 1978, when many politicians were working against Moi's appointment as president. Leading this support was Sharif Nassir, and it was largely because of his efforts that most Muslims enthusiastically backed Moi as Kenyatta's successor. Supkem announced its support for Moi in the press, and Muslim delegations from different parts of the country arrived to express to him their loyalty.[25] In December of that year, Supkem organized an enormous delegation of 3,000 Muslims representing all Muslim sects and communities for a meeting with the new president to convey to him their allegiance. They promised that they would follow Moi and would support the policy of Nyayo that he had declared. Moi, for his part, repeated that freedom of religion as laid down in Kenya's constitution would be preserved and that Muslims could build mosques wherever they wanted.[26] In the 1992 elections, a majority in Mombasa voted for the opposition, but in the Coast

Province as a whole Kanu's efforts succeeded and it won a clear majority of delegates (see Chapter 13).

Before the parliamentary and presidential elections in December 1997, the government attempted to improve its standing in Mombasa. Despite its misgivings about the coastal Muslims, the government took further steps to demonstrate its consideration for Muslim demands. Among these steps were the banning of Salman Rushdie's book *The Satanic Verses* and an increase in the foreign currency allowance of pilgrims traveling to Mecca for the hajj. No similar increase was given to Christians wanting to go on pilgrimage to holy places in Israel or to visit the Vatican. The government's argument was that the hajj was obligatory for Muslims whereas visiting holy place was not compulsory for Christians.

In conclusion, under both Kenyatta and Moi, a number of measures were taken to placate the Muslims to ensure their support. These, however, did not satisfy their aspirations or allay Muslims' many complaints about discrimination. Their discontent was expressed especially on the eve of the first multiparty elections in 1992, when the Muslim opposition grew (Chapter 14 deals with the emergence of Muslim extremism in Kenya).

5

Religious Leadership and Muslim Solidarity

The government's desire to control the activities of the Muslim community, manifested by the establishment of Supkem, was also conspicuous in the government's assuming the exclusive authority to appoint the chief qadi. This, the highest Muslim religious post in Kenya, was created in the colonial period. At that time, the chief qadi was appointed by the British authorities to act as a link between them and the Muslims, and he received his salary from the government. This practice continued in independent Kenya, and the office of chief qadi is enshrined in the constitution. The chief qadi serves as the government's adviser in all matters pertaining to Muslims—inheritance, marriage, divorce, and *waqf* (an endowment set aside for religious purposes) property—that are decided in the shari'a courts. The qadis of different areas such as Mombasa, Kisumu, Lamu, Malindi, and Garissa are appointed by the chief qadi, and they assume their posts after they have been approved by the president and their appointments have been published in the official gazette.[1] In 1996, the president approved the appointment of the qadi of Nairobi, Shaikh Hammed Kassim; during that year, the number of qadis reached fifteen.[2]

The chief qadi is the one who announces the start and end of the Ramadan fast according to the sighting of the moon. He receives messages, including telephone messages, from Muslims who say they have seen the moon, and he decides on their veracity and whether to allow them to announce it to members of the community. In Mombasa, the beginning and end of the Ramadan fast are marked by cannon shots from Jesus fort (located on the seacoast).

The chief qadi is the Muslims' senior representative to the authorities. Like the heads of the Christian churches, (and as a representative of the traditional religions), he is invited to official functions.

From time to time the government tries to bolster his prestige by participating in events that he organizes or is connected with. An important and respected chief qadi was Shaikh Abdallah Saleh al-Farsy, who came from Zanzibar, became a Kenyan citizen, and served as qadi during the years 1968–1982. Shaikh Farsy was known for his wide expertise in matters of Islam and his many writings. He commented on the Qur'an and translated it into Kiswahili, in reaction to the Ahmadiya translation of the Qur'an into Kiswahili, which, it was claimed, was falsified. The Shaikh was among the religious leaders who hailed the reforms of Islam and objected to local practices such as saint veneration and the costly ceremonies of Maulidi (see Chapter 6). He was very careful not to intervene in politics and other matters that could bring about a conflict with the government, and some of his detractors claimed that for this reason he could not supply the Muslims with dynamic and charismatic leadership. Moreover, he felt himself to be a foreigner because of his Zanzibari origin.

Shaikh al-Farsy resigned voluntarily, citing his advanced age and his wish to rejoin his family in Zanzibar. Senior government officials took part in the farewell ceremony organized for him, and they made speeches hailing his efforts to unite the Muslims and his helpful counsel to the high court of appeals in matters of Islamic law. The shaikh, for his part, took the opportunity to call on the Muslims to be loyal to the state and to increase the study of Islam and the Arabic language, which, to his regret, were not sufficiently studied in schools and madrasas.[3]

On the occasion of the appointment of his successor, Shaikh Nassor Nahdi, formerly qadi of al-Nairobi, a large reception was organized. Government representatives who participated called on the Muslim community to respect the new chief qadi and promised him full government backing.[4] During Shaikh al-Nahdi's time, as a result of the democratization process in Kenya, opposition parties were established and there was greater freedom of speech; the chief qadi's position was therefore not as strong as before. In the 1990s, there was severe criticism of him by Muslims demanding a reduction in his authority and changes in the method of his appointment.

Muslim Celebrations and Muslim Solidarity

One illustration of the government's desire to win the support of the Muslims was the declaration of 'Id al-Fitr, the end of the Ramadan fast, as a national public holiday. This holiday is enthusiastically celebrated not only in Muslim centers on the coast but throughout

Kenya, especially in the large cities. In Nairobi, for example, the main mosque, the Jamia Mosque, cannot hold the tens of thousands of worshipers who went to the mosque, and they overflow into the adjoining streets. President Moi and government representatives throughout Kenya send greetings to the Muslims for the festival, mentioning the freedom of religion that exists in the country and promising to work for the Muslims' well-being. Muslim leaders, especially those in key posts, repeatedly avow their loyalty to the president and praise his relationship with them.[5] In the major cities the holiday is celebrated with festive Maulidi processions organized by the National Maulidi Committee.[6] All major newspapers publish special supplements for the festival, which are financed by Muslim companies. In these supplements Muslims also publish information about their businesses and extend greetings to the Muslim community. The supplements also offer commentaries on Islam in general and on the importance of Ramadan and of 'Id al-Fitr in particular. Special programs are devoted to these topics on radio and television.

The most famous Muslim celebrations occur in the ancient city of Lamu, whose residents are predominantly Muslim. These festivals, such as the Maulidi, which marks the birthday of the Prophet Muhammad in the month of Rabi' 'al-Awal, are attended by tens of thousands of Muslims arriving from all parts of Kenya and from abroad, because the way the Maulidi is celebrated in Lamu is unique in the Muslim world.[7] During the weeklong Maulidi festivities there is a very colorful procession (the Matwari), with singing and the scattering of perfume accompanied by flutes and drums, toward the grave of Sharif Habib Swalih bin Alwi, a religious leader who came to Lamu in 1880 and established the tradition of this procession. Afterward there are prayers and recitations in Lamu's central mosque, the Riadha Mosque, and traditional music and dancing until dawn.[8] Among the myriad activities are donkey and dhow races and, for young girls, henna-dye competitions (henna is a reddish dye made from flowering shrubs and applied to hands, feet, and hair). Later we look at orthodox Muslims' opposition to this kind of celebration.

Other impressive Muslim events are the celebrations in honor of pilgrims who go to Mecca to perform the Hajj. About 1,500 Kenyan Muslims each year make the pilgrimage, and the need to look after their welfare was one of the reasons a Kenyan embassy was established in Riyadh.[9] Even though the government stringently restricts the acquisition of foreign currency and does not allow Christians to obtain it for their visits to holy sites abroad, Muslims have been able to obtain it—even in increasing amounts over the years—for their pilgrimages to Mecca.

These various celebrations strengthen Muslim solidarity and highlight the Islamic way of life in Muslim centers. Although the Muslim community has many divisions, its solidarity comes to the fore whenever they suspect that the sanctity of Islam is threatened. This happened, for example, when a letter to the editor was published in the *Standard* (newspaper) supporting the ideas of Salman Rushdie and the distribution of his book *The Satanic Verses*. This letter, which was signed "Disturbed Muslim," pointed out among other things that the Prophet Muhammad borrowed many ideas from the Jews and the Christians. The *ka'bah* (the holy site in Mecca), according to the writer, was established by the patriarch Abraham and therefore Jews also had the right to claim it. In his opinion, Islam, as propagated by Muhammad, "was dead and those who brandish this form of frozen Islam are even more dead."[10] This letter sparked fierce protest by Muslims of all organizations, who bitterly condemned both the writer and the newspaper. Among the leading critics were Supkem, Assistant Minister Sharif Nassir, and various qadis and imams. There were calls to boycott the newspaper, and its office in Mombasa was set on fire. The *Standard*'s editor published an apology for printing the letter, admitting that it had been a mistake and asking Muslims for forgiveness.[11] Some Muslims felt they could accept the editor's apology and consider the matter closed, but others could not, and the issue stayed in the headlines for months with Muslims of all categories condemning the letter.

The Propagation of Islam

A primary goal of all Muslim organizations is to strengthen and propagate Islam by building Muslim schools, mosques, and madrasas and by demanding that Islamic studies be included in the curriculum of government schools. To raise money for these purposes, Muslim leaders, including assistant ministers and the chief qadi, periodically organize harambe.[12] Muslims of Asian origin, whose economic situation is better than that of African Muslims, are among the chief donors. Representatives of Muslim countries such as Kuwait, Saudi Arabia, Abu Dhabi, Egypt, Libya, Pakistan, and Iran also sometimes make contributions, both to strengthen the Muslim community and the Islamic faith and also to counterbalance Israel's activities. Contributions by Supkem or other Muslim organizations, or by visiting Muslims from other countries, are highlighted in the press (see Chapter 11).

Among other activities to strengthen and propagate Islam, the journal *Nurul-Islam*, published in Nairobi, collects information on the position of Muslims in Kenya and around the world and discusses Islamic issues. An organization called the Qur'an Dissemination Institute distributes tapes of readings from the Qur'an and lectures on Islam. Some shaikhs devote their time to conversion, especially among practitioners of traditional religions. Famous among these shaikhs are Khamis Ahmad Said and Muaalim Said bin Ahmad al-Qumari, both of Mombasa. They work primarily among the Giriama tribespeople, who live near the coastal strip. For illiterate converts to Islam, they present the *shahada* on a sheet for the convert to mark with his thumbprint (the shahada is the confession of faith that constitutes the first pillar of Islam). They also see to it that the convert undergoes circumcision in the hospital, and they take care of him financially until he recovers.[13]

Conversion is also carried out during festivals and colorful processions such as 'Id al-Fitr and the Maulidi. During the 'Id al-Fitr celebrations in Lamu in 1994, for example, about 2,000 goats were slaughtered, worth 3.4 million shillings and contributed by Muslim welfare organizations. On the same occasion, dozens of worshipers of traditional religions converted to Islam and took part in the feast and festivities. In the same year, there were about 500 new converts in the town of Isiolo alone.[14] (In Uganda and Tanzania as well, many people convert to Islam during the Maulidi celebrations.) Non-Muslims who come to these festivities are impressed by the dancing, singing, and enthusiasm of the believers and by the spirit of solidarity, and they often convert. Participation also enables them to enjoy the free delicacies that are provided as well as the rice, cloth, clothing, and household utensils that embassies and Muslim businesses contribute.

6

Religious, Political, and Personal Divisions

Although there are factors that strengthen Muslim solidarity, religious, political, ethnic, and personal divisions among the Muslims weaken their overall position. Muslim leaders are well aware of this, and periodically they warn of the danger posed by fractiousness and emphasize the need to adopt a unified stance vis-à-vis the authorities.[1] But these warnings have had little influence, and the divisions persist and even continue to grow. Only in specific cases, when an outside danger is perceived as threatening all Muslims and hindering the expansion of Islam—such as the case of Salman Rushdie's book or of hurtful statements by Christians or the government—do the Muslims display solidarity (see Chapter 10). The large number of Muslim organizations reflects the sharpness of the divisions. Religious differences are often connected to personal competition for leadership.

On the other hand, in Uganda, especially before independence, personal and religious differences were not as divisive, because there was one recognized leader who had the prestige of coming from the royal family of Buganda and could rally around him most of the Muslims. Such were Prince Nuhu Mbogo, brother of King Mutesa I, and after him, from 1921, the prince's son Badru Kakungulu. In Kenya, the Muslims did not have such strong local leaders with traditional prestige and authority. Kenya's Muslim leaders are aware of this and take every opportunity to point out that their community lacks "proper leadership."[2]

Religious Differences

One of the problems that continue to cause serious religious disagreement among the Muslims concerns when to set the time for the start of the Ramadan fast and when to declare its end (marked by 'Id al-Fitr). This problem, which also exists in Uganda, Tanzania, and elsewhere, has been particularly pronounced in Kenya and further exacerbated by personal differences.

In the colonial period, the British recognized the chief qadi as the sole authority for deciding the times for the onset and termination of Ramadan. He did this according to the sighting of the moon, and the Muslims usually accepted his ruling. There were, however, a few groups that went according to the calendar and celebrated the festival on another day. But the differences of opinion were not serious and did not disturb the Muslim community or the authorities.

After independence, the Muslims reiterated their request that 'Id al-Fitr and 'Id al-Hajj be recognized as national holidays. As we have seen, their request was finally granted by President Jomo Kenyatta in 1971, but only with regard to 'Id al-Fitr, and this was in the framework of Kenyatta's policy of making certain concessions to the Muslims to allay their feelings of discrimination. As in the colonial period, the chief qadi was granted exclusive authority to determine the timing of the Ramadan fast and the feast of 'Id al-Fitr, according to the sighting of the moon.

The making of 'Id al-Fitr into a national public holiday not only benefited the Muslims but also caused discord and, ultimately, nationwide divisions. The government contended that the whole nation could not wait for the announcement of the date of the festival only after the sighting of the moon, because members of other faiths in factories, government offices, and schools needed to know a reasonable time in advance when the holiday would occur in order to adequately prepare for it.

Indeed, immediately after President Kenyatta announced his decision about "Id Day" there was a debate on the subject in parliament. Toward the end of Ramadan, on 17 November 1971, the assistant minister in the president's office, a Christian named Kamwithi Munyi, announced to parliament that after the chief qadi had decided on the onset of Ramadan according to the sighting of the moon, the public holiday of 'Id al-Fitr would be set for twenty-nine to thirty days after that, with no connection to the actual sighting of the next new moon. After consultations with the chief qadi, it was decided that the festival and the holiday would fall that year on 20 November 1971. The assistant minister added that if the moon was sighted before or after that date, the Muslims could receive an extra day's holiday from their employers on that day, so that they could fulfill their religious obligations. He stressed that the whole nation was now affected by the issue, not only the Muslims.[3]

Several Muslim members of parliament objected to this ruling, claiming that it went against Islam and even contradicted what had been published in the official gazette. But the government did not alter its decision. To forestall disputes in the coming years, the government agreed to set up a Hilal (moon) Committee, composed of several Muslim leaders, the chief qadi, and government representatives, to discuss the issue further. The committee decided to accept the government's line, that is, to determine in advance the date of 'Id al-Fitr but to allow Muslims an additional day's holiday according to the sighting of the moon. Thus it was agreed that the national public holiday would fall thirty-one days after the beginning of the Ramadan fast. At this time, the chief qadi was Shaikh Abdallah Saleh al-Farsy, who was accepted by most Muslims and considered very knowledgeable in Islam and Islamic law. The chief qadi would announce the start of the Ramadan fast after he had received evidence as to the sighting of the moon, and the government, in line with his decision and with that of the Hilal Committee, would declare the date of the holiday.

In 1982 Shaikh al-Farsy completed his term of office, and the government replaced him with Shaikh Nassor al-Nahdi. During his term, disputes among Muslims about the festival increased, and many did not accept the chief qadi's ruling about the dates of the Ramadan fast, so that 'Id al-Fitr was celebrated by Muslims on different days. The conflict worsened in the early 1990s after the appointment of Shaikh Ali Mohammed Shee as imam of the central mosque of Nairobi, the Jamia Mosque. Imam Shee was a strong personality, with independent and uncompromising views, and he sparked off further disputes among the Muslims during his tenure. He had no respect for the chief qadi, and relations between them were tense. In 1994, the imam decided to declare the end of the Ramadan fast and the beginning of 'Id al-Fitr himself, after—according to him—he had received telephone reports of the sighting of the new moon from reliable Somali Muslim witnesses from the northeastern part of the country and also from Mombasa and Zanzibar. The chief qadi rejected this decision and declared that the fast should continue until an announcement came from him. The Muslims in Kenya were confused, some of them heeding the imam and some the chief qadi. Shee took this opportunity to issue a strong attack on al-Nahdi. He claimed that the same Somali Muslims from the Northeastern Province had informed al-Nahdi earlier about their sighting of the moon but he had not taken them seriously; hence the Somali Muslims had turned to Imam Shee. The imam accused the chief qadi of prejudice against the Somalis, arrogance, and an unwillingness to cooperate with other leaders. According to Shee, the chief qadi's authority as defined by the Kenyan constitution encompassed issues of marriage, divorce, and inheritance but did not relate to the sighting of the moon and the end of the Ramadan fast.

But the main thrust of Shee's criticism was that al-Nahdi had not been elected by Muslims but had been appointed by the government. He was a government "stooge" who did as he was told and lacked the stature that the imams enjoyed among the Muslims. He added that the current chief qadi could not lead the Muslims like his well-respected predecessor, al-Farsy. Moreover, the arrogant al-Nahdi did not consult with imams and learned Muslims and acted arbitrarily.[4] Even in areas that were under his jurisdiction, such as marriage and divorce, al-Nahdi dragged his feet.[5]

Even some of the leaders of Supkem expressed dissatisfaction with al-Nahdi's performance. Fatma Hyder, for example, who was serving as director of women's affairs, criticized al-Nahdi during a seminar in 1994 in Nairobi. According to her, the chief qadi had to be an expert in Muslim law and acceptable to most of the Muslims, whereas al-Nahdi was a political appointee who lacked the necessary qualifications; she added that even the regional qadis he had appointed were not well versed in Islamic law. She demanded that the Muslim community have a say in the chief qadi's appointment.[6]

In 1995, too, the Muslims celebrated 'Id al-Fitr on different dates, and Shee's attacks on the chief qadi intensified. Al-Nahdi's supporters, for their part, criticized Supkem, claiming that it was not doing enough to find a solution to the Muslim dispute. In response, Supkem assembled about ninety religious leaders to try to settle both matters, that is, 'Id al-Fitr and the chief qadi's role. The assembly set up a body called Majlis al-'Ulamaa (the Council of Religious Leaders), the fifteen members of which were assigned to study the issues from every angle and to propose solutions. A well-known shaikh, Ustath Harith Swalih, was elected chairman of Majlis, Imam Ali Shee was appointed his deputy, and Ahmad Muhammad Msallam of the Saudi embassy was designated as secretary of the council. The Majlis was authorized to publish rulings (*fatwa*) "on every issue that concerns Muslims including religious, social, economic, political and cultural matters," and to consult with the government on such matters. A respected guest at this assembly was the Kuwaiti ambassador, Muhmad Said Yusuf al-Badr, who promised to work to strengthen Supkem and stipulated that from now on all requests to his country for assistance must come through that organization.[7]

The chief qadi's supporters, especially on the coast, saw in the Majlis assembly and, particularly, Imam Shee's senior position an infringement on al-Nahdi's authority and a successful move to weaken him. In particular, they feared Shee's increasing influence over Supkem. In any case, it seems that even the Majlis was unable to bridge the differences over either 'Id al-Fitr or the chief qadi's position. During 1996, Shee's supporters repeatedly stated that they did not recognize al-Nahdi's authority and called on him to resign so that the Muslims could choose an acceptable leader instead of a "government official" who was unable to unite the Muslim community, the ummah.[8] The qadi of Nairobi, Shaikh Hammed Kassim, formerly qadi of Mombasa, also joined in these demands. Some opponents of the chief qadi went even further in vilifying him, claiming that he had become senile and had lost his powers of judgment.[9]

Imam Shee's attitude toward Supkem was not consistent. At the start of 1996 he fiercely criticized the council, asserting that it was just an organization doing the government's bidding, demanding that its constitution be changed to make it more democratic and representative of Muslim opinion. He advanced a new idea, namely, that the leader should be chosen by the Muslims and not appointed by the government and that he should receive the title of khalif.[10] In opposing the chief qadi and Supkem, and claiming that they were government agents, the imam put himself in opposition to the government, though he did not join any of the opposition parties.

Supkem rejected all of the imam's proposals, and Ahmad Khalif, who had been its secretary-general since 1982 and was also at that time an assistant minister in the government, issued an announcement supporting the chief qadi and opposing demands for his resignation. Furthermore, he vigorously opposed Shee's call for the election of a khalif, declaring that there was no place for khalifs in Kenya, which was a secular state with different religious groups.[11] However, the secretary-general agreed that there was a need to augment the chief qadi's authority in matters of personal law, that is, marriage, divorce, and inheritance.[12] To set the dates of the Ramadan fast, Supkem would set up a special committee for sighting the moon that would operate throughout the country. The information would be conveyed immediately to Supkem, which would notify the Muslim public; thus, Supkem's position would be strengthened at the expense of the chief qadi. It is interesting that Supkem, which is under the government's influence and serves as its instrument for directing Muslim affairs according to its wishes, acted here to reduce the chief qadi's authority, if not for the benefit of opposition elements such as Shee then at least for the benefit of Supkem itself.

The secretary-general emphasized that he agreed with the request that Supkem's constitution be changed, but he argued that it should be done in a way that would ensure the organization a more central role in directing Muslim affairs in Kenya. He said that prior to the Supkem elections, which were scheduled for 1996, he would invite the chief qadi and the other 15 qadis, learned Muslims, intellectuals, and representatives of the different Muslim organizations to discuss the issues of altering the constitution, sighting the moon, and generally preventing disputes.[13]

As of the end of 1999, the qadis have not met and there has been no change in the constitution. Yet the elections to Supkem did take place on 26 May 1996. This time the elections reflected the conflicts between the opposition parties and the ruling Kanu Party since, with the introduction of the multiparty system, Supkem's members included Muslims belonging to the opposition parties. Ahmad Khalif was reelected as secretary-general. The chairman of Supkem's branch in the Somali area of Mandera was Muhammad Rashid, who belonged to the opposition party Ford-Asili. He and several other members claimed that the elections had been rigged, accused Khalif and his colleagues of turning Supkem into a tool of Kanu, and demanded new elections.[14] Here again divisions based on party or personal rivalries held sway among the Muslims.

Concerning 'Id al-Fitr, the current practice is that it falls thirty-one days after the start of the Ramadan fast, which is declared by the chief qadi. 'Id al-Hajj remains a holiday only for Muslims.[15] The government rejected Supkem's request that it be ascribed the task of proclaiming the start of 'Id al-Fitr.

As for Imam Shee's idea about a khalif, not only Supkem but other Muslim circles strongly rejected it. The Nairobi Muslim Youth Organization, for example, attacked Imam Shee for this proposal and asserted that he was influenced by Shi'a ideology, which gives wide religious and political authority to the religious leader—an undemocratic practice.[16]

Imam Shee's ideas about the relationship between Sunni and Shi'a also sparked controversy among the Muslims. In several sermons, the imam—who is a Sunni—called for a closer dialogue between Sunnis and Shiites and for establishing good relations with the Iranian embassy. On 26 February 1996, a congress of thirty-two learned Muslims was held under the sponsorship of the cultural attaché of the Iranian embassy, the main topic being "The Unity of Islam and the Enemies of Islamic Unity." Among the Iranian participants was Ayatollah Waiz Zade Khorasani, head of an organization called the Association for Closer Links Between Muslim Sects. The Iranian ambassador to Kenya, al-Haj Hamid Moayer, also participated. Imam Shee headed the Kenyan delegation. The congress is reported to have discussed means of Sunni-Shiite cooperation.[17] Even so, Imam Shee did not mince words during the congress, attacking the chief qadi and demanding his resignation and the election of a Muslim leader acceptable to all Muslims. This congress was undoubtedly part of the Iranian embassy's activities among Sunnis, especially in Nairobi and Mombasa, aimed at bringing the Sunnis closer to Shi'a or even converting them to it. These Iranian activities are carried out with the help of influential Muslim figures, and some Sunnis have in fact converted to Shi'a in the service of the Iranians (see Chapter 11).

Imam Shee's work on behalf of the Shiites was opposed by some Sunni leaders, sponsored apparently by Saudi Arabia, which did not look favorably on Iran's activities and Shee's position on various issues. Shee's tenure as imam of the Jamia Mosque in Nairobi was due to end in February 1995. Three months earlier, the committee in charge of the mosque announced that it had no intention of renewing his contract. It was claimed, among other things, that in his sermons he had blurred the distinctions between Sunni and Shi'a and, for political motives, had worked against the chief qadi. The imam was also accused of financial irregularities, opportunism, and inconsistency. Shee's opponents asserted that, on the one hand, he opposed the chief qadi, claiming that it was a political appointment, while on the other hand he had recently tried to curry favor with the Kanu Party because of his ambition to serve as chief qadi himself. As an example they cited a Friday sermon in which the imam had attacked the establishment, by Richard Leakey, of the opposition Safina Party. Shee reproved Leakey for using an Arabic name (*safina* means ship), to obtain Muslim support for getting his party registered according to law.[18] The government eventually agreed to recognize the party on the eve of the 1997 elections, in which it won three seats.

Imam Shee's opponents included Asian Sunnis, who are among the main contributors to the Jamia Mosque. Shee, for his part, accused the Asians of trying to appoint an Asian imam, or one of Arab origin, and raised the problem of the exclusion of Africans from key positions by wealthy non-Africans.[19] The imam's supporters pointed out that the Mosque Management Committee was in fact run by Punjabi Asians, who composed a majority of fourteen members as against six non-Asian members. According to them, the committee made decisions on a "racial basis" and awarded contracts for work at the mosque only to Asians; moreover, Asian religious functionaries were appointed to mosques throughout the country despite ignorance of Kiswahili or the local tribal language. These supporters of Shee maintained that the Asians' rancor toward him derived from his work to increase the African Muslims' consciousness of their rights. They pointed out that since Shee's appointment as the mosque's imam, the number of worshipers had increased to an average of 7,000 on Fridays and 2,000 on other days.[20] At one stage, a compromise was reached between the Mosque Management Committee and Shee, through the intervention of Assistant Minister Sharif Nassir and other Muslim MPs.[21]

Nevertheless, during the course of 1996, the continuing dispute between Shee's supporters and detractors led to violent clashes that called for police intervention. In May of that year, it was reported that Shee had agreed to accept compensation and resign and that he would be replaced as imam by Shaikh Khalfan Khamis.[22] But according to the opposition newspaper *The People* (17–23 May 1996), Shee had not resigned of his own free will but had been pressured to sign a letter of resignation by a police officer, at the request of the Mosque Committee.

Among the subjects that gave rise to disputes was the question of whether it was permissible to use drums (*tambour*) and other musical instruments in mosque services. The dispute was particularly intense among the Swahilis on the coast in the 1950s, when some Swahilis opposed the use of drums. The Muslims were further divided on the question of whether it was necessary to add the afternoon prayers (*salat az-zuhr*) to the Friday prayers (*jum'a*).[23] The issue of Friday prayers was also a cause of continuing dispute among Ugandan Muslims, and there it also involved political matters and a leadership struggle.[24]

Conservatives Versus Progressives

With the spread of secular education among the Muslims and the increase in the number of Muslims studying at universities in Kenya and abroad, serious conflict has developed between conservative circles—representing primarily the older generation—and progressive circles—representing primarily the younger generation. The conservatives want to preserve the traditional Islamic ways in education, family, and daily life; the progressives demand that Islam be adapted to modern life. Muslim religious leaders warn that young Muslims are slavishly imitating European practices in dress, behavior, food, drink, and entertainment, and are neglecting their religious duties of prayer and fasting.[25] Conservative religious leaders refer to changes and reforms as *bid'ah*, heretical. In contrast, those with progressive views argue that Islam and Muslims will suffer severely and continue to lag behind the rest of the population if they shut themselves off from the modern world.

Demands for modernization were made among Muslim groups on the coast even in colonial days. They were prominent in the teachings of Shaikh al-Amin al-Mazrui, who lived in the early part of the twentieth century and served as chief qadi of Kenya (he died in 1947). He was influenced by Egyptian reformists such as Muhamad Abdul Rashid Rida and al-Afgani.[26] Shaikh al-Amin al-Mazrui was among the Kenyan 'ulamaa who worked to introduce reforms into Islam and to eliminate customs that in their view contravened the spirit of Islam, such as saint worship and the elaborate and expensive celebration of the Maulidi. He demanded that modern, secular, and technical subjects be included in education and that Muslim women be provided an education. This did not reflect feelings of Muslim inferiority vis-à-vis Western-Christian civilization and a desire to imitate it, but rather a concern to enable Muslims to compete with Western technology. Shaikh al-Amin propagated these ideas in seminars, sermons, and articles. His ideas were more fully elaborated in the latter half of the century by some of his students, including Shaikh Abdallah Saleh al-Farsy who, as we have seen, served as chief qadi.

After independence, the demand for changes was raised by a number of writers, journalists, academics, and organizations, including student organizations. Education was a key point of contention; whereas the conservatives feared the Christian influence in the public schools and instead sent their children to Muslim schools (*chuo*)—where they memorized the Qur'an and concentrated on the study of religion—the progressives sought to provide their children a modern, technical education and also sent their daughters to school.

Prominent among the progressives in recent years has been the writer Faraj Dumila. In a pamphlet called "Is Kenya Culture on the Move?"[27] he entreats young Muslims to focus on acquiring a secular education. In various articles he warns about old-fashioned customs that are harmful to Muslims; for example, he complains that the Maulidi celebrations take place not only on the Prophet's birthday but also on various social and political occasions and that much money is wasted on food and drink. It would be better, he says, for the money to be invested in improving education and the condition of the family. Dumila demands changes in the position of the woman in the family. He calls for Muslim girls to receive a secular education, to be able to choose a professional career, to join women's organizations, and to take part in politics. He condemns the custom whereby parents arrange a marriage for their daughter. Furthermore, the wedding festivities last a week or more and entail a heavy financial burden on the family; he suggests, instead, giving the money to the young couple so that they can set up a home. Dumila asks for the abolition of some mourning ceremonies, such as the *matanga* and the *eda,* in which the family has to prepare lavish, expensive dishes for the guests. He severely criticizes conservative leaders for resisting change.[28]

Among the Muslim politicians who came into conflict with conservative religious leaders was Juma Boy, who served in the 1970s as secretary-general of the Central Organization of Trade Unions (COTU). He, too, called on young Muslims to acquire a secular, technical education and to take part in academic life. He censured the traditional Islamic system of education in which teachers are restricted to teaching the Qur'an, warning that they were helping to keep Muslims weak and backward. Not surprisingly, Juma Boy was fiercely attacked by religious leaders.[29] A similar opinion was voiced several years later by the minister of state in the president's office, Hussein Maalim Mohamed, who requested that young Muslims be encouraged to acquire a secular education, and accused conservative Muslims of wishing to preserve the system of education in the chuo and the houses of religious leaders and to limit education to the study of the Qur'an. He claimed that ignoring other subjects led to unemployment among the Muslims.[30]

At the meeting of the Muslim Education and Welfare Association (MEWA) in Mombasa in April 1994, sponsored by the Ford Foundation, several speakers addressed the issue, and academics such as Mohamed Bakari and Hassan Mwakimako warned against Muslim organizations that emphasize the building of madrasas and mosques while neglecting secular studies that could help young Muslims find work, not only as civil servants but in the liberal professions. They demanded that funds contributed within Kenya and from abroad be used to improve the standard of living in Muslim areas, for example, by drilling wells to supply clean water.[31]

An interesting and veteran organization that tries to introduce reforms into Islam is the Islahil Islamiya, or Society for Islamic Reformation (see Chapter 2). At a meeting in September 1994, the organization called for adapting Islamic law to the spirit of the times, thus arousing the ire of shaikhs and imams.[32] Supkem also reacted harshly, warning that the head of the organization, Mohamed Amana, and his colleagues were close to heresy.[33] This dispute clearly demonstrated the conflict between the two Muslim organizations and Supkem's desire to be the only decisionmaking body on such matters. Supkem also rejected Shaikh Amana's demand that the chief qadi be elected by a certified group of Muslims who would check that he had the necessary qualifications, thus enhancing his prestige.

Among the issues on which religious leaders opposed change were those related to family planning. The UN Conference on Population and Development, held in Cairo in September 1994 to deal with issues of birthrates, abortion, and family planning, aroused strong reactions among Kenyan shaikhs who opposed its decisions, especially on abortion and the equal distribution of inheritance between sons and daughters. One of the fiercest opponents was Imam Shee, who decried the conference even before it met and urged that it be boycotted.[34]

The Islamic law of inheritance was another issue on which educated Muslims in Kenya saw a need for reform. Thus, for example, a Muslim scholar named Mohamed Mbwana argued in an article that the law of inheritance should be adapted to the times and that, in light of the progress that had been made in woman's position in education and in society, girls should be given an equal part.[35]

There were also generational differences concerning the Maulidi celebrations, particularly in the Tana region, where the elders insisted that the ceremonies take place within the mosque, while the young people demanded they be held in the courtyard after prayers and include drums and other musical instruments. Younger Muslims' desire to share in the local Muslim leadership also contributed to this conflict.[36]

In the Swahili coastal area of Watamu north of Mombasa, disputes between Muslim groups arose in the 1980s and 1990s in which young Muslims played a significant part. Prominent among the groups were two that prayed in different mosques: the Swahili Islam, which was more conservative, celebrating the Maulidi extravagantly with songs praising the Prophet and supporting the sharif of the town of Lamu; and the Halali Suna, a reform movement that demanded greater equality among believers and opposed the hegemony of the sharifs. The two groups disagreed, among other things, about burial rites and about the method of sighting the moon, and they celebrated 'Id al-Fitr on different days. The second group had many outside supporters.[37]

The Tabligh movement, which came to Kenya from Pakistan in 1990 and established branches in Nairobi, Mombasa, and Malindi, also reached Watamu. Calling for Muslim unification, it worked to bridge the gaps between the two groups and succeeded to a large extent. The Tabligh group in Watamu numbered no more than twenty to thirty people. The men grew beards, wore long gowns, and always held prayer beads as they walked; the women wore robes that covered their whole bodies and veils over their faces—attire that was much more modest than the *buibui,* the black gown and veil worn by Swahili women on the coast.

The Tabligh movement succeeded especially among the youth, who saw it as an invigorating alternative to the existing situation. After Watamu became a tourist center and many hotels were built there, the drinking of alcohol and even drug use became widespread in the area. Opposed to the frequenting of bars, the youth of Tabligh set fire in 1994 to a number of places where alcoholic drinks were sold, and some of their members were arrested by the police. They opposed the appropriation of land and its allotment to wealthy individuals from outside the region, and they requested assistance to local people for setting up businesses. Young men were also attracted to this movement because it offered financial help to those willing to devote all their time to studying the Qur'an. This new movement demanded extreme meticulousness in religious law, but unlike the IPK, which arose at the same time in Mombasa, it was more wary about coming into conflict with the authorities. (The Tabligh movement also came to Uganda, but there it was more violent and did come into conflict with the authorities; it was declared illegal in 1994.)

In recent years, progressive and educated Muslims have become increasingly disappointed with the existing Muslim leadership in Kenya, particularly Supkem and the chief qadi, whom they regard as failing to fulfill their main task of improving the education and economic situation of the Muslims. This disappointment came to a head at the Islamic congress organized by MEWA in April 1994 in Mombasa. In his speech, a young University of Nairobi lecturer, Hassan Mwakimako, reiterated the complaints against the current Muslim establishment. He characterized Supkem as a government agent that carried out the will of the regime and was not concerned about Muslims' real interests. He advocated making the IPK a legal political party and attacked Supkem for opposing this party just as the government did. In general, Mwakimako asserted, Supkem in its present form could not unite the fractious Muslim community. Other speakers made similar claims, also criticizing Muslim parliamentarians (members of Kanu) for caring only about their seats and toadying to the government at the expense of Muslim interests.[38]

Modern 'Ulamaa Versus Traditional 'Ulamaa

An interesting article by Mohamed Bakari, "The New 'Ulamaa in Kenya,"[39] describes the emergence of the modern 'ulamaa in Kenya, especially in the 1960s and 1970s, as reflecting both the influence of Shaikh al-Amin al-Mazrui and the fact that Muslim students had begun receiving grants to study in universities in Arab and Islamic countries. There they broadened their education and were exposed to new ideas. On their return to Kenya they expressed opposition to the traditional Islamic system of education, at the head of which were mostly shaikhs of Hadramaut origin. Bakari gives some examples of traditional and modern shaikhs, of which I mention only a few here.

Prominent among the moderns was Muhammad Salum Badamana, a lecturer in the Faculty of Veterinary Medicine at Nairobi University. He was born in Lamu in 1940 and, as was customary, received his Islamic education in the chuo and in the al-Riyadha madrasa. He then decided to study agriculture at the University of Egerton in Kenya, after which he left to study veterinary medicine at the University of Musul in Iraq. He received his doctorate in veterinary medicine from the University of Nairobi, then began to concentrate on Islamic issues. He organized seminars on Islam with the cooperation of Muslim organizations and broadcast programs on Islam on Kenya radio in which he advocated, in the spirit of Shaikh al-Amin al-Mazrui, such reforms as introducing modern technical studies into Islamic education and promoting the status of women.

Another instance of a shaikh who acquired a modern education was Hamid Mohammad Kassim, who served as qadi of Lamu. Shaikh Kassim went to universities in Iraq, Saudi Arabia, and Nigeria and studied physics as well as Islam. In his lectures and sermons, he too opposed the traditional Islamic system of education of the Hadramaut school and asked for modern studies to be introduced, for girls to be educated, and for other changes to be made.

Indeed, all of the modern 'ulamaa mentioned in Bakari's article, after studying Islam in Kenya, went abroad to study and were influenced by modern ideas. On their return, they demanded changes in education and in the role of Muslim women and opposed customs such as saint worship and extravagant Maulidi celebrations. These 'ulamaa came into conflict, of course, with the traditional 'ulamaa from the Hadramaut madrasas (whom Bakari mentions in detail in his article), such as Said Ali Badawi, who was appointed chief qadi for a short period in 1947 after the death of Shaikh al-Amin, and Said Ali's brother, Sharif Khitami, a more aggressive opponent of modernism. Among other things, Khitami attacked Shaikh al-Farsy and described him as a foreigner who had come to Kenya to sow divisions in the Muslim community.

Africans Versus Arabs

A political-ethnic division that damaged Muslim solidarity as early as the precolonial period was that between Arab Muslims who saw themselves as being of "pure" Arab origin, and African Muslims, that is, African tribespeople who had converted to Islam. For the Swahilis, who had mixed Arab and African blood, it was always difficult to define themselves as belonging to either of these two groups.[40] In the period of Omani rule in Zanzibar and on the East African coast in the nineteenth century, the Arabs treated the Swahilis as racially inferior to them, like the local Africans, and the administration on the coastal strip was solely in Arab hands.

In the 1880s, with the growth of competition between Germany and Britain over spheres of influence in East Africa, changes occurred in the position of the sultan of Zanzibar and in that of the local Arab rulers in the coastal region, such as the Mazrui family from Oman, which in fact ruled several areas where the sultan's sovereignty was only nominal. In October 1886, the Anglo-German agreement on the division of influence in East Africa was signed, in which it was stipulated that the sultan would retain control of Zanzibar, Pemba, and a strip of 10 miles on the coast from Muingani in the south to Kipini in the north. In May 1887, William Mackinnon received from the sultan a concession for his company, the British East Africa Association (afterward called the Imperial British East Africa Company, IBEA), to administer and develop the coast under the sultan's sovereignty.

The IBEA did not manage to hold its ground and suffered financial losses, partly because of revolts by local Arab rulers and partly because of the Mazruis, who opposed European penetration. The British government decided to replace the trading company and on 1 July 1895 declared the establishment of the East Africa Protectorate. As commissioner of the Protectorate they appointed Arthur Harding, who was also consul general of Zanzibar. This meant that, under his leadership, the protectorate was again run from Zanzibar. In 1895–1896, Harding succeeded in finally crushing the rebellious Mazruis and thereby achieved full British control of the coast, ending local Arab ambitions of hegemony. Even so, the special position of the Arabs and the Swahilis was preserved under the new administration, for several reasons:

- Harding had a positive attitude toward Islam and Muslims. Having served in the past in several Muslim capitals, including Cairo and Istanbul, he had an understanding and sympathy for Muslims that are also evident in his writings.[41] Immediately after the suppression of the revolts, he showed a readiness to be considerate toward the Muslims and the traditional leadership. He tried to allay Muslim suspicions that Christian missionaries active on the coast would damage their religion and economy by attempting to free slaves who worked on their farms. Immediately after the declaration of the protectorate, Harding called a meeting in which he announced to the Muslim dignitaries that Islam would remain the local religion, shari'a law would be kept, and traditional leaders and functionaries would continue in their posts. The current situation concerning slaves would also be maintained, that is, slavery would not be completely banned.[42]

- Because of divisions among them, a large proportion of Arabs and Swahilis on the coast cooperated with the British in putting down the revolts, and it was necessary to reward them.
- For Harding, in setting up a new administration it was convenient to rely on the experience and knowledge of the Arabs and the Swahilis in the areas of administration, jurisdiction, and communications, especially because they were literate and knew the local conditions well.

Harding, then, tried to integrate the traditional Muslim administration and the British administration. Officers of the sultan such as the *liwali*, the *akida*, the *mudiir*, the qadi, and other functionaries became officers of the British government. The Arabs and the Swahilis now had to regard the British as their masters instead of the sultan. At the same time, a double administration was created, Arab alongside European. The protectorate was divided into four provinces, three of which were on the coast, which shows the importance that the British assigned the coast at the beginning of the protectorate. The 10-mile-long coastal strip was called Sayyidieh (the province of the sayyid, that is, the sultan), and the British area extended from Vanga in the south to Kipini in the north. At the head of every province was a British subcommissioner. In Mombasa and other important centers, Harding appointed Arab liwalis with judicial and administrative authority over the non-European residents; they acted as intermediaries between the British and the populace. Harding also appointed qadis in each province and gave them judicial authority in religious and personal matters such as marriage, divorce, and inheritance. In 1897, he also appointed a chief qadi for the whole coastal area, with his center in Mombasa, to judge appeals that came from the qadis' courts. The first chief qadi was Sherif Abdul Rahman bin Ahmad, who had earlier been the qadi for the Siu region.

It is significant that already, at the start of setting up their administration, the British differentiated between Arabs and Swahilis. The latter generally were given less senior posts than the former, and this further strengthened Swahili feelings of being discriminated against by the British and the Arabs.

Furthermore, during the colonial period, the British gave the coastal strip, which they had inherited from the sultan, a special status within Kenya, and the Omani policy of granting citizens' rights according to their ethnic origin was continued, except that now the Europeans were the superior race, and after them the Arabs and Swahilis, who were small in number but whom the British regarded as more "civilized." At the bottom of the ladder were the black Africans, most of whom followed traditional religious beliefs and who formed the majority in the area under British rule. There were local Arab leaders who decided which Muslims were counted as Arabs and which as Africans, the main problem being to determine in which category the Swahilis belonged. Generally speaking, the Arabs saw the Swahilis as Africans, whereas the Africans regarded them as Arabs. Schools too were separate, and Swahilis who were defined as African could not study in Arab schools. Hyder Kindy, a leading Swahili personality both in the colonial period and during independence, dwells in his book bitterly and at length on the Arabs' humiliating attitude toward the Swahilis. He recounts, among other things, how Arabs were angry at him because he took a name that could give the impression that he was an Arab.[43] Kindy also decries the fact that Arabs married Swahili women but opposed Swahilis marrying Arab women. When Kindy himself married an Arab woman against her father's wishes, infuriated Arabs considered it "a disgrace and shame."[44] In contrast to Kindy, who was proud of his Swahili origins, many Swahilis tried to be regarded as Arabs so that they could enjoy more rights.

The two groups, Arabs and Swahilis, had separate organizations. In 1927, Swahili leaders founded the Afro-Arab Association; it was replaced in the 1950s by a more active body called the Afro-Asian Youth League, whose chief demands were that Swahilis be granted rights to vote for the institutions representing them and that their educational system be improved.[45] The same Swahilis, when they were employed by the British outside the coastal strip within Kenya—for example, as clerks in Nairobi or as workers in military camps, tended to treat the black Africans with scorn. Swahilis were, in fact, the first residents of Nairobi, and until 1920 they formed a majority there. Even African tribespeople, such as the Kikuyu and the Kamba, who came to Nairobi and converted to Islam, were not considered equals by the Swahilis. They called them Mahaji in a pejorative sense (Mahaji comes from hajj, i.e., those who made the pilgrimage to Islam). In contrast, they nicknamed themselves Wazaliwa (those who were born Muslims). There were even separate mosques for African Muslims and Swahilis; the Africans' mosques were called tribal mosques. The Swahilis even organized separate Maulidi celebrations.

The British also treated the Swahilis as superior to Africans who had converted to Islam. They regarded African Muslims as people who had been "detribalized" and hence did not give them land in the regions of the tribes from which they had come.[46] Just as the Arabs' attitude toward the Swahilis poisoned the atmosphere between them, so the Swahilis' attitude toward the African Muslims had a negative influence that manifested itself after independence.

The differentiation between Swahilis and Africans became even more conspicuous in the 1950s, when there was a change in the political position of the former. In 1952, the Swahilis in Mombasa, nicknamed "the Twelve Tribes," were officially recognized as Arabs, and in the local elections of 1957 and 1961, they were registered as Arabs and distinguished from the Africans. During the same period, there were already thoughts about approaching independence, and the Swahilis faced a dilemma—whether, with the end of colonialism, to identify themselves as Arabs in their political demands or to support the black Africans. This was a difficult problem for them because, on the one hand, they did not enjoy the full support of the Arabs and, on the other, they were not liked by the African leaders, especially the Christians among them. This dilemma intensified on the eve of independence, when the fate of the coastal strip became the main political issue for its inhabitants.

It should be pointed out that Kenya's coastal strip was run by the British as a protectorate in which the sultan had at least some formal authority, and the red flag of Zanzibar flew next to the British flag. Residents of the coastal strip were considered "British protected persons." The inland territory of Kenya was regarded as a colony, and its inhabitants were "British subjects." These differences in status caused problems on the eve of independence. The Arabs and some of the Swahilis supported *mwambao,* that is, the separation of the entire Coast Province from Kenya and its unification with Zanzibar, so that the inhabitants' special rights would be preserved. They formed the Coastal Peoples Party, which rejected the 1895 agreement between the British and the sultan and contended that, once the British conquerors left the region, it should revert to its former owners. Another group of Swahilis who in general supported mwambao used this slogan as a bargaining chip to ensure the rights of the minority in independent Kenya. They were prepared to settle for autonomy for the entire Coast Province, including the 10-mile area outside the strip. In contrast to these two groups, there was a group of conservative and less militant Swahilis who founded the Coastal League, which would have settled for autonomy for the coastal strip alone. The request common to all of these groups was to receive a special status on the coast.[47] Black Africans, including Christians, Muslims, and animists, wanted the Coast Province to become an integral part of Kenya and were joined in this by the Twelve Tribes.[48]

On the eve of independence, the British government decided to send to Kenya Sir James Robertson, formerly governor-general of Nigeria, to check the situation on the spot and recommend to the British government and to the sultan of Zanzibar what changes should be made in the 1895 agreement that had been signed between them concerning the coastal strip. Robertson found that the coastal strip was not economically viable on its own and that Mombasa was an essential port for Kenya and its western neighbors, Uganda and Rwanda. He stressed that, despite the different status of the coast, it had been governed for a long time as part of Kenya, and therefore he recommended that the coastal strip be annexed to Kenya and that the sultan receive suitable compensation for it. He also recommended that Kenya's new constitution include guarantees of human rights and freedom of religion, including the Muslims' right to follow shari'a law in matters of religion and personal status, and that in independent Kenya the shari'a courts administered by qadis continue to function. In 1963, the British government and the sultan of Zanzibar signed an agreement endorsing Robertson's recommendations. The British repeatedly promised the sultan that the chief qadi's authority and the shari'a courts would be preserved and would continue to govern matters of personal status among Muslims even after independence. In the case of a lawsuit between a Muslim and a non-Muslim, the general law would apply. Following this, the sultan agreed to waive all of his authority over the coastal strip.

At the negotiations on the constitution between the Kenyans and the British in London, there were also representatives of a political movement on the coast calling itself the Mwambao United Front ("mwambao" means coast in Kiswahili). They emphasized again and again that the Muslim inhabitants of the coast were a "distinct social group" and should be granted autonomy or the option of seceding from Kenya and establishing a separate state, or "rejoining" Zanzibar.[49]

In 1963, when Kenya became independent, the coast's hopes for a separation or autonomy vanished, although they reemerged from time to time in different forms. Independent Kenya abolished the traditional administrative posts held by Muslims, such as the liwali, the akida, and the mudiir, which were considered remnants of the Zanzibar sultanate. Religious posts, such as the chief qadi and the other qadis and religious authorities, were maintained, although attempts were made to change them, which caused agitation among the Muslims.

The Mwambao affair and the coastal Muslims' aspiration to secede from Kenya fostered government suspicions of the Muslims, which entered deeply into the hearts of the Christian African leadership and are still felt today. The distrust between the two sides is mutual, the Muslims feeling that the regime discriminates against them and considers them second-class citizens. This has negative practical ramifications, which is discussed later.

The ethnic-political division between Arabs and Swahilis who identified with them on the one side, and African tribespeople who had converted to Islam and Swahilis who identified with them on the other, continued after independence and still exists, even if the topics of disagreement have changed somewhat. No serious practical attempts are being made today to secede from Kenya. The dispute between the two groups concerns, rather, leadership issues and relationships with Arab countries.

In the 1960s, 1970s, and 1980s, the Arab-Swahili group, whose orientation in the Middle East conflict was pro-Arab, had as its leaders assistant ministers, Mohamed Jehazi and Shaikh Salim Balala, and later Sharif Nassir, assistant minister and chairman of the Mombasa branch of Kanu. These leaders were supported by funds received from Arab countries. Among the leaders of the African-Swahili group were Abdallah Mwidau (an MP who served in the 1970s as mayor of Mombasa) and Hyder Kindy. The dispute was personal and came to the fore during elections to the city government of Mombasa, to parliament, and to the leadership of Kanu's branch on the coast. The African-Swahili group objected to the intervention of Arab countries and demanded that Kenyan Muslims not intervene in the Middle East conflict. Arab support for the Arab-Swahili group, involving both funding and activities, was very pronounced during the 1960s and 1970s and came especially from Egypt, Saudi Arabia, and the Gulf oil-producing states such as Kuwait and Abu Dhabi; it later in the 1970s and 1980s, came from Libya. Leaders of this group were invited to visit Egypt and other Arab states, and through them funds and grants flowed in, with the purpose of garnering support for the Arab countries (see Chapter 11).

The rivalry between the two groups influenced Muslim attitudes toward Israel. The African-Swahili group, headed by Hyder Kindy and Abdallah Mwidau, maintained neutrality toward the Middle East conflict and held contacts with the Israeli embassy in Nairobi and with the local Jewish community. The group came out against anti-Israeli declarations and stressed that the Arab-Israeli conflict was not a conflict between Judaism and the Islamic world. This group even cooperated with the Jewish community in advancing education by means of the creation of a joint fund, the African Muslim-Jewish Education Fund (AMJEF), which distributed scholarships to Muslim students. African Muslim personalities such as Juma Boy, head of the trade unions, and Ibrahim Mwaruwa, a Kanu leader in Mombasa, also criticized the Arab countries' direct support for Muslim political leaders and requested that all Arab aid pass through the government.

Muslims of African origin have also charged that most of the top religious posts, such as qadis and imams, are given to Muslims of Arab extraction. An organization called the Baladia Muslim Mission issued an announcement to the press expressing exasperation at the situation and warning that if it continued, Islam would be weakened by division and would lose supporters.[50] In 1994, in the Kibwezi area where the Kamba tribe lives, a dispute broke out between Muslim tribespeople and Muslims of Arab and Asian origin. The Africans complained that the Arabs discriminated against them because of their skin color and prevented them from appointing an imam to the main mosque in the area, the Zahir Mosque, on the grounds that the Africans were not sufficiently conversant in Islam.[51]

As we have seen, there have been similar disputes in recent years between the imam of the Jamia Mosque in Nairobi, Ali Shee, and his non-African Muslim opponents, who tried to get him removed from his post. From time to time, Shee's followers called on the Muslim Arab embassies not to intervene, hoping to avoid a deepening of the ethnic divide among the Muslims. The vice-chairman of the Mosque Management Committee, Maulidi Jasho, issued a statement in July 1994 in which he asserted that attempts to remove the imam only intensified the breach between Muslims of African origin and those of Arab origin.[52]

The African-Arab division was illustrated more vividly in recent years in the violent conflict between supporters of the IPK, which the government refused to recognize, and its opponents from the United Muslims of Africa (UMA) organization, which is described below. Here it will suffice to give one striking example, from the by-elections to parliament in the constituency of Kisauni in Mombasa, held in 1993. There were two contenders for this seat: Rashid Mzee, from the opposition Ford-Kenya Party, who was supported by Shaikh Khalid Balala, leader of the IPK; and Emmanual Maitha, from the ruling

Kanu Party. Rashid Mzee had the votes of the Muslims who were members of the IPK and of the Arabs, whereas Maitha received the support of the African tribespeople known as Mijikenda and of the African Muslims. In his election propaganda, Maitha contended that Rashid Mzee represented the Muslims of Arab origin. Mzee won the election, but the conflict between the two candidates again reflected the poor relations between the two camps.

The ethnic divide among the Muslims can also be seen in the differences between the Arab and Swahili residents of the coastal strip and Muslim converts from African ethnic groups living in the other part of the Coast Province (the Mijikenda) such as the Giriama, the Taita, and the Pokomo. The latter group has contended that jobs are given mainly to Muslims living on the coastal strip. Specifically, it is claimed that the influential assistant minister Sharif Nassir, who is of Arab origin, allocates jobs primarily to Arab and Swahili residents of the coastal strip, ignoring members of African ethnic groups, both Muslim and non-Muslim. In an interview, Reuven Tsuma, a Christian and member of one of the Mijikenda tribes and an active member of the ruling party, stated that he was organizing a pressure group within Kanu to demand that the government recognize the importance of the Mijikenda and give them senior posts in the government as well.[53]

Sunnis Versus Shiites

As we have noted, the number of Shiite Muslims in Kenya is small. Until recent years they were not a party to disputes because of their marginal position. With the growth of Iranian political and religious activities in Kenya, however, differences arose between Sunnis who opposed the propagation of Shi'a and those who changed their religion and became Shiites or were Shiites by birth. Between these two extremes were shaikhs, such as Ali Shee, who tried to moderate between the Sunnis and the Shiites.

One of the religious leaders who worked against Shi'a and considered it a heresy was Shaikh Ahmad Msallam. He translated from Arabic to Kiswahili books condemning Shi'a and was helped to publish them by a Saudi Arabian organization in Kenya called Dar al-Iftah.[54] Badamana, who studied in Iraq and came into contact with Shiites, also played an important role in the fight against Shiite influence. In lectures throughout the country he warned that Shi'a contravened Islam, and he stressed among other things that Shi'a opposed the first three khalifs, Abu Bakir, Omar, and Othman. He attacked Muslims who accepted Shi'a, charging that they did it for financial gain.

His chief opponent was Shaikh Abdullahi Nasr, a Shiite convert from Sunni. He worked to disseminate Shi'a throughout Kenya with lectures and the publication of pamphlets explaining the origin of Shi'a and emphasizing that it did not contradict Islam. He stressed that he regarded Sunnis and Shiites as brothers in one religion and that they should work together. His ideology, as expressed in his lectures, was disseminated by means of cassettes that were sold throughout East Africa.[55]

Another interesting Muslim figure who moved from Sunni to Shi'a is Ahmad Khatib. Born in Lamu in 1949, he studied Islam in Zanzibar and Khartoum, then went to Paris to study economics. There he befriended pro-Khomeini Iranian students and became a Shiite. When Khomeini returned to Teheran, he joined his entourage. He later returned to Paris but was expelled to Kenya on suspicion of activities against anti-Khomeini dissidents. On his return to Kenya he was arrested for a short period and interrogated. Today he lectures on Islam in various places in Kenya. (For more on Iranian activities in Kenya, see Chapter 11.)

Personal Disputes Among the Muslim Leadership: The Activities of Sharif Nassir

An especially serious split in the Muslim leadership derives from the rivalry between Muslim personalities on the coastal strip, particularly in Mombasa. The conflict concerns the Muslim leadership and its representation in government and the fierce competition to win seats in parliament. During President Moi's tenure, the dispute has worsened as Sharif Nassir has gained prominence; he today stands at the center of the political tensions among the Muslim leadership. Nassir, of Arab origin, became extremely close to Moi when, immediately after President Kenyatta's death in August 1978, he expressed his fervent and unequivocal support for the election of Moi, then vice-president, to the presidency. At that time a number of candidates were competing for the top post; Nassir, who was already a leading figure in Kanu, succeeded in recruiting many coastal Muslims to support Moi. When Moi was elected president, he appointed as assistant minister Nassir, who was also chairman of Kanu's branch in Mombasa.

Since then, Nassir's political activities have displayed certain characteristics. For one, he expresses unequivocal support for President

Moi in his public statements. Because of his closeness to Moi, and also because of his organizational abilities and wealth (he has managed to collect money from local Muslims and from Arab countries), he has been able to organize mass gatherings in honor of President Moi whenever he visits Mombasa. In his speeches, Nassir exhorts his listeners to be loyal to the president and to follow his Nyayo ideology. During the opposition's struggle for the multiparty system, Nasser supported the president in opposing it, using all sorts of arguments to persuade his audience that such a system was not suitable for Kenya. Because of his unswerving loyalty to the president, he acquired the nickname of "President Moi's watchdog."[56]

Nassir also shows an uncompromising ambition to be the only well-known Muslim political leader in Mombasa and the coastal region and to be the decisive influence in the coastal branch of the party, the municipality, and the trade unions. He fights hard and with all the means at his disposal against anyone he regards as a rival, and in the process he often exploits his government connections. He works just as hard to get his supporters into parliament and into key positions in the government and in public institutions. In the 1979 elections to parliament, for example, Nassir ran against Mohamed Jehazi (who was married to the daughter of Hyder Kindy), a well-known coastal leader who had served as assistant minister since the early 1970s. Nassir managed to defeat him and to replace him as representative of the Mombasa-Central constituency. It should be noted that Mombasa has four seats in parliament and, up until the first multiparty elections in December 1992, they were all won by Kanu, the only party, after intra-Kanu contests. Since then, Nassir has succeeded in retaining the Mombasa-Central seat.

Similarly, when Kassim Mwamazandi, assistant minister of foreign affairs, was elected in April 1979 as chairman of Supkem, Nassir feared that Mwamazandi would amass too much influence and therefore worked against him. Nassir declared that it was impossible for someone involved in politics as an MP to lead an organization that was essentially religious. There was an ongoing dispute between the two rivals, in which Mwamazandi accused Nassir, among other things, of receiving money from Arab countries to use against his competitors.[57]

Nassir waged a particularly cruel and bitter struggle against his rival Abdallah Ndovo Mwidau, who served in the 1970s as mayor of Mombasa and later was elected to parliament for the constituency of Mombasa-South. Mwidau, a Swahili and a well-mannered, educated man, acquired great influence among the Swahilis in Mombasa. Nassir feared his influence and regarded him as a rival. In the framework of the historic conflict between Arab Swahilis (those who regarded themselves as Arabs) and African Swahilis, Mwidau considered himself first and foremost an African and expressed strong opposition to Arab countries' involvement in Muslim affairs in Kenya, particularly the intensive Libyan activity in the 1970s aimed especially against Israel. Mwidau, for his part, like Hyder Kindy, did not hesitate to cooperate with Kenya's Jewish community, which he respected and whose support he sought for the advancement of educational institutions in Mombasa. Nassir, who at that time was working for the Libyans and expressing anti-Israeli views, succeeded in obtaining the president's support in his fight against Mwidau. On Moi's orders, Mwidau was fired from the company that employed him in Mombasa, which seriously damaged his livelihood.[58] To Nassir's chagrin, however, Mwidau managed to be repeatedly reelected to parliament as representative of Mombasa-South (until Mwidau's death in 1986).

Nassir also intervened in the Mombasa municipal elections, and here he came into conflict with the mayor and with the minister of local government in the 1980s, Charles Rubia.[59] Nassir's involvement in trade union affairs was criticized by Juma Boy, head of COTU, who called on Nassir not to intervene in this area and to cease trying to infiltrate his supporters into COTU.[60]

Nassir's activities also went beyond Mombasa. In Lamu, for the 1979 parliamentary elections, he worked against MP Abu Baker Mohamed Madhboti and supported his opponent Mazamil Omar. After Madhboti won, Nassir slandered him before President Moi, and Moi, on a visit to Lamu in October 1979, strongly criticized Madhboti and called him a "smuggler" and one who had bought votes. Madhboti was taken aback by this and hotly denied the accusations, finally managing to meet with Moi in order to prove his innocence.[61] It is interesting that Nassir also accused Madhboti of working for Israel against the Arab countries, a charge that Madhboti denied.

In the violent conflict that took place in Mombasa between the IPK and the UMA, Nassir also operated against the UMA leaders even though they supported the government. Nassir again feared that the UMA leaders might shunt him aside. In addition, the UMA opposed the Arabs and the Muslims of Arab extraction, of whom Nassir was one.

Nassir's never-ending battles against his opponents reached new heights in his conflict with one of the veteran Muslim political leaders on the coast, Said Hamed. Hamed, an active member of Kanu, was an MP representing Mombasa-North. In Kanu's internal elections in November 1992, before the parliamentary elections, Hamed lost his seat to another Kanu member; as compensation Moi appointed him ambassador to Saudi Arabia. When Hamed ended his term in Saudi Arabia early in 1996, he decided to oppose Sharif Nassir, whose protégé he had been, and to compete in the forthcoming 1997 elections for Nassir's seat in parliament representing Mombasa-Central. There was a fierce competition between the two, both of them trying to win the support of the president and party leaders. Nassir, despite his good connection with the president, was at that time in one of the worst crises of his political career. People such as the mayor of Mombasa (Ahmad Mwidani), African Swahilis, and Muslims from the Mijikenda supported Hamed, as did, apparently, leading government figures who were tired of Nassir's arrogance and intrigues.[62]

Nevertheless, Nassir's most dangerous rival in the 1990s was Rashid Sajad, like Nassir one of the president's favorites.[63] Sajad, an Asian Shiite, was a Mombasa-based tycoon and one of the big commodity traders. In 1993, President Moi appointed him to parliament, and he gradually became one of the most powerful persons on the coast; his task was to bring Kanu back from the reversal of the 1992 general elections. In those first multiparty elections, Kanu won only the Mombasa-Central constituency, where Nassir ran, out of the four Mombasa constituencies. The fact that Sajad had the confidence and favor of the president was again manifested early in 1994, when he was appointed chairman of the Kenya Port Authority. Although he was removed from this post a year later because of the port's deteriorating performance, his power and influence did not wane. He continued to be deeply involved in Mombasa politics, and it is no wonder that he clashed with Nassir. The Nassir-Sajad conflict was a conspicuous part of the IPK-UMA disputes during 1992–1994 (see Chapter 14).

Later, in an attempt to undermine Nassir's position, Sajad formed his own group of Kanu leaders while trying to keep to the background himself. Prominent among this group were Suleiman Shakombo, vice-chairman of Kanu's Mombasa branch and a perennial Nassir rival; Mohamed Jehazi, a prominent coastal leader; Emmanuel Maitha, an outspoken Kanu activist and one of the UMA's leaders; Rajab Sumba, a former mayor of Mombasa; and Said Hamed, a challenger of Nassir.

In September 1995, the group staged a "coup" and announced that Nassir had been replaced as Kanu district chairman by Shakombo. The heated conflict among Kanu leaders eventually led President Moi to intervene on Nassir's side, advising the protagonists to await the calling of new Kanu elections. As it happened, in the December 1997 general elections, Nassir again won the Mombasa-Central seat and remained the district Kanu chairman. Moreover, in 1998, Nassir was promoted to a ministerial post and became the second Muslim minister in Moi's new cabinet along with Hussein Maalim Mohamed. As for Sajad, he too remained one of Moi's favorites and in 1998 was reappointed as MP in the new parliament.

7

Muslims and the State

Kenya defines itself as a secular state and insists on the separation of church and state. The establishment of political parties based on religion is prohibited, although the government repeatedly emphasizes that the constitution guarantees freedom of religion.

Until 1992 Kenya was a one-party state, the sole party being Kanu. The only channels for criticism of the government were the churches and some nongovernmental organizations. In the struggle for democratization and specifically for instituting a multiparty system, the main churches, Protestant and Catholic, cooperated and often sharply criticized the government—sometimes in open letters in the press—for its arbitrary behavior and human rights abuses. In response, the regime threatened members of the clergy and even arrested some of them. Many church leaders objected to the government's insistence that the church not get involved in political affairs, stressing that they were duty bound to safeguard the citizens' wellbeing in political as well as religious matters.

The churches exert great influence in education, health, welfare, development projects, and other areas, and the conflict between them and the government was generally much fiercer than that between the Muslims and the government. Since independence, the Muslims, as a minority, have generally been very careful not to antagonize the government by criticizing it publicly, although many Muslims of all circles have been angry about discrimination, especially vis-à-vis the Christians (see Chapter 13). Even when Muslims dared to voice their grievances, they usually did so moderately. In some cases, Muslim criticism came from generally progovernment politicians, such as Sharif Nassir or Kanu members, who wished to show that they were representing the interests of their coreligionists who had voted for them, or that they were frustrated with their marginal role in decisionmaking. Even when criticizing the government, however, they emphasized that Muslims were loyal to the president.

In contrast to the Muslims' restraint, Christian religious leaders had already begun strongly criticizing the government in the 1970s, and this criticism increased during President Moi's rule. They demanded that he adopt a multiparty system, honor human rights, allow freedom of expression and assembly, and hold free and fair elections. They condemned the government when it failed to satisfy these demands. The umbrella organization of the churches, the National Christian Council of Kenya (NCCK), demonstrated that it supported political opposition groups in their criticism of the government.[1]

One of the government's most outspoken opponents was B. Njoroge Kariuki, an Anglican clergyman of the Kikuyu tribe. In a seminar held in Nairobi on 15 June 1990, he argued that the church had to be involved in politics because, in the absence of political opposition parties that could prevent government excesses, the church remained the only nationwide body with the institutional strength and the commitment to public morals and social justice to enable it to

> speak and act in implicitly political ways. . . . The social evils of our time, for example corruption, tribal patronage in employment, interference of the state with basic human freedoms, electoral rigging, detention without trial, torture, gagging of the press, etc., are so great . . . that Christians with any compassion cannot be indifferent to or complacent about the effects of such evils upon human lives in Kenya.[2]

Kariuki repeated the demand that the church be made independent of the state and called for the abolition of Article 2A of the constitution, which prohibited the establishment of parties other than Kanu.

Kariuki was not the only member of the clergy to make such demands. Among the leading bishops who shared his views on religion and state was David Gitary, also a Kikuyu, who in 1995 became the Anglican archbishop; he claimed that Kanu did not truly represent the people and accused the government of rigging the 1988 general elections.[3] Bishop Henry Okullu, a Luo, also demanded the abolition of Article 2A and called for limiting the presidency to two terms.[4]

Among the sharpest critics of the government was the Anglican bishop Alexander Muge of the Nandi tribe (which, like the president's tribe, belongs to the Kalenjin ethnic group). On the eve of the 1988 elections, Muge objected to the cancellation of the secret ballot system and the introduction of the "queueing" system, in which voters queue behind the candidate of their choice. The Catholics joined him in this protest. Muge also accused the government of corruption in the distribution of foreign relief aid.[5] He asserted that the church should monitor government activities and called on the ministers not to exceed their lawful authority.[6] When in 1990 Bishop Muge was killed in a road accident, the government was suspected of involvement, especially since only days earlier a government minister had warned him to fear for his life if he continued to disobey its injunctions.

Church leaders also harshly criticized the government during the intertribal clashes that broke out in several areas, especially the Rift Valley, in 1990–1992. The Catholic bishop Mwana Onzeki accused the authorities of inflaming the situation, and opposition groups made similar charges.[7] Later, Onzeki claimed that he had clear proof that the government was providing military training to several groups in the forests of Molo, a region whose inhabitants suffered during the disturbances. The different churches joined forces in warning the government to desist from such actions. Thus, during the conference of NCCK-affiliated churches in May 1992, the Anglican archbishop Manasses Kuria, together with Bishops Gitary and Okullu, called on their followers to initiate civil disobedience if the government continued to violate law and justice, since in that case "the Christians have no obligation of loyalty."[8]

On the eve of the 1997 elections, it was the church leaders who headed the opposition groups that formed the National Convention Executive Council (NCEC). To ensure free and fair elections, they demanded reforms in the constitution and the abolition of all restrictions on freedom of speech and assembly. Only after violent disturbances did the president consent to some of the demands, but he also succeeded in shunting the NCEC aside by relegating the issue of reforms to parliament. To resolve the constitutional impasse, the Inter-Party Parliamentary Group (IPPG) was established.

Even after Article 2A was abolished and a multiparty system instituted, the church continued its political involvement on the principle that politics is an integral part of its responsibility to the people. Thus, when ethnic violence again broke out in January 1998 in Laikipia and Njoro in the Rift Valley, after the general elections in which President Moi was reelected and his Kanu Party won the majority of parliamentary seats and formed the government, the church again joined hands with the opposition parties. In a "Call to End the Violence," the Catholic bishops implied that the gangs who had attacked the Kikuyu homestead and killed dozens of people were Kanu supporters taking revenge on the inhabitants for supporting the opposition parties. The bishops did not accept the government's claim that the attackers were cattle rustlers and declared that "the government appears to have given [the attackers] a go-ahead with its loud silence to date." They appealed to the president "to fulfill the pledges that he made to Kenyans as he sought their votes, to unite the country and to bring lasting peace . . . to put an end to the violence immediately, because we know that he is able if he so wishes . . . to respect the oath of office that he took barely three weeks ago."[9]

The government was well aware of the church's strength and was careful not to take strong action against its leaders as it did against leaders of the opposition parties. It did, however, issue periodic warnings in which it accused the church of inflaming antigovernment sentiment, fomenting demonstrations, and spreading false accusations. In September 1988, for example, Vice-President Joseph Karanja warned during a debate in parliament, "We cannot accept that the pulpit be used to lambast the government and the elected leaders of the people. . . . They have to know that we are not South Africa. They are not Bishop Tutu. There is no apartheid here to fight. We are not Latin American republics where peasants are landless and priests use confrontational theology to fight the system."[10] The national chairman of Kanu, Peter Oloo Aringo, accused the leaders of the (Anglican) Church of the Province of Kenya (CPK) of being tools of the opposition.[11]

President Moi himself repeatedly warned the church to stay out of politics, while stressing that Kenya had no intention of undermining freedom of religion.[12] Moi dealt especially severely with foreign Christian missionary activities, even threatening to expel those who got involved in politics ("I say to all of them: Go back home, except those who respect the government"); eventually some foreign missionaries were in fact expelled.[13] Moreover, certain church publications were banned. For example, on 16 March 1988, the NCCK's newspaper *Beyond* was banned because it protested the rigging of the 1988 general elections, which it described as "a disgrace to democracy."[14] In 1995, a Catholic newsletter in Swahili called *Inooro* was banned.[15] There was, in fact, an element of tribalism in the church's positions: criticism of the president and the government came primarily from Kikuyu and Luo religious leaders, whereas church leaders (such as the head of the Inland Church) who belonged to the president's ethnic group or groups close to it generally supported Moi and his policies.

Moi himself is, indeed, a devout Christian, a Protestant belonging to the Inland Church. His regular Sunday attendance of church is prominently broadcast on radio and television. He maintains good relations with several religious figures, especially from his church. He makes a point of showing that he seeks to strengthen Christianity and opposes only those who exploit religion as a political weapon against his government. In his book *Kenya African Nationalism*,[16] he emphasizes that his Nyayo ideology is based on both African tradition and the Christian faith. He acknowledges the importance of Christianity and of the church's role as an institution in Kenya, while stressing that the church must be loyal to the government and restrain its criticism.

For a long time the Muslims refrained from the kind of harsh criticism of the government voiced by non-Muslim church leaders. Public statements by Muslims, such as those of Assistant Minister Sharif Nassir, generally supported the government and its policies. For example, when the church opposed the queueing system in the 1988 elections and demanded a secret ballot, Nassir came out in favor of the abolition of the secret ballot.[17]

In an effort to maintain control over the Muslims' various organizations and activities, the government established Supkem, a progovernment, umbrella Muslim organization. It was generally headed by people close to the government, including assistant ministers (see Chapter 5), who made sure to praise the government's activities as benefiting Muslims and repeatedly exhorted Muslims to be unconditionally loyal to it. Like the chief qadi, also a government appointee, Supkem always supported the government's policies and the separation of religion and politics. Supkem ratified a detailed resolution supporting government policies and a decision that "Muslim institutes and organizations must not involve themselves in political activities."[18] Thus, the main Muslim religious organization, in contrast to the main churches, generally supported the government's policies.

As discussed in Chapter 4, the government also sometimes made a point of conciliating the Muslims, especially at election time, by granting them favors, such as declaring 'Id al-Fitr a public holiday and appointing some Muslims to senior positions. The government also agreed to periodic increases in the foreign currency allowance of pilgrims to Mecca.

In Kenyatta's time, the issue of religion did not prove divisive, partly because of his charismatic personality as "father of the nation" and partly because he himself did not publicly assert his Christian identity. Moreover, during his rule there was no serious advocacy for democratization. Even when Kenyatta described the Muslim residents of the coast as lazy and as despising manual labor, and granted members of the Kikuyu tribe large tracts of land in the Coast Province, there was no outspoken criticism during his lifetime.[19]

In contrast to those Muslim leaders who cooperated with the government and generally supported its position that religion and state be kept separate, there were Muslim academics who during the 1990s espoused opposing positions, though they were not as outspoken as the church leaders. Mohamed Bakari, professor at the University of Nairobi, argued that religion and state should not be completely separated because this weakened the Muslims politically, and that political activities by Muslim parties and organizations should not be prohibited.[20] Hassan Mwakimako, lecturer in religion at the University of Nairobi, also publicly favored the formation of a Muslim political party. In a 1994 lecture at a seminar sponsored by the Muslim Education and Welfare Association (MEWA) at the Muslim Centre in Mombasa, Mwakimako maintained that separation of religion and state was one-sided and operated primarily against Muslims, suppressing their freedom of expression and preventing their advancement. Mwakimako contended that the president, by showing in different ways that he was a devout Christian, in fact made a connection between church and state. Mwakimako pointed out that Christian religious figures from abroad were allowed to hold public meetings and to preach in public places, activities prohibited to the Muslims. Indeed, Muslim preachers, even those working within mosques, were sometimes arrested and accused of incitement. When Christian politicians criticized the regime, their religion was not publicized, only their names and their political views; but when Muslims expressed political opinions, their Muslim identity was highlighted. The NCCK, in fact, publicly proclaimed its political views and criticized the government in the name of Christianity; a Muslim organization that behaved the same way would be severely punished.[21] Mwakimako also accused the Muslim leadership of cowardice and subservience. It is interesting that his lecture was reported in the press with the anodyne title "Muslim NGOs and Community Development: The Kenya Experience." Outside the academic world, Mohamed Galgalo, member of parliament and assistant minister, also asserted in an interview in May 1994 that there should be no separation between religion and state.[22]

Among those who advocated allowing the Muslims to form a political party and supported the registration of the IPK was Ali Mazrui. In a number of articles and lectures given on visits to Kenya, Mazrui contended that religion had never undermined the stability of African governments and pointed out that there were Christian political parties in Europe (for Mazrui's views, see Chapter 13).

Although there were both Christian and Muslim leaders who favored allowing religious figures to enter politics, there was never any cooperation between them on this issue.

There is no doubt that the Kenyan government, headed by Christians, held deep suspicions toward the large Muslim minority that reflected historical and political factors and greatly influenced government policy toward the Muslims. These fears were rooted in the coastal Muslims' aspirations on the eve of independence to secede from Kenya and join Zanzibar, or at least obtain autonomy (the government's suspicions toward the coastal Muslims were discussed at length in Chapter 6).

The Somali Muslim Factor

In addition, the government distrusted the Somali Muslims in the Northeastern Province, who indeed desired to join Somalia, with whom they had ethnic, linguistic, social, and religious affinities. The Somalis, like the coastal Arabs, were proud of their race and saw themselves as superior to the black Africans. They claimed Arab origins and, according to their tradition, were descendants of the Quraish tribe, the tribe of the Prophet Muhammad. The special position of the coastal Arabs during Omani rule and later during the colonial period, and their demands to secede from independent Kenya, encouraged the Somalis to demand a special position for themselves and to work for union with Somalia, particularly after it gained independence on 1 July 1960. In the British colonial period, the Northern Frontier District (NFD) was given a special status and Somali political parties were allowed to operate in it. On the eve of independence, the British government sent a special committee to Kenya to investigate the situation in the NFD. In its report of December 1962, the committee emphasized that most of the area's residents, especially the Somali Muslims, wanted to break away from Kenya after independence and unite with Somalia. The report also stressed that daily life in the area, residents' political attitudes, and their relations with non-Muslims were greatly influenced by Islam.[23]

After the British decided to include the area in independent Kenya, the Somalis boycotted the 1963 general elections that set the stage for independence. There was unrest in the region, including violent clashes between Somali guerrillas, known as Shifta, and the Kenyan security forces. Somalis also attacked convoys and police stations, and the Kenyan government declared a general emergency and mounted a campaign against both the guerrillas and the residents. Among the leaders of the underground groups was Deghow Ma'alim Stanbul, who fought for the cause of a Greater Somalia. Stanbul was captured in 1963 and held until 1969; since then he has ceased violent activities and has claimed that he seeks to achieve his aims by nonviolent persuasion. In recent years, as Kenyan Somalis' complaints about discrimination have increased, he has issued statements criticizing the government and asserting that Somalis are treated as second-class citizens.[24]

Somalis periodically complain about discrimination and the lack of development projects in their region. In November 1980, for example, the MP from Garissa, Abdi Kader Hassan, claimed during a parliamentary debate that Kenyan security forces were attacking Somalis and had even destroyed settlements and mosques in the region. G. G. Kariuki, minister of state in the president's office, responded that the Northeastern Province was still a security area and that the settlements that were destroyed had been built illegally.[25]

The government's suspicious attitude toward the Somalis also affects Kenyan-Somali relations, which have generally been hostile and alternate between periods of high and low tension. Kenya accused Somalia of assisting the Somali underground in its operations. Although tension was reduced when the two countries signed an agreement in 1967 and Somalia declared that it had no territorial claims against Kenya, the latter's fears remained. In the first decade of Mohamed Siad Barre's military rule in Somalia (spanning 1969–1991), tension between the two countries increased again and Kenya eventually accused Somalia of seeking to conquer the Northeastern Province as it had conquered the Ogaden region of Ethiopia in 1977. This, in turn, reinforced Kenya's suspicion toward its Somali residents. In the 1990s, the continuing civil war in Somalia and the flood of refugees crossing the border only intensified the government's concerns. Moreover, from time to time information was published that the radical Islamic organization Al-Ittihad al-Islami, which was based in Somalia, was trying to operate among the Kenyan Somalis. In recent years, President Moi has worked to bring the opposing sides in Somalia to the negotiating table. At a meeting between the leaders of these groups in Nairobi in October 1996, Moi succeeded in working out a cease-fire, although like previous cease-fire agreements it was breached several days later.

During President Moi's tenure as a whole, however, there has been a certain mellowing toward the Somalis, especially after the attempted coup against Moi in August 1982, which was aborted largely by an officer of Somali extraction, Mahmud Mohamed, who was later appointed chief of staff. His brother, Hussein Maalim Mohamed, was then the only Muslim minister in the Kenyan government (see Chapter 3). Even so, complaints about discrimination against Muslims were often heard from Somalis, whose presence among the senior echelons of the Kenyan regime did little to allay the deep mistrust toward them.

Monitoring Islamic Activities and the 1987 Disturbances

The authorities, in general, closely monitor Muslim political activities and take sharp measures when these activities seem to threaten the government. The Islamic activities of foreigners are watched especially closely. In 1980, for example, the government banned the activities of the Muslim Student Association of the University of Nairobi. Although no official reason was given for this step, a Muslim activist named J. Omari claimed that the ban was connected to the organization's links with various Arab embassies. Through the embassies the association occasionally invited Arab lecturers who spoke to the students, and the government apparently looked askance at this.[26]

Until the appearance of the IPK in the 1990s, the mutual suspicions between the government and the coastal Muslims seldom mounted to violent confrontation. Such a confrontation occurred, however, in November 1987 after five imams who had arrived from Tanzania were expelled from Kenya. The Christians claimed they were expelled because in their sermons they had slandered the Bible and asserted, among other things, that only the Qur'an was a holy book. The Muslims rejected that claim and said the expulsion resulted from the Christians' anger at the spread of Islam, especially since among the converts to Islam there was a priest.[27] It seems that several other events precipitated the expulsion. Shortly before it, during the Maulidi procession, some young Muslims had assaulted Assistant Minister Sharif Nassir and Mayor Mwidani of Mombasa, who were participating in the event. In reaction, the government at the last moment revoked the permission it had granted Muslims to hold an assembly at the Tonomoka stadium, which had been organized by figures who opposed Nassir. Immediately after the expulsion, about 4,000 Muslims demonstrated against it and against the cancellation of the assembly, damaging cars and government property; the security forces reacted harshly. About twenty people were injured and about 100 arrested, including Said Hamed, Nassir's political rival; the well-known theologian Shaikh Sharif Ahmad Badawi; and several Kanu members who were known to oppose Nassir. Clearly, personal factors played a role in this confrontation. After a short while, those arrested were released and the situation quieted. But in an emergency meeting of Muslim leaders, including the chief qadi, it was agreed that preachers from outside Kenya who wanted to enter the country would first be thoroughly checked by both government representatives and Muslim leaders.

Although this confrontation in 1987 was trivial compared to the clashes between Muslims and the government during 1992–1994, which is analyzed later, it clearly illustrates the government's fears of any organized Muslim opposition.[28]

U.S. Embassy Bombings in Nairobi and Dar-es-Salaam

The twin bombings of the U.S. embassies in Nairobi and Dar-es-Salaam on 7 August 1998 again raised the issue of the relations between the Muslims and the government. In these simultaneous bombings, more 250 people were killed in Nairobi, including twelve Americans, and some 5,000 were injured; eleven were killed in Dar-es-Salaam and about seventy were injured. According to U.S. government sources, the U.S. embassy in Kampala was also targeted, but U.S. and Ugandan intelligence officers were able to foil the plot.[29] Investigations by the U.S. Federal Bureau of Investigation (FBI) and the Kenyan Criminal Investigation Department (CID) are still proceeding, but it seems that most of the suspects are Muslims, both foreigner and local.

One of the first questions to be raised was why Nairobi and Dar-es-Salaam were targeted. A reasonable answer was that both places appeared to be soft targets for terrorism because of lax security arrangements at seaports and airports and the thousands of miles of porous borders with countries in a state of war. The U.S. embassies were, moreover, centrally located and easily accessible by road. It was also emphasized in the press that the U.S. ambassador to Kenya, Prudence Bushnell, had repeatedly asked the State Department to build a new embassy, warning of the embassy's "extreme vulnerability."[30]

But it also seems that the nonlocal perpetrators took into consideration the recent religious tensions in these countries and the existence of Islamic extremism among some circles, manifested in Kenya by the riots that occurred in Mombasa and other coastal towns a few years earlier. They believed these local militants would be prepared to cooperate with them against "the enemies of Islam." It should be noted, however, that immediately after the bombings, Muslim leaders in Kenya hastened to distance themselves from the actions and the perpetrators and, like other Kenyans, expressed shock and outrage.

The prime non-Kenyan suspect is Usamah bin Laden, whom the United States views as the likely mastermind behind the attacks. Bin Laden, a Saudi construction tycoon turned terrorist, runs and finances from his mountain refuge in Afghanistan a number of Muslim extremist groups—in the Middle East and elsewhere—that are devoted to jihad against the United States and Israel.[31] One suspect connected to bin Laden was Mohammed Saddiq Odeh, a Palestinian from Jordan who was captured in Pakistan soon after his arrival from Nairobi on 7 August, the day of the bombings. Odeh had lived in Kenya since 1994 and was married to a local woman. He resided first in Malindi and then in Mombasa, both towns being Muslim centers on the coastal strip. His wife and her relatives described Odeh as a simple fish merchant and a carpenter, a devout Muslim who prayed five times a day. His arrest in Pakistan, they claimed, came as a surprise to them. Pakistani authorities, however, said Odeh had confessed that he played a major role in preparing the car bomb that devastated the U.S. embassy in Nairobi and that bin Laden was his supreme commander. On 14 August he was deported to Kenya, and from there the FBI took him to the United States for further investigation. There, Odeh denied any involvement in the bombing. Among the other prime non-Kenyan suspects was Abdallah Mohamed Fadhul of the Comoro Islands, described as an explosives expert; the United States offered a $2 million reward for information leading to his arrest.

Among countries other than Afghanistan that the United States suspected of having a link to the bombings was Sudan, repeatedly accused of being a training camp and crossroads for the world's terrorist organizations. The Iranian embassies in Nairobi and Dar-es-Salaam were also suspected of involvement. Indeed, a U.S. spokesperson in Nairobi said that Iran "is on the list of the main suspects." The Iranian embassy in Dar-es-Salaam hurriedly dismissed this as a "baseless allegation."[32]

As for the Kenyan suspects, one was Ali Salim, a mechanic from Mombasa who was arrested on suspicion that his garage was used to prepare the car bomb. Another Kenyan arrested was James Nganga, manager of the Hilltop Lodge in Nairobi, owned by a Lebanese and frequented by Muslim businessmen; it is suspected that the bomb was assembled there.

On 12 August 1998, President Moi announced that the security forces had arrested a number of people in connection with the bombings but did not divulge their nationality.[33]

From all the information available, it seems that the main suspected perpetrators and executors of the bombings were non-Kenyan Muslims, but it is reasonable to assume that they were helped by a few local antigovernment militants. The government's suspicion that both local and non-Kenyan Muslims were involved was clearly evident in its decision to ban several Muslim NGOs. This became another bone of contention between the regime and the Muslim community and reflected aspects of the relations between the Muslims and the state.

On 8 September, nearly a month after the bombings, the government shut down five Muslim NGOs: the Mercy Relief International Agency, the al-Haramain Foundation, Help African People, the International Islamic Relief Organization, and the Ibrahim bin 'Abd al-'Aziz al-Ibrahim Foundation. A sixth NGO that was not recognized by the government but operated illegally, Rabitat al-Islam, was also ordered to close. Most of the banned NGOs operated in the Northeastern Province, but their headquarters were in Nairobi. Soon after the bombings the offices of the Mercy Relief International Agency in Nairobi were raided by a combined force of FBI and CID agents, who confiscated documents and other items. The government also deported those nonindigenous workers of the NGOs, who were suspected of links with radical Middle Eastern organizations. The head of the government's NGO coordinating office, John Etemesi, justified the crackdown on the Muslim NGOs on the grounds that they posed a threat to security. The government even claimed that the terrorists might have imported bomb parts disguised as relief supplies through the Mercy Relief International Agency.[34] Some officials also charged that the NGOs were not doing much charitable work but were mainly engaged in proselytizing. The *Weekly Review,* a government organ, said Christians feared that some of the Muslim NGOs "had as their main goal making Kenya an Islamic country within the next two or three decades."[35] Indeed, even before the bombings, President Moi had expressed concern about the NGOs and threatened to ban some of them for involving themselves in politics. In November 1997, the police arrested for investigation ten Muslim NGO workers, among them Sudanese, Pakistanis, and Kenyans, and searched their homes before releasing them on condition that they limit their work to charity and welfare.[36]

Although some of the allegations about the NGOs seem to be gross exaggerations, they reflect the fact that both the government and the churches were alarmed by the recent surge of Islamic fervor in Kenya. The growing Christian-Muslim antagonism was also cause for concern.

As for the Muslim community, it was enraged by the crackdown on the NGOs, and leaders of all persuasions formed a united front against the government's action. Muslims felt that by shutting down only Muslim NGOs immediately after the bombings, the government had put the onus on the Muslim community. Accusing the authorities of demonizing Muslims and Islam and of yielding to U.S. pressure, they directed especially bitter criticism at the vigorous actions of the FBI agents, who arrived in Kenya to investigate the bombings and received wide publicity.

A letter to the editor from a Muslim published at the time aptly expresses the deep indignation felt by many Muslims. The writer asserted that by singling out Muslim institutions for suspected connections to the bombings, the government lent credence to the false accusation that "Islam is a global threat," adding that "many of us are victims of this Western bias." As for the charge that the banned NGOs were involved in proselytism, he retorted: "Do we have underground laws that prohibit the propagation of Islam? . . . Our Christian counterparts are doing the same and more aggressively than the Muslims."[37]

Among the protesters was Minister Hussein Maalim Mohamed, who maintained that the banned NGOs had been doing valuable charitable work. He was joined by other MPs from the Northeastern Province, who even threatened to sever all ties with the government. Even Supkem, usually moderate and proestablishment, was among the loudest protesters against the ban, apparently fearing that it would continue to lose support and be severely criticized, especially among Muslim youth, for its progovernment stance, as occurred during the IPK's struggle for registration. Hence, this time Supkem joined other Muslim leaders in calling on all Muslims to stage mass demonstrations throughout the country on 2 October 1998 to protest the banning of the NGOs. These demonstrations were meant to be a major expression of Muslim unity and strength.

As the day of the demonstrations drew nearer, however, the Muslim leaders split between radicals and moderates. The radicals were headed by Shaikh Ali Shee, now chairman of the Imams and Preachers Council of Kenya. The moderates were Supkem leaders who feared that Shee would dominate the demonstrations and overshadow them and that the rallies would turn into violent antigovernment displays that might lead to clashes with the security forces. They decided, therefore, not to participate in the demonstrations. Eventually the demonstrations did take place, mainly in the Muslim strongholds of the coastal strip such as Mombasa, Kwale, Kilifi, and Malindi, and in Garissa in the Northeastern Province. In Mombasa, where about 10,000 Muslims gathered, Shee read a strongly worded antigovernment and anti-American set of resolutions and gave the government a fourteen-day ultimatum to reinstate the banned NGOs. He fiercely attacked the "great American Satan" and called on the Muslims to boycott U.S. products.

Supkem officials and other Muslim leaders, however, preferred to meet with President Moi to discuss Muslim grievances. At the head of the Muslim delegation were Supkem's chairman, Abdulghfar al-Busaidi, its secretary-general, Ahmad Khalif, and its organizing secretary Sharif Hussein Omar. The president agreed to set up a committee of Supkem officials and other Muslim leaders to examine the work of the banned NGOs and forward to him their recommendations. (At the time of writing their recommendations have not yet been published.) The government also agreed that the banned NGOs could appeal against the proscription; furthermore, it announced the deregistration of eleven non-Muslim NGOs, a step widely regarded as a conciliatory gesture to the Muslims.[38]

In conclusion, the aftermath of the bombings of the U.S. embassies reflected several important characteristics of relations between Muslims and the government in Kenya:

- Government suspicions of the Muslims
- The Muslims' ability to temporarily form a united front when they feel that non-Muslims are vilifying Islam and condemning all Muslims as partners to global terrorism
- The government's tendency to retreat when confronting a strong, relatively united Muslim reaction, and to placate the Muslims with conciliatory steps
- Mistrust between Christians and Muslims
- Radical Muslims' animosity toward the West in general and toward the United States in particular
- The cleavages in the Muslim community, of which the rift between Supkem and Imam Shee is paradigmatic

In that regard, one must agree with the *Weekly Review*'s comment that "the apparent Muslim unity that was evident immediately after the banning of the NGOs, has been shattered and a rift has again been opened between Muslim radicals and conservatives who seek dialogue and accommodation with the government."[39] This rift, no doubt, is one of the factors that weaken the Muslims in their confrontation with the government.

Fears of Muslim Separatist Tendencies

The government's and the Christian community's distrust of Muslims was again in evidence in 1999. This time it was in connection with Majimbo: an ethnic-based system of government. ("Majimbo" in Kiswahili is the plural of "jimbo," which means province.) Majimbo was discussed in Kenya in the 1990s in the context of demands for constitutional reforms by several leaders and ethnic goups.

In February 1999 some political and religious Muslim leaders from the Coast Province met to discuss the Muslim response to future constitutional reforms. The news was leaked to the press that the participants had recommended that only Muslim public administrators be posted to Coast Province and that the meeting had called for the creation of a "Muslim jimbo where sharia laws would prevail."[40] This news caused an immediate uproar among Christians and government circles. Although the mayor of Mombasa, Najib Balala, who was one of the participants, denied that the meeting had proposed an Islamic jimbo, his disclaimer was not accepted.

The strongest reaction came from the minister of state in the office of the president in charge of internal security and provincial administration, Marsden Madaka, who warned against "separatist tendencies" that could harm Kenya's national cohesion and unity. He called the idea of a Muslim jimbo "impractical, misplaced and dangerous," and demanded a total condemnation of the notion of a Muslim Coast jimbo, declaring that the "Coast is not for Muslims alone. It is a secular multi-racial province whose institutions cannot be based on a theocratic foundation."

Leaders of the majority Christian and other non-Muslim communities in the Coast Province expressed anxiety and sharply ciriticized what the Muslims were alleged to have said at the meeting, complaining that the meeting was "another deliberate attempt" to Islamize Mombasa and the Coast Province and warned that such ideas were likely to bring about religious and ethnic tensions.

This strong reaction to the recommendations of the Muslim meeting, whether or not they were actually made, again shows how deeply suspicious the Kenyan government and the Christians are of Islamic radicalism and Muslim separatist tendencies.

8

Muslims and the Law

As early as the 1895 agreement between the sultan of Zanzibar and the British government, which laid out the arrangements by which the British would rule the coastal strip, the British promised to preserve the "Islamic way of life" (see Chapter 6). Therefore, during British rule in Kenya, a law was proclaimed (the East African Order in Council, 1897) under which a triple court system was set up: common courts, native courts, and Islamic shari'a courts. When both parties to a dispute were Muslims, Islamic law was applied, but when the case was between a Muslim and a non-Muslim, common law was used. In the 1931 Court Ordinance, the authority of the shari'a courts was limited to matters of the personal status of Muslims—inheritance, marriage, divorce, and waqf affairs.

On the eve of independence, Governor Sir James Robertson was sent to Kenya to examine the prospective arrangements after independence and, following his recommendations, an agreement was signed in 1963 between the British government and the sultan that would maintain the authority of the chief qadi and the shari'a courts in independent Kenya as in colonial times, with Islamic law applying in matters of personal status when both parties to a dispute were Muslims, and common law when only one party was a Muslim.

The subject of Muslims and the law was raised at the Constitutional Conference in London. Muslim leaders feared that in independent Kenya, under a Christian government, they would not be able to continue to live under Islamic law. On the coast, a political movement, the Mwambao United Front, was formed primarily to protect Muslim religious interests. The movement sent two prominent Muslims to the conference in London, Shaikh A. Nasir and Q. S. Basadiq. These representatives emphasized in their arguments before the conference that Muslims should be regarded as a "distinct social group," and they even requested that they be granted autonomy or be allowed to join Zanzibar. The Somali Muslims in the Northeastern Province actually boycotted the elections that were held in 1962, before independence.[1]

The 1963 constitution of independent Kenya therefore addressed the issue of Islamic law and ensured Muslims' right to decide personal matters according to the law of the Qur'an. The Qadis' Courts Act stipulated that the jurisdiction of the qadis' courts would extend not only to the coastal area, which was heavily populated by Muslims, but also to other Muslim areas such as Nyanza, the Rift Valley, the Western Province, and the Northeastern Province. The authority of the chief qadi and of the other qadis was safeguarded accordingly (see also Chapter 5).[2]

After independence, differences of opinion sometimes arose between the authorities and the Muslims about Islamic law. These differences reflected the opposing attitudes of the government and the Muslims toward the legal system, the mistrust between Muslims and Christians, and also disagreements among the Muslims themselves.

In 1967, a severe dispute emerged, which would reach a climax only in 1981. Already at the start of independence, the Kenyan government wanted to unify the laws and eliminate the existing three-tiered system of common law, customary or native law, and Islamic law. On 17 March 1967, the Commission of Inquiry was set up, headed by the speaker of the National Assembly, Sir Humphrey Slade, to look into the possibility of "harmonizing" all the laws of succession in the country. In August 1968, the commission presented its recommendations for unification, which were not liked by the Muslims, neither Sunnis nor Shiites. The law declared that every citizen had to make a will concerning inheritance, whereas the Muslims claimed that there was no need for a will since the Qur'an already specified how to arrange an inheritance. When the proposed bill, drafted according to the commission's recommendations, was brought for its second reading before parliament in 1970, and Muslim members of parliament again opposed it, the attorney-general, Charles Njonjo, decided to postpone the debate and first to present the law to a council of ministers for discussion. The subject came up again in parliament in 1972 and the law was passed, but because of a storm of protest by Muslims, its implementation was postponed.

The subject came up again on 1 July 1981 when the government decided that the law should finally become operational. Again, Muslims reacted with anger and harshly condemned the law at public meetings and in the media. The organizing secretary of Supkem, Mohamed Amana, who was also the secretary of Kanu in Lamu, asserted that the law contradicted both Kenya's constitution, which ensured freedom of religion, and the Qur'an.[3] Muslim MPs also came out against the law, including former assistant minister Mohamed Jehazi. Particularly vehement in his pronouncements was Shaikh Abdullahi Nasr, a famous publisher, whose sermon in the central mosque in Nairobi, before thousands of worshipers, called on them to defy this law and even warned that anyone who obeyed it would be a Muslim heretic. He protested that the law's purpose was to force Muslims to act against their beliefs (on Nasr, see also Chapter 6).[4]

The dispute became even hotter when the attorney-general, Joseph Kamera, attacked the Muslim opposition and warned them to comply with the law. He declared that the law corrected "outmoded" customs, and its aim was to unify rules of succession so that they would be the same for all citizens. He stressed that Muslim law was similar to outmoded tribal customs and that the Muslims had no right to be given preference over others. Muslims who wanted to act according to the laws of the Qur'an should write in their wills, but they had to make a will.

The attorney-general's words poured oil on the fire. Muslim leaders expressed outrage that he had compared the laws of the Qur'an, which were the laws of God, to tribal laws, which were made by man, and had dared to assert that Islamic law was "outmoded." The qadi of Mombasa, Ali Mohamed Ali Darani, threatened that all the qadis would resign if the law was enforced.[5] In an article in the *Daily Nation,* Mohamed Hyder Matano, lecturer in zoology at the University of Nairobi, averred that the attorney-general's words were an insult to Islam and that his attitude was apparently influenced by his Western Christian education, which did not accept the idea that Islam determines everything in the lives of Muslims. Matano warned that the law would polarize the communities and proposed a compromise according to which Muslims would be exempted from writing a will, but those who wanted to could do so.[6]

Muslims in the government and in the Kanu Party also expressed opposition to the law, albeit more moderately. Thus, Kassim Mwamazandi, chairman of Supkem and also assistant minister of energy, agreed that the law was contrary to Islam but, unlike Shaikh Amana, tried to placate the Muslims by telling them they could rely on Supkem to explain the Muslims' case to the president.[7] Assistant Minister Sharif Nassir, who was also chairman of Kanu in Mombasa, supported the position that Muslim and tribal law could not be compared and that Muslims had first and foremost to obey the Qur'an because "God's law was higher than man's law." He asserted that the Qur'an constituted the Muslims' will and there was no need to make another will.[8] Nevertheless, like Mwamazandi, Nassir asked the Muslims to calm down, be loyal to the president, and trust him to find a fair solution; he also accused some Muslim leaders of exploiting the affair to promote their position among the Muslims.

Muslim leaders, however, continued to issue pronouncements against the law that appeared in the media. Some Muslims even attacked Sharif Nassir in letters to the newspapers, asserting that they did not have to keep quiet about the matter and that Muslims had the right to react vigorously.[9] Some Muslim MPs, headed by Assistant Minister M. O. Soba, put most of the blame for what had happened on the chief qadi, Shaikh Abdallah Saleh al-Farsy, for not exerting pressure on the government soon enough, and they demanded his resignation.[10] The chief qadi responded that it was not his job to intervene on his own initiative; he advised the government on Muslim matters only when asked, and he was not the spokesperson of the Muslims.[11]

In response to the request of Muslim leaders who supported the government, such as the chief qadi and Sharif Nassir, President Moi agreed to receive on 15 September 1981 a delegation of Muslims, including Assistant Minister Mwamazandi, Assistant Minister Nassir, the chief qadi, and Muslim MPs. The president did not make a decision on the issue but suggested setting up a committee to meet with the attorney-general to work out a fair solution. In addition, he criticized those who demanded the chief qadi's resignation and warned again that religion should not be mixed with politics.[12] Meanwhile, it was agreed that the law would not be put into effect until the committee had made its recommendations. Supkem then set up a committee of six members, including the chief qadi and three jurists; yet the whole subject again disappeared. The status quo continued, and there were no substantial developments in the law of succession.

In this whole saga, the divisions within the Muslim community emerge as the starkest element; each side strongly asserted its views, some of which harshly criticized the chief qadi and the head of Supkem. An interesting editorial in the *Daily Nation* accused the Muslim leadership and Supkem of failing to act systematically and effectively in opposing to the law or to explain the Muslims' position adequately to the government; such effective action might have convinced the government to set the law aside for good. The article remarks that "they woke up at the eleventh hour," in 1981, only after the government had decided to put the law into effect. Moreover, it claims, if one wants to have a society founded on equality, one cannot ignore the arguments of the attorney-general; it is therefore incumbent on

Muslims to act democratically by persuasion rather than threatening to break the law.[13]

Christian MPs and prominent figures, for their part, generally expressed support for the law of succession. One such was Wangari M. Mathai, a professor who served as chair of the National Council of Women and in recent years has worked for the democratization of the regime.[14] Supkem tried to recruit the Christian umbrella organization, the National Christian Council of Kenya, to support the Muslim position but without success.[15] In general, among the Christians one did not hear expressions of understanding for the Muslims' claims.

Another, less pronounced legal dispute broke out in April 1994 when Attorney-General Amos Wako announced that he was preparing a law according to which a woman could sue her husband and accuse him of rape if he pressured her to have sexual relations with him against her will. The law, he said, would become operational in 1996. This time Shaikh Ali Shee, imam of the central mosque of Nairobi, came out against the law, asserting that it "would cause many problems in African society" because it "damaged the institution of marriage and respect for it" and contravened the spirit of the Qur'an.[16] By the end of the 1999, no such law has been brought before parliament for its approval.

9

Muslims and Education

The Muslims in Kenya are considered the least advanced sector in the area of modern, secular education, as compared to the Christians, the Asians and, especially, the Europeans. The problem of the Muslim educational system and how to advance it greatly occupies leading Muslims and Muslim institutions and sometimes causes difficulties in the relations between Muslims and the government.

In the colonial period, the British continued to maintain the social hierarchy that was in place during Omani rule, which greatly affected education. Someone who was classified as a Swahili, for example, could not gain admission to an Arab school, and the Swahilis had separate educational institutions.[1] Muslim leaders accused the colonial authorities of putting the education system in the hands of Christian missionaries with the aim of stopping the spread of Islam and disseminating Christianity.[2] Muslim parents, fearing to send their children to the public schools, instead sent them to *chuoni* schools—established in mosques and in the houses of shaikhs or teachers—where they learned the Qur'an by heart.[3] The older students studied *hadith* (tradition), *fiqh* (Muslim law), or other Islamic subjects in madrasas. In the chuoni schools and the madrasas, there were no secular studies, which were regarded as unlawful (*haram*).[4] Shaikhs even forced parents to take their children out of the public schools. Muslims accused the government of discrimination and of not providing financial aid to support madrasas and to train Muslim teachers. The government responded that the Christians had set up nongovernmental institutions that bore most of the financial burden, and they urged Muslims to do the same.

Religious leaders from Hadramaut established prominent madrasas. Habib Salih Jamal al-Lail was very active in this field, setting up the well-known Riyadha Mosque College in 1889 (see Chapter 1), which produced renowned religious teachers and served as a model for other institutions. Among present-day prestigious madrasas that provide religious education from kindergarten to secondary level is Madrasatul Munawarrah, set up in Nairobi in 1990; about 700 students studied there at the time it was founded. Some of the madrasas include in their curricula secular studies as well, such as English, mathematics, and history—but only to a limited extent. In the colonial period, a few of the Arab schools, such as the Arab Secondary School, introduced secular subjects into their curricula. In the 1930s the Swahilis succeeded in persuading the colonial authorities to set up a junior-level secondary school in the coastal region, to which both Swahilis and African Muslims were admitted.

A factor that assisted Islamic education in the colonial period was the Aga Khan's East Africa Muslim Welfare Society (EAMWS), which established a branch in Mombasa in 1945. The society, whose aim was to improve the condition of Muslims in general, established schools and mosques and even paid the salaries of Qur'an teachers. It also distributed Muslim literature and educational books and provided educational scholarships.[5]

An important step in the field of Islamic education was taken in 1948 with the setting up of the Institute of Muslim Education. The idea stemmed from the Aga Khan's suggestion to establish a Muslim university in East Africa. His idea was not implemented at the time, when it became clear that the cost was too high and the students would not be able to make substantial financial contributions. It was decided instead to set up an institute that would give Muslims a general education with emphasis on technical skills. A clause in the new institute's constitution stipulated that, within the framework of the institute, a secondary school for general education for Arabs would be established. This was done under pressure from the sultan of Zanzibar, who was chiefly concerned about the Arab community, which had enjoyed special rights during his rule. The sultan, the Kenyan colonial government, and the Aga Khan jointly sponsored the financing of this institute, the construction of which began in 1948, whereas the government alone financed the establishment of the secondary school for Arabs. The school officially opened on 16 March 1950, with a ceremony in which the sultan participated. The institute itself opened on 9 May 1951 with 108 students; by 1958, there were 200.[6] In 1964, the government of independent Kenya took responsibility for running the institute and turned it into a technical school. By that time, Muslims formed only 10 percent of the school's students. The Muslims' hope that the institute would in time become a university was foiled, although, as we shall see, their aspirations to set up a Muslim university in the coastal region continued.[7]

With independence in 1963, the government introduced changes into the entire education system and nationalized all the schools. The Kenya Education Commission, established in 1964, recommended promoting equality in education and preventing schools from becoming centers of religious propaganda and proselytization. The same year, the government set up a commission to look into the state of Muslim education and to recommend ways to improve it. The commission found that the Muslim education system was poorly organized, especially compared to that of the Christians; it recommended that Muslim religious matters should be studied as a subject in schools and that textbooks should be written by professional educators. In 1968, the government issued a law declaring that general religious education should be taught as a regular subject in every school. In 1970, the Ministry of Education took a further step in this direction by appointing a commission to prepare a low-level program for secondary schools called Islamic Religion Education, along the lines of the existing Christian Religion Education program. The Islamic program was approved in 1971 and first introduced as an experiment into an Arab secondary school in Mombasa, which changed its name to the Khamis Secondary School; it was later introduced in other schools as well. It was difficult to implement the program because of a shortage of teachers of Islam. Gradually the subject of Islam was also introduced into primary schools, though it was not compulsory to take examinations in it.[8] But even after Islamic studies could be found in the curriculum, a considerable proportion of Muslim students continued to study in the traditional chuoni and madrasa system.

Over time, a number of Muslim organizations arose whose purpose was to modernize and improve Muslim education and to introduce reforms and secular subjects into the madrasas. Among them was the Ansaar Muslim Youth, set up in 1976, and—more important—the Muslim Education Welfare Association (MEWA), established in 1986, which focused on Muslim education and tried to include secular studies in Muslim schools and madrasas. Both these organizations claimed that Muslims were discriminated against in the field of education, but they emphasized that the blame for Muslims' backwardness was not the government's alone. They asserted that the Muslim leadership and Muslim members of parliament devoted insufficient effort to promoting education in general, and secular education in particular, among the Muslims.[9]

Supkem has also tried to promote Muslim education by organizing courses for teachers in Islamic subjects, improving the program of studies in Islamic schools, introducing secular subjects, and pressuring the government to increase the budget for Muslim education. Supkem also maintains contacts with Muslim Arab countries that provide financial aid to schools as well as scholarships. The following are some examples of its activities in this area.

In October 1971, a course for teachers of Islamic education in primary schools concluded. Ahmad Abdallah, one of Supkem's leaders who also served as deputy governor of the Central Bank of Kenya, took this opportunity to call on the government to introduce the subject of Islam into the curriculum of every school in Kenya to promote greater understanding among the country's citizens. For this purpose he requested that the Ministry of Education assist in the printing of suitable textbooks on Islam.[10]

Muslim intellectuals, some of them leaders of Supkem, publish articles to inform Kenya's citizens about the principles of Islam. Notable among them is Farouk Muslim, a law lecturer at the University of Nairobi and secretary of Supkem in the late 1970s, who in 1977 published a wide-ranging article on Islam and its relation to education. He stressed that it was not Islam that had caused Muslims' backwardness; Islam, he maintained, did not oppose progress and the study of modern, secular subjects. Instead, he attributed the Muslims' deteriorating situation to mismanagement, lack of support for the advancement of Muslim education, and other social and institutional problems. He emphasized in his article Supkem's exceptional efforts in the area of education, specifically the training of Muslim teachers and the improvement of the status of women. He mentioned that Supkem had managed to obtain from the city of Nairobi a plot of land on which the organization planned to establish a large school for 900 students at a cost of U.S.$10 million.[11] Like many other plans of Supkem, however, this one has not yet been implemented.

The head of Supkem's Education Department in the 1980s, Mohamed Quraishi, also tried to make it clear to Muslims that Islam did not oppose general education; on the contrary, it encouraged education and especially valued *talab al-'ilm* (the acquisition of knowledge).[12] In general, Muslim leaders and intellectuals devote great attention to this theme and try to overturn the ban on general education issued by extremist conservative religious leaders.[13]

Another of Supkem's important activities is to improve the position of the Muslim woman in Kenya. To this end, Supkem's Department of Women's Affairs periodically organizes meetings and seminars to discuss the issue. For example, the head of the department,

Fatma Hyder, organized a seminar in Nairobi in October 1994, with the participation of women from around the country; the seminar considered ways to advance Muslim women and to gain them entry into the educational system.[14]

Among those institutions that work to introduce secular education into Qur'anic schools are the Aga Khan Foundation[15] and the Islamic Foundation. The latter is an international organization, with a branch in Nairobi, that publishes pamphlets and textbooks on Islam in English and Kiswahili and, for a time beginning in 1976, published the quarterly *Al-Islam*, which dealt with Muslim issues and developments in the Islamic world. The organization also assists in efforts to reconstruct mosques and to establish schools.[16]

Some Muslim academics—whose number has grown in recent years, albeit slowly in comparison with Muslims' percentage in the population and with the Christians—devote themselves to researching Muslim education and suggesting ways to improve it. Even though they fiercely criticize both the colonial authorities and the government of independent Kenya, they do not refrain from also condemning Muslim leaders and organizations, including Supkem, for not doing enough to improve Muslim education.

Notable among Muslim professors are Mohamed Bakari and Saad Yahya, who actively participated in the seminar on Islam in Kenya organized by MEWA 1994, which dealt to a large extent with the question of education. Bakari is associate professor of linguistics at the University of Nairobi, where Yahya also lectures in the Department of Economics. Among other Muslim professors and lecturers at the University of Nairobi who work to advance Muslim education are Mohammed Hyder of the Zoology Department; M. H. Abdulaziz of the Linguistics Department; Hassan Mwakimako of the Department of Religions, who worked on a doctorate on Islam and is one of the strongest critics of the government and of Supkem; and Shirin Walji of the History Department.

In the field of Islamic education, Kenya's Muslims are assisted by contributions from the Arab world, primarily from the oil-producing Arab countries. Particularly large contributions were made in the 1970s and 1980s. In 1978, for example, Abu Dhabi donated $5 million for the establishment of a technical secondary school for Muslims;[17] Saudi Arabia assisted in the founding of Mombasa's Institute for Islamic Education, or Dar al-'Ulum (house of learning); in March 1981, Saudi Arabia contributed 752,000 shillings (about $100,000) to the Association for the Study of the Qur'an (Jam'iyat Ta'lim al-Qur'an). According to the chair of the association, in 1981, 550 students were studying at the Institute of Islamic Education.[18] In 1983, the Egyptians assisted in the founding of a center for teachers of Islam in Muranga in the Kikuyu area. (For Arab-Islamic activities, see also Chapter 11.)[19]

In general, since independence, with the help of the above organizations and assistance from Muslim bodies abroad, there has been a certain advancement of Muslim education. A number of colleges for teachers of Islam have been set up, like those at Muranga and Mikindani. The Kenyan government has granted Supkem 50 acres in the region of Voi to set up another college for Muslim teachers, and Supkem's spokesman announced in 1983 that they had already begun planning the college, which would cost 6 million shillings.[20] A Muslim school in the Huruna section of Nairobi became the Kenya Muslim Academy in the 1980s; Minister Hussein Maalim Mohamed and Assistant Minister Sharif Nassir have organized harambe gatherings to raise money to expand it.[21] In the field of girls' education there has also been some progress: a number of schools for Muslim girls have been established in Muslim centers, such as the Al-Huda madrasa in Mombasa, which also organizes seminars and assemblies for women.[22]

The idea of establishing an Islamic university in Kenya arises from time to time, but to date nothing substantial has been done to realize it. Thus, in 1994, Supkem's chair, Ali Shaikh Amin, announced that the organization was going to establish an Islamic university with the assistance of Muslim countries such as Saudi Arabia; as we shall see, Iran has also recently shown an interest in the proposal.

This process of establishing Muslim educational institutions has generally been slow, however, and Muslim leaders continue to complain about discrimination against Muslims in the field of education, especially when compared to Christians. The gap in education between Muslims and Christians is one of the reasons for the uneasy relationship between these two communities and for the tension between Muslims and the government.

10

Muslim-Christian Relations

Just as the Christian regime in Kenya harbors suspicions toward the Muslims—suspicions rooted in historical and modern events—so do many Muslims lack faith in a government headed by Christians and mistrust the Christian churches. This attitude is expressed in Muslim complaints about discrimination. The competition between Islam and Christianity in East Africa has, in fact, existed since Christianity first appeared in the region. The two world religions were ambitious to propagate themselves at the expense of traditional African religions, and they came into conflict with each other. As the Muslims, who were the first to arrive in the area, increasingly feared being displaced by the Christians, the Muslim-Christian dispute became not only religious but also political and economic.

Under the Christian colonial regime, Muslims lost their political superiority on the East African coast and gradually their commercial and economic privileges as well. Christian missionaries monopolized general education, and the authorities both directly and indirectly assisted the dissemination of Christianity. During this period, the Muslims occasionally protested against the government and accused it of trying to damage Islam and drive it out of Kenya. For example, in 1931, Muslim representatives sent a memorandum to the British authorities pointing out that colonial policy in Kenya was aimed at preventing the spread of Islam, as was occurring under British rule in Uganda. The memorandum noted that the British government in Kenya had invested a vast amount of money in the propagation of Christianity and Western culture by supporting the Christian missionaries.[1] In the colonial period, Asian Muslims, as well as Arab and African Muslims, mistrusted Christianity. In 1935, Asian Muslims who were wealthier, established the Muslim Missionary Movement, whose purpose was to check Christian missionary activity.[2]

Since independence, government leaders headed by the president, especially President Moi, have emphasized their Christian identity, even though the principle of the separation of church and state is entrenched in law, and Kenya's status as a secular state is periodically mentioned. Nevertheless, since independence, there have been no serious episodes of violence between Christians (who form about 70 percent of the population) and the Muslim minority, such as occurred in Uganda in the precolonial period and during Idi Amin's rule (1971–1979), or in Tanzania in recent years. Sometimes Kenya's Christians and Muslims express their mistrust of each other, mainly in written and spoken declarations by political and religious leaders. Yet when violence did break out in recent years, it was between Muslims and the authorities or among the Muslims themselves, as is described later.

It would seem at first glance that the Christian and Muslim organizations have common interests against the government. For instance, following the Christian-led campaign for a multiparty system there were requests to register the Islamic Party of Kenya (IPK) as legal within the multiparty framework. Calls for greater democracy and respect for human rights were heard from both sides. But the attitude and influence of the two groups were different, and they made no serious attempt at cooperation in this area. Muslim-Christian competition for the souls of the population rendered all their common interests irrelevant.

Muslim Complaints and Activities Against Christians

Muslim complaints against Christians in general, and against Christian churches and organizations in particular, usually resemble Muslim complaints against the government:

- They complain that the Christians relate to the Muslims as if they are foreigners who do not belong in the country and identify them with the Arabs (Muslims in Uganda make a similar complaint).
- They contend that Christian missionaries control education and direct it to spreading Christianity, and that even the government universities are used to propagate Christianity. The Department of Religious Studies at the University of Nairobi is, Muslims assert, no more than a branch of the missionary organizations. Indeed, Hannah Kinoti, head of the university's Department of Religious Studies, said in an interview in 1994

that for a long time Muslim students were prevented from registering in the department, and even Muslim teachers expressed reservations about joining the academic staff. She stressed that, for her part, she had made a great effort to recruit Muslim lecturers, including Mohamed Bakari.[3]
- Christian missionary leaders mention in public and among students that Muslims were slave traders.[4] Muslims complained that this belief was strengthened by a statement President Moi made on the subject at the Madaraka celebration (the receiving of internal self-government) on 1 June 1992. This was a preelection period, and several Muslim leaders were campaigning for the establishment of an Islamic party, hurling accusations against the government, and stirring up unrest in Mombasa (see Chapter 14). In his speech in the central stadium of Nairobi, before a large crowd, the president warned Islamic "fundamentalists" against harming the unity of the people and appealed to moderate Muslims to rein in the extremists. He said that in the end the disturbances would harm the Muslims themselves, because violence would revive bitter memories of the period when the coastal Muslims were slave traders. In this connection, an interesting article by Mohamed Bakari, "What Ails the Muslims?" attributes Muslims' lower status to Christian missionary propaganda in Kenya and its strong influence on the public.[5]
- Muslims claim that government leaders, headed by the president, stress the Christian foundations of their political ideology. They cite as an example President Moi's statement in his book that his philosophy of Nyayo is based on African tradition and the Christian faith.[6]
- Muslim leaders refer to Christian missionary activity against Islam during the colonial period, when "all the missionaries without exception were full of suspicion and hate towards the Muslims." They assert that this attitude still exists today in independent Kenya among many Christian officials, and is clearly evident in the area of education.[7]
- Christian judges and jurists do not take Islamic law into account. Muslims cite the examples of Attorney-General Joseph Kamera and, after him, Charles Njonjo, who tried to abolish the Islamic law of inheritance.[8]
- Christians put pressure on the government to prevent foreign Muslim religious leaders and preachers from entering Kenya and demand that those who have arrived in Kenya be expelled, whereas Christians are allowed to invite religious personalities

from outside. In this connection, Muslims recall the expulsion of five Muslim preachers from Tanzania, which they claim the Christian churches induced by pressuring the government; the expulsion caused serious disturbances on 30 October 1987.[9]

- Christian missionaries belittle the holy objects of Islam and even desecrate them. Muslim shaikhs and leaders in the town of Wajir, for example, published a letter in the opposition newspaper *Society* in which they protested that Christian missionaries working in their area had desecrated 500 copies of the Qur'an and caused interreligious tension. According to them, when the Muslims staged a protest rally and demanded that missionaries in the area cease their anti-Islamic activity, government forces dispersed the rally and even shot and wounded several demonstrators. Wajir's Muslim leaders demanded in their letter the cessation of all missionary activity in their region and threatened that if it did not stop, "they would take the law into their own hands."[10] A further example is the demonstration that took place in July 1993 in the Somali area of Isiolo, organized by local Muslim leaders after Friday prayers to protest against the administration of a local school that had forbidden Muslim girl students to wear a veil and Muslim dress that covered their whole bodies. Muslims claimed that Islam demanded that every girl over the age of fifteen cover her face and legs in public. Here too the district commissioner intervened on behalf of the Christian administration and warned the protesters not to harm the school or the teachers.[11] (On the government's contrary decision on this matter, see Chapter 4.)

Muslim community leaders do not content themselves merely with complaining; they also engage in propaganda aimed at stopping the spread of Christianity. In this propaganda they recall in particular the cooperation between the churches and the British colonial authorities and emphasize Christianity's "Western-imperialist" orientation and how this harmed African aspirations for independence.[12] Indeed, a primary objective of organizations such as Nukem and Supkem has been to counter Christian activity against Islam (see Chapter 3). In this fight the Muslims also expect assistance from Arab and Muslim countries. Thus, for example, the Egyptian embassy in Nairobi announced to the administration of al-Azhar University that Muslim organizations in Kenya were asking to be sent teachers and preachers "in order to withstand attempts to convert them to

Christianity and the Vatican's intensive activity in Muslim centres in Kenya." In response, Shaikh al-Azhar promised to provide help, "so that Muslims in Kenya could withstand the onslaught of Christian missionaries," by sending books, teachers, and preachers and also providing scholarships for study at al-Azhar.[13] (These Arab-Muslim activities are further discussed in Chapter 11.)

One of the claims made by the leaders of the IPK was that since all the other parties were led by Christians and did not concern themselves with the welfare of Muslims, there was a need for an Islamic party. In the disturbances that took place in Mombasa during 1992–1994, anti-Christian preaching was prominent in the propaganda of IPK supporters. Some Muslim circles did not look favorably on the pope's visits to Kenya, whose purpose, they believed, was to stimulate missionary activity. During Pope John Paul's third visit to Kenya, several Muslim organizations boycotted the mass prayer ceremony held in his honor on 19 September 1995 in the presence of hundreds of thousands of the faithful. The imam of the central mosque of Nairobi, Shaikh Ali Shee, was supposed to give a speech at the ceremony but did not appear.[14] One of the organizers of the visit, Father Stephan Okello, accused Muslim leaders of spreading malicious rumors that "the Catholic church had a plan to Christianize the whole of the African continent by the year 2000." Shaikh Ali Shee assented to this in an interview with Reuters and averred that the pope's visit was connected with "a secret plan to drive Islam out of Africa."[15]

Christian Complaints and Activities Against Muslims

Christian religious leaders and public figures reject the Muslim claim that discrimination by Christians is to blame for the Muslims' weakness in Kenya. They attribute the Muslims' complaints to their not being ready to acknowledge their minority status in a Christian-dominated state. Blame for Muslim backwardness, they assert, should be assigned to the Muslims themselves for opposing the modernization of education. Some mention the chewing of the intoxicating drug *miraa*, which is common among the Muslims and causes indolence and loss of a sense of reality and which—according to the Christians—is one of the reasons for widespread unemployment among the Muslims.[16]

Counter to the accusation that Christians work against Islam, Christians claim that Muslims disseminate anti-Christian propaganda in schools and public places. They cite the distribution of the anti-Christian pamphlet "The Gospel of Barnabas."[17] It is the Muslims who try to "buy" Christians for Islam, they assert. In October 1987, for example, Archbishop Manasses Kuria of the Church of the Province of Kenya (CPK) strongly criticized Muslim activity against Christianity and warned that their incitement could ignite a religious war. Muslim leaders, including Supkem, reacted to this criticism with a fierce denial; Sharif Nassir pointed out that Islam forbade the use of money to "buy" people from other religions and said the archbishop's purpose was to incite Christians against Muslims.[18]

The mutual suspicions and denunciations came to a head with the formation of the IPK in 1992, which led to outbreaks of violence on the coast. Christian fears of Muslim extremists were expressed in statements and articles, especially in the Christian press. For example, the July 1993 issue of the *JPR*, the journal of the umbrella organization of the Protestant churches, the National Christian Council of Kenya (NCCK), was devoted to Christian-Muslim relations in Kenya. Jeff Mbure, an NCCK activist, in an article entitled "Focus on Christian-Muslim Relations in Kenya: Rising Tension as Fundamentalism Sets In," expressed apprehension that Kenya was becoming an arena for Muslim-Christian conflict and that Islamic fundamentalism threatened the country's future. The tension, he warned, would intensify, and what was happening in North Africa would be child's play compared to the conflicts in store for Kenya. He noted that, according to information reaching the churches, there was a real possibility that the fundamentalist Islam spreading over North Africa would also reach East Africa. He quoted Ali Mazrui, who called this process "the third wave of change" that succeeds Western imperialism and neocolonialism (according to Mazrui, the stance of Kenya's Christian regime toward the Muslims is an aspect of neocolonialism). Mbure noted the rise in recent years of Muslim groups that were more aggressive and less tolerant, even among themselves. He suspected that as the number of Muslims in Kenya increased, so would their demands. Although, when the Muslims were still a small minority, there were attempts at Christian-Muslim rapprochement, this phenomenon would, in his view, start to vanish altogether with the appearance on the scene of the IPK. Mbure maintained that one of the causes of Muslim extremism in Kenya was the influence of inflamatory decisions by Muslim congresses calling for jihad. Also blamed were the activities of Arab and Muslim countries among the Kenyan Muslims, which included the financing of Muslim organizations in Kenya and the dispatching of religious teachers and preachers. Mbure expressed amazement that the Kenyan government allowed Muslim countries to operate in Kenya, whereas in these same Muslim countries the Christian minorities were regarded as infidels and forbidden to engage in missionary work.[19]

Similar statements about the activities of Muslim countries were published in an article, "There Is Also Arab Neocolonialism," that appeared in the 7 December 1995 issue of the Catholic journal *Avenire*, which is published in Rome in Italian. The writer warns about the dangers posed by the Islamic activities of Iran and other Muslim countries, such as the building of mosques and madrasas, and by extremist religious preaching, as in Tanzania. The 1992–1994 disturbances in Mombasa, which erupted in the background of Muslim requests to set up an Islamic party (see Chapter 14), also drove some Christians to issue warnings about the danger posed by Islamic fundamentalism. A Catholic circular distributed in 1993 mentions the civil war in southern Sudan, which broke out because of the Sudanese government's ambition to Islamize the south, and maintains that Muslim extremists in Kenya, such as the leaders of the IPK, display similar extremist tendencies.[20]

Mazrui's statements, supporting the establishment of an Islamic party in Kenya and attacking the government for what he considered its unfair treatment of the Muslim minority (see Chapter 13), elicited responses from Christian intellectuals and journalists, such as William Ochang, a professor, and the journalist Barak O. Muluka, who accused Mazrui of defending Arab actions aimed at acquiring a decisive influence in Africa, ignoring the damage that Arab slave traders had caused Africa and supporting Islamic fundamentalism. Muluka, in his article "Mazrui: From Universalist to a Crusading Sectionalist: Ethnic and Islamic Particularism," charged Mazrui with having become a lobbyist for the Arab and Muslim community on the coast, a community that was working to Arabize and Islamize the province. He attacked Mazrui for demanding that the West pay compensation for the slave trade while not demanding the same from the Arabs because, Mazrui contended, it would damage Afro-Arab unity. Muluka characterized Mazrui's activism and preaching as encouraging rifts in Kenyan society.[21]

The cardinal Maurice Otunga caused a storm of protest over statements he made at a conference of Christian representatives from African countries (SECAM, Secretaries of the Episcopal Conference of Africa and Madagascar, 12–16 January 1993) in Nairobi. The cardinal's words reflected Christians' anxiety about Muslims. He called on the representatives to fight the spread of Islam in Africa. He asserted that the Muslims were determined to destroy Christianity and to turn Africa into a Muslim continent, and the time had come for Christians to wake up and take action against this menace. The Muslims, in his view, were obligated by their religion to wipe out Christianity, and if the Christians did nothing to block this ambition, Christianity in Africa would "die a natural death."[22]

The cardinal's words infuriated Muslim organizations and leaders. The Muslims were particularly incensed over an assertion Otunga made that the Muslim belief in Muhammad as the last prophet was based on a lie, because Jesus was the last prophet. Muslims and Christians conducted a vehement debate in the letters-to-the-editor columns. Muslim religious and secular leaders even accused the cardinal of igniting a religious war in Kenya. Imam Ali Shee, for example, stated that the cardinal's words reflected factors that prompted Christians to discriminate against Muslims, discrimination that Muslims had endured for many years. He noted that many Christian organizations had waged a ceaseless struggle to prevent the dissemination of Islam but so far had failed. Cardinal Otunga's words were a continuation of this struggle, and they drove a wedge between Christians and Muslims that could lead to conflict. Imam Shee even contended that the warnings about what people called Islamic fundamentalism were nothing more than a pretext for those calling themselves fighters for freedom and equality, led by the United States, whose real purpose was to justify the war against the spread of Islam. Similarly strong statements were made by Muslim organizations, including Nukem, whose leader Shaikh Ali Amin al-Hinawi demanded that the government take steps against the cardinal. Supkem's leaders made similar declarations, and the unregistered IPK threatened to take measures to avenge these inciteful statements.[23]

In response, Kenya's Catholic Church published a clarification, signed by the archbishop, that claimed the cardinal's meaning had been distorted and that he had not been speaking against "true Islam" but against "Islamic fundamentalism," which "is making a lot of noise today, causing so much distrust and hostility." All the cardinal had said, according to the archbishop, was that the two religions had to coexist in peace and harmony. The church's announcement also stressed that it could not ignore the negative phenomenon of the growth of Islamic fundamentalism, which prevented any possibility of interfaith dialogue in an atmosphere of mutual respect. The announcement noted that Islamic fundamentalism was disseminated by Arab and Islamic countries and was influenced by extremist decisions taken at Islamic conferences. As an example it cited the resolutions of the Organization of Islamic Conference (OIC) in January 1981 in Mecca, which called for a jihad against "infidels," to "liberate the territories" in which Muslims live and to propagate Islam. The bishops repeatedly warned against such dissemination of Islamic fundamentalism and called on Christianity to arise and fight against the phenomenon.[24]

But the distrust of extremist Islam only intensified after the violent confrontations sparked by the formation of the IPK, and pronouncements by Christian leaders that enraged Muslims did not cease. For example, trouble again arose after the Anglican bishop of Eldoret, Stephan Kewasis, declared on 28 August 1994 that there was a need to increase missionary activity in the Northeastern Province in order to check the spread of Islam emanating from that area. He pointed out with alarm that mosques were being built all over the country, and urged Christians to build churches everywhere, including in Muslim areas such as the Northeastern Province and the Coast Province. Kewasis was speaking at a conference with many participants, including the Archbishop Kuria Manasses of the CPK and representatives from Kenya, Tanzania, Sudan, and Rwanda, who came to mark the 150th anniversary of the beginning of evangelism in the region.[25] These statements were publicized in the press, and Muslims again warned that such expressions constituted incitement and would cause conflict between Christians and Muslims, the more so since this time there was mention of missionary activity in Muslim areas.[26]

Indeed, several attempts were made to erect churches in Muslim areas. The CPK, for instance, embarked on a plan to build a large cathedral in the town of Lamu in the north, which is almost 100 percent Muslim. Local residents asked the government to intervene to stop the building plans, contending that the site designated for the cathedral was a Muslim cemetery and that there were already several churches in the area and no need for more. The district commissioner did intervene and halt the project and appointed a Commission of Inquiry in which council members from Lamu, the CPK, and government representatives took part.[27] By the end of 1999, the commission had not yet submitted its recommendations.

Together with these warnings and threats from both sides, there were also sometimes attempts at conciliation, chiefly when the danger of a flare-up increased. For example, Reverend Gatanga, editor of the NCCK's organ *JPR*, published in June 1995 an article titled "Christian-Muslim Relations: Let's Have Better Understanding." In it he called for a dialogue between Christian and Muslim leaders and for an emphasis on cooperation by means of providing appropriate information in the education system and to the public at large. He warned that if the situation continued to deteriorate, it would end with the outbreak of severe hostilities as in Sudan and Nigeria.[28] President Moi also makes pronouncements from time to time warning of the dangers of Christian-Muslim conflict.[29] During the pope's visit to Kenya as part of his 1995 tour of Africa, he devoted part of his address to the need for Muslim-Christian dialogue, especially at a time when religious radicalism was on the rise.[30]

Muslim leaders also sometimes call on Muslims and Christians to cooperate for the good of the whole population. Assistant Minister Sharif Nassir, for example, though he repeatedly complained about discrimination against Muslims, asked for the matter to be dealt with through negotiation. Even his response to Cardinal Otunga's words was relatively moderate. He said that he could not believe his ears and called on the cardinal to study and understand the Qur'an and to work for Christian-Muslim unity. He remarked that he himself was working to instill respect in his community for Christianity and Christians.[31]

Sometimes Muslim leaders point out interests common to Christians and Muslims, such as the opposition of both the Catholic Church and Muslim leaders to family planning. Indeed, in September 1995, Cardinal Otunga and Imam Shee organized a joint ceremony at which they publicly burned contraceptive devices in one of the squares in Nairobi.[32] At Muslim and Christian festivals, such as 'Id al-Fitr or Christmas, the leaders sometimes publish mutual greetings. On 'Id al-Fitr in 1983, for example, the archbishop of the CPK, Manasses Kuria, sent greetings to the Muslims.[33] But such cooperation is rare and has not succeeded in removing the tensions and suspicions between the two religions.

Those suspicions were again illustrated on the eve of the 1997 general elections, when the heads of the churches, together with opposition groups, set up the National Convention Executive Council (see Chapter 7) to pressure the government to carry out constitutional reforms. Supkem set up a similar council, called the Muslim Consultative Council, to discuss and present Muslim demands for administrative and constitutional reforms. Attempts to achieve cooperation between the two bodies did not go smoothly; the Muslims repeatedly complained that they were not given sufficient representation in the reform movement.[34]

Both Muslim and Christian leaders cause religious tension by making provocative statements, such as that of Cardinal Maurice Otunga calling for a struggle against the spread of Islam in Africa, and the alleged Muslim demand for a Muslim jimbo (province) on the coast, where the sharia would prevail (see Chap. 7). Although both sides often issue denials after the event, the damage has already been done, and mutual fears have been heightened.

11

Arab-Islamic Activities

One of the factors that has influenced the political and religious standing of Kenya's Muslims has been Arab-Islamic activity. In some ways these activities have been beneficial to Kenya's Muslims, in others detrimental.

On the positive side, several Arab countries have contributed financially to Islamic organizations and to the advancement of Muslim education, although not to the extent that Muslims had expected. On the negative side, the assistance was provided to specific Islamic bodies and not through a central organization, and this caused anger and jealousy among rival Muslim organizations and personalities. In addition, rivalries between some of the contributors themselves sowed further divisions among the Muslims. Moreover, aid that was not donated via governmental institutions increased the suspicions of the government and the Christian organizations.

Kenya was an important venue for Islamic political activity, mainly on the coastal strip, even during the colonial period. It was Egyptian president Jamal 'Abd al-Nasir who, in his book *The Philosophy of Revolution,* emphasized the importance of the use of Islam for political objectives. Nasir delineated three circles of influence—Arab, African, and Islamic—and he exploited them to promote Egypt's interests in its conflict with the West and with Israel.[1] In December 1953, the East African Islamic Conference met in Nairobi with Egypt's support. The Egyptian press emphasized that the conference's aim was "to discuss the establishment of a Muslim political force in Africa."[2] The British authorities, however, successfully contained Nasir's ambitions in Kenya as in other places.

Immediately after Kenya's independence in 1963, the Egyptians worked energetically and openly among the coastal Muslims. This caused apprehension among Christian organizations and the government, which openly expressed its concerns. Since then, the Egyptians have managed their Islamic operations much more cautiously.[3]

In the 1970s, Nasir's legacy was continued, to a large extent, by Libyan President Muammar Qadhafi, who was more aggressive in using Islam as a political tool in African countries, including Kenya. Qadhafi's fanatical outbursts against the West and Christianity, and against African regimes that did not toe his policy line, created tension between himself and many African governments. Libyan embassies in numerous African countries were closed or Libyan diplomats expelled.[4] In Kenya, the Libyans operated among the coastal Muslims and forged links with the leaders of Supkem and other Muslim bodies through the Libyan organization Propagation of Islam (al-Da'wa al-Islamiya). The Libyans even intervened in internal conflicts among the Muslim leadership, such as the dispute between Assistant Minister Sharif Nassir and Abdallah Mwidau, in which they supported Nassir.[5] Such blatant intervention provoked angry letters to the press warning against this interference; one letter accused Libya of inciting and helping Somali groups to act against the Kenyan government while reminding readers of Libya's subversive activity in other parts of Africa.[6]

Kenya was suspicious of any direct link between Arab-Islamic organizations and the Muslim community and insisted that all of their activities be channeled through the government. Thus, when the Libyan Taher Shweihidi, secretary-general of the Joint Organization for Establishing Islamic Cultural Centres, visited Kenya in September 1983 to open an Islamic cultural and educational Center in Nairobi, the government reacted with reservations. Attorney-General Mathew Muli reminded Shweihidi that Kenya's educational system was run by the government and certain standards had to be safeguarded; he demanded that Shweihidi consult with the ministries of education, health, and culture before establishing any center in Kenya. Muli, moreover, expressed concern that a center providing services to one faith, the Muslims, might provoke resentment among others and warned that "Kenya could not accommodate any sort of segregation in public institutions." The center was not established.[7]

In March 1988, the government banned distribution of the bulletin *Voice of Kenya*, published by the Libyan embassy, because of its incitement against Christianity. In December of the same year Kenya ordered the closure of the Libyan embassy, accusing Libya of inciting the Muslims during the 1987 riots and of assisting underground, antigovernment organizations such as Mwakenya.[8] The closure came in the wake of confessions by university students that Libyan diplomats had paid them to foment disturbances on the campuses. At that time, Kenya was also apprehensive about growing military ties between

Libya and Uganda. In 1992, at the time of the intratribal riots on the eve of the first multiparty elections, Kenya accused Libya of fanning the flames of those riots and of training young Kenyans in Libya and Uganda to overthrow the regime.[9]

In general, in the 1970s and 1980s Arab countries' Islamic and political activity in Kenya intensified, especially to prevent the renewal of Kenyan-Israeli diplomatic relations and to halt the economic cooperation that continued to exist between the two countries (as it did between Israel and other African countries such as Nigeria, Cote d'Ivoire, Ghana, and Cameroon) despite the severance of diplomatic relations. In Nairobi there were usually thirteen Arab embassies, as well as embassies of the Arab League and the Palestine Liberation Organization (PLO).[10] In addition, several Muslim organizations centered in Arab countries were active in Kenya, chief among them the World Islamic League (Rabitat al-'Alam al-'Islami); the Islamic Development Bank, whose main task in Kenya was to provide scholarships for Muslims to study in Arab countries;[11] and Kuwait's Islamic Endowment Fund for Kenya. To these can be added the Kenya-Arab Friendship Association, in which all the Arab embassies participated. Islamic propaganda also reached Kenya from the Islamic Propagation Centre in Durban, South Africa, which disseminated pamphlets about Islam, such as "What the Bible Says about Muhammad," which was reprinted in Nairobi and distributed by the Jamia Mosque of Nairobi. Another organization, which all of the Muslim embassies in Kenya established together in the 1980s, is the Ambassadors' Association of Muslim Countries.

This is not the place to deal with the whole range of the Arab countries' political, economic, and propaganda activities;[12] the focus here is specifically on Islamic activities.

The primary aims of Islamic activity in Kenya were to

- disseminate Islam, thereby strengthening the Muslim minority's position;
- strengthen the standing of Arab countries both with the government and with the Muslims;
- drive Israel out of Kenya, where, even after diplomatic relations were broken off, Israel had a considerable presence, with access to the government and to the Muslims; and
- pursue rivalries between Arab countries or between some Arab countries and Iran; for example, Iraq and Iran competed for the support of the government and the Muslims, as did Saudi Arabia and Iran, Egypt and Iran,[13] Saudi Arabia and Libya, and Egypt and Libya.

The Arab countries tried to achieve their objectives in Kenya in different ways, for example, by:

- Penetrating Islamic organizations such as Supkem. For example, in the assembly of Muslim leaders (Majlis al-'Ulamaa) which convened in August 1994 to resolve the bitter dispute among Muslims about determining the date of 'Id al-Fitr, the Saudis took part, and a diplomat from the Saudi embassy was appointed secretary of the assembly.[14]
- Contributing funds for setting up mosques and Muslim schools. One of the important Muslim schools founded in Mombasa was the Shaikh Zayed Bin Sultan al-Nahayan Secondary School, which was financed by the United Arab Emirates (UAE) in the early 1980s. The president of the UAE visited the school in April 1984 and was received with great deference by the president of Kenya and Muslim leaders.[15]
- Sending teachers and religious functionaries.
- Financing seminars and conferences on Islamic topics to which lecturers from Arab countries are sent.
- Inviting Muslim leaders to visit Arab countries.
- Encouraging the study of Arabic in schools.
- Organizing quizzes on the Qur'an.
- Providing scholarships to Muslim students to study in Islamic countries.
- Founding clinics and cultural centers.
- Setting up welfare and charity organizations.

In the 1980s, Libyan Islamic activity in Kenya was banned, but Saudi Arabia, Kuwait, the UAE, Oman, Iraq, Sudan, and (later) Iran became very active in the country.

In the various activities mentioned here, Saudi Arabia has played a prominent part since the 1960s. Among its important contributions, apart from financial donations for the founding of Muslim centers, schools, and mosques, was the setting up of a branch of the World Islamic League in the 1970s. The chairman of the Kenyan branch was Assistant Finance Minister Shaikh Mohamed Salim Balala, who was in fact the operational arm of the Saudis.[16] The Saudis also founded a secondary school for Islamic studies in the town of Machakos and sent teachers from Saudi Arabia to work in it.[17] A Saudi delegation that arrived in the 1970s under the auspices of Saudi Arabia's Educational Delegations to the Middle East (Ba'that al-Mamlaka al-'Arabia al-Sa'udia al-Ta'limiya Fi'l-Shark al-Awsat) had already in the 1970s prepared study programs on Islam and Arabic for schools in

East Africa.[18] In May 1994, the chair of the Kenyan Muslim organization Nukem announced a Saudi plan to establish an Islamic university.[19] Saudi Arabia and Iran have competed in efforts to setting up such a university on the coast, but the government has prevented them from carrying out this project.

In general, Saudi Arabia's Islamic activity, in contrast to Libya's, is carried out quietly through large Muslim organizations and is combined with general Saudi aid to the Kenyan government; hence, it does not cause the government concern. In the 1980s, there was considerable quiet competition between the Saudis and the Libyans to obtain Muslim support, and in recent years there has been similar competition between Saudi Arabia and the Gulf states on the one hand, and Iran on the other. There was a noisier and more public rivalry in the 1980s between Iran and Iraq, who were at war and vied for the moral support of Kenya's Muslims with mutual denunciations in the press. Late in 1982, Iran's activity increased when it invited some Muslim leaders to an international Islamic conference to be held in Teheran. Among those who attended were the qadi of the town of Kisumu, Shaikh al-Amin, and one of the leaders of Supkem, Farouk Muslim. This visit prompted criticism within Supkem and from other Muslim leaders, who warned against being identified with either of the two sides. Supkem's leaders merely expressed sorrow at the Iraq-Iran War and stressed the need for peace between the two Muslim countries. In several places, such as Lamu, the Muslims were divided between supporters and opponents of Iraqi president Saddam Hussein.

Iran's Activities in Kenya

Over the past decade, Iran has become more active in the sphere of Islamic politics in Kenya. Apart from wanting generally to strengthen its position in Third World countries, Iran has certain goals in Kenya:

- Iran wants to exploiting the ongoing tension between Kenya and Western countries, especially the United States, which sharply criticizes Kenya for human rights violations, corruption, repression of the opposition, and the lack of real democracy. The propaganda is anti-Israel as well as anti-West. the economic benefits for Kenya of cooperating with Iran are also emphasized.[20]
- Iran wants to disseminate Islam, including the Shi'a and the ideas of the Khomeini revolution, while exploiting the Muslim

community's feelings of being discriminated against. Thus, Ali Akbar Nataq Nuri, then speaker of the Iranian parliament, said that Iran placed special emphasis on the "revitalization" of Islam in Africa. The journal *West Africa*, which quoted this statement, recalled the document published in Lusaka, Zambia, according to which Iran had set up an Islamic organization called Islam in Africa, one of whose tasks was to establish at least one Islamic party in every African country, with Kenya chosen as a center of Islamic activity in East Africa.[21] According to Iran's ideology, every struggle that is carried out in the name of Islam is a credit to the Iranian revolution, a sign of its success in exporting its ideas, and a demonstration to the Islamic world of its importance. As Jawad Larjani, a member of Iran's Supreme Council for National Security, put it: "Our honor and glory in the world depend on . . . the diffusion and the revival of Islam." Thus, Iran is duty bound to give material and moral support to genuine Islamic movements everywhere, to spread its ideology and lead the Islamic world.[22]

Iran has carried out its Islamic activity in Kenya more cautiously than Libya so as not to arouse fears among the government and the Christian organizations. The great majority of Kenya's Muslims are Sunnis, and Iran seems to have used the services of Sunni Sudan. This assumption is strengthened by a number of declarations by leaders of both countries. During a visit to Iran in December 1986, for example, Sudan's then prime minister, Sadiq al-Mahdi, spoke about cooperation in spreading Islam in the world and in Africa, and about strengthening "ideas of the Islamic revolution" of Iran and Sudan. The speaker of Iran's Islamic Consultative Assembly and later president, Hashemi Rafsanjani, declared during that visit: "We believe that, if a strong foundation for revolutionary Islam is established in Sudan, it could fulfill a useful role in Africa."[23] In his visit to Khartoum in December 1991, Rafsanjani declared, referring to General Omar Hassan al-Bashir's military coup of June 1989, that the "Islamic revolution of Sudan . . . can doubtless be the source of inspiration to movements and revolutions throughout the Islamic world."[24] Later, in June 1994, Sudanese president Hassan al-Bashir declared after talks with the Iranian ambassador in Khartoum that "Sudan and Iran take an identical position and they will continue to be the chief stronghold of the Islamic faith"; he added that Sudan would strengthen its ties with Iran because this would serve the interests of Islam and Muslims all over the world.[25] In the Kenyan context, this practice of using Sudanese cooperation does not seem to have been very effective because of the chilly relationship between Kenya and Sudan. Sudan frequently complains that Kenya assists the southern Sudanese underground and allows them to open offices in Nairobi. For its part, Kenya accuses Sudan of trying to spread extremist Islam in its country and has even accused Sudan of subversive activities.[26]

The following paragraphs provide examples of Iran's activity in Kenya.

Islamic Cultural Center

The Islamic cultural center that Iran has set up in Nairobi is called the Al-Rasul al-Akram Islamic Centre. It has a reading room and a large library with much Islamic material, including many anti-Israeli texts. There are also videos that can be borrowed, some of which have been shown on television. The center organizes meetings and seminars, such as, the First Muslim Women's Seminar, to which Fatma Hyder, Supkem's head of Women's Affairs was invited, and at which, among other things, the tradition of wearing a veil (*hijab*) was extolled. The wife of the Iranian ambassador remarked in her speech that "those who follow the path of Islam would not be infected by AIDS."[27]

The center also organizes exhibits on Iranian culture, which are advertised in special supplements in the newspapers;[28] distributes books on Islam to Muslim students;[29] and offers free courses in Islamic subjects and in Arabic and Persian. On the anniversary of the Ayatollah Khomeini's death, the center conducts assemblies in Nairobi and Mombasa that glorify Khomeini and highlight his struggle against the West. The Centre also holds ceremonies at which prizes are awarded to students for writing the best essay on "The Imam Khomeini as I Know Him."[30]

Embassy

Iran has set up a large embassy in Nairobi, and the Iranian ambassador and his staff frequently visit Mombasa and Muslim centers throughout the country. The embassy also distributes food, clothing, and medicine on the occasion of Muslim festivals such as 'Id al-Fitr.

Furthermore, the Iranian embassy in Kenya publishes a free newsletter called *The Guide,* which consists mainly of quotations from Khomeini's speeches, interviews with Muslim leaders, and material against Israel, Iraq, and Christians and in favor of Sunni-Shiite cooperation.[31] The articles are written by local Muslims recruited for this purpose. In this connection, an article in the Iranian journal *Salaam*

(3 April 1996), on the occasion of President Rafsanjani's visit to Africa, asserted:

> There have been many efforts by Christian missionaries and Zionist groups to change the cultural-social identity of the African peoples. In order to stand up to these schemes, it is necessary to strengthen the links between Iran—an important country in the Islamic world—and African countries, and to stop the infiltration of Christianity and Zionism, which are working to drive Islam out. Our hope is that the visit of President Rafsanjani to Africa, where about 400 million Muslims live, will mark the beginning of stronger ties between Iran and African governments.

Pan-African Propaganda

Early in 1995, Iran increased its propaganda in Africa and began radio broadcasts in two widespread African languages, Kiswahili in East Africa and Hausa in West Africa.[32] Iranian leaders and ambassadors in Africa repeatedly stress the importance that Iran attributes to its relations with African countries. For example, in his farewell meeting in November 1997 with the outgoing Kenyan ambassador Salim Juma, President Mohamed Khatami said that strengthening ties with African nations is of special importance in Iran's foreign policy,[33] and such statements were repeated in nearly all the courtesy calls to the different ministers by the new Iranian ambassador to Kenya, Hassani Tabatabai. By the end of the decade Iran had more than twenty embassies in Sub-Saharan Africa.

Propagation of Shi'a

Iran seeks both to disseminate Shi'a Islam in Kenya and to foster cooperation between Sunnis and Shiites. Iran has succeeded in converting to Shi'a several notable Muslims, such as Ahmad Hatib and Shaikh Abdullahi Nasr. The latter owned a publishing company and distributed free booklets on Shi'a.[34] Just as Iran recruits Lebanese Shiites for its operations in West Africa, it recruits Shiites, especially members of the Ithna'ashari Shi'a minority, to advance its interests in Kenya. Among these is MP Rashid Sajad, who is close to the country's leadership (see Chapter 6). Iran hopes that with the help of these Shiites, and by making contributions to Muslims, it can influence a wider segment of Sunnis. Iran also exploits the fact that the differences between Sunni and Shi'a are not so clear to many Muslims in Kenya, especially the young and the less conversant in Islam, who can be influenced especially in conditions of unemployment and economic hardship. An example of Iran's efforts to blur the differences between Sunni and Shi'a and to be accepted by Sunni groups was a conference, "The Unity of Islam and the Enemies of Islamic Unity," held in Nairobi on 26 February 1996 and sponsored by the Iranian Cultural Council, in which learned men and religious leaders from Iran and Kenya participated. The Iranian delegation was led by Ayatollah Waiz Zade Khorasani, chairman of the Society for Closer Links between Muslim Sects; heading the Kenyan delegation was the imam of the Jamia Mosque in Nairobi, Shaikh Ali Shee, who was criticized by some Sunni religious leaders for his attempts to blur the distinctions between Sunni and Shi'a. The Iranian ambassador to Kenya, al-Haj Hamid Moayer, also took part. Imam Shee's speech included a call to Supkem to integrate into its activities all the Muslims in the country and not just the Sunnis.[35]

Iran also supports and helps finance the setting up of mosques and Islamic institutes in Kenya.[36]

Exchange of Distinguished Visitors

Iran brings important Iranians to Kenya on visits, such as the visit in 1990 by the Iranian minister of culture and cultural guidance, Sayed Mohamed Khatni, who repeatedly cited Iran's desire to forge closer cultural ties with Kenya. Apart from religious figures, the visitors also frequently include statesmen and economists, such as Foreign Minister Velayeti in April 1994 and the assistant minister of agriculture in June 1994.[37] A particularly important visit was that of President Rafsanjani, who came to Kenya in September 1996 in the framework of an extensive tour of Africa that included Uganda, Sudan, Tanzania, Zimbabwe, and South Africa. The president was accompanied by an entourage of 200, including the ministers of foreign affairs and of industry and trade as well as business leaders and economists. One of the purposes of the visit, which took place less than a month after President Clinton had confirmed the imposition of partial sanctions on Iran, was to counter U.S. efforts to isolate Iran. During the visit, Iran and various African countries signed many economic agreements. The agreement with Kenya included increasing the amount of oil Kenya bought from Iran, which now totals about 15 percent of its needs. In addition, Iran agreed to provide technical and financial aid to Kenya to renovate its refineries in Mombasa. The visit took place at a time when Kenyan-U.S. relations had deteriorated because of the latter's pressure on Kenya for greater democracy. Rafsanjani exploited this situation, making a speech before a Muslim audience in Mombasa in which he stressed Iran's interest in cooperating with African countries to limit the West's influence.[38]

Iran also invites Kenyan Muslim personalities to visit Iran. Particularly wide publicity was given to the June 1994 two-week visit of Rashid Mzee, a Sunni member of parliament and vice-chairman of the opposition Ford-Kenya Party, who had won his parliamentary seat thanks largely to the support of the militant leader of the Islamic Party of Kenya, Shaikh Khalid Balala, who clashed bitterly with the authorities (see Chapter 14). Mzee, a lecturer in veterinary medicine at the University of Nairobi, was accompanied by another MP from his party, Farah Maalim, to take part in the events marking the fifth anniversary of Khomeini's death. During the visit, Mzee met with ministers and other senior officials. On his return to Kenya, he remarked at an assembly convened in his honor that, following his discussions, the Iranian government had agreed to assist Ford-Kenya financially—because it was the largest opposition party, popular outside Kenya as well—and to help Kenyans enjoy real democracy under a multiparty system. When Mzee commented that during the visit he had learned "new tricks" that would strengthen the party, his words met with thunderous applause.[39] He also asserted that Iran had promised to found an Islamic university in the Coast Province and that an Iranian delegation was about to arrive in Kenya to carry out a comprehensive study on the subject. He added that Iran was donating, through him, twenty scholarships to Muslim Kenyan students to study in Iran.[40] The *Kenya Times,* mouthpiece of the ruling Kanu Party, reacted harshly to Mzee's speech, stating that the Iranian government must respond and clarify its position on the professor's statements and that if they were true, they indicated gross intervention in Kenya's affairs.[41] Mzee's words in fact embarrassed the Iranian embassy in Nairobi, which operated cautiously and tried not to provoke the government. (Iran had not forgotten that, in the late 1970s, Kenya had closed its embassy in Nairobi and accused Iran of sabotage and interference in Kenyan affairs.) The Iranian ambassador immediately called a press conference and vigorously denied the professor's claims, calling them "total rubbish"; he further accused Mzee of endangering Kenyan-Iranian relations. The ambassador emphasized that his country's policy was based on noninterference in other countries' internal affairs and that it wanted strong, mutually beneficial relations with Kenya. As for setting up an Islamic university in the Coast Province, the ambassador said he had not heard of the idea and stressed that Mzee had not been invited to Iran by the government but by the Committee to Mark Five Years Since the Death of Khomeini.[42]

Economic and Technical Cooperation

To allay suspicions, Iran repeatedly declares that it does not seek to spread Islamic revolutionary ideals; it acts to build friendly relations and to demonstrate goodwill.[43] In this context, Iran engages in economic and technical cooperation and trade activities by means of which it can, in fact, spread its ideas and garner support without raising suspicion. Thus, extensive coverage was given to the opening of the Iranian Medical Center in Nairobi in October 1997; the Iranian ambassador declared in his speech that other medical centers would be opened in other places for the benefit of all Kenyans.[44] Iran frequently stresses, especially during visits of important Iranians to Kenya, the economic benefits that can accrue to Kenya from good relations with Iran, such as the supply of oil, the development of the oil industry, and the importation of Kenyan goods. On 15 August 1995, for example, an Iranian delegation of twenty businessmen headed by Foreign Minister Velayeti arrived in Kenya. The Iranian embassy in Kenya gave wide publicity to the visit and took the opportunity to point out that seven Iranian companies were working in Kenya and had invested millions of dollars. Furthermore, Iran Airlines has opened a direct flight between the two countries, and in recent years there have been three fairs of Iranian industrial and agricultural products in Nairobi, during which much propaganda material was also distributed. In the third fair, which opened on 5 September 1995, seventy Iranian companies displayed their products and Iran's assistant minister of trade participated. As noted, Rafsanjani's visit in 1996 saw the signing of economic agreements.

* * *

Despite Iran's caution in its activities in Kenya, they have already indirectly led to disagreements, albeit minor, between Sunnis and Shiites about mosques. When Iran has donated money to mosques, Shiites have claimed that this gives them the right to run them; Sunnis deny this.[45] Leading Muslims have also criticized Iran's Islamic activity for possibly leading to a split within the Muslim community. As for the government, it takes an ambivalent attitude toward Iran's Islamic activities. On the one hand, the government expects to benefit economically from cooperation with Iran in the areas of oil supply and the export of Kenyan goods to Iran, and the Iranian government encourages these expectations and stresses that it can also provide technical aid in agriculture and industry.[46] President Moi visited Iran in November 1988, and Kenya opened an embassy in Teheran that is usually staffed by Muslims. Nevertheless, it appears that Kenya closely monitors Iran's Islamic activity to ensure that it remains within reasonable limits.[47]

Reactions of the Government and the Christians

Arab-Islamic activity in general arouses misgivings among the authorities and among Christians. The government fears the influence of fanatical Islam coming from Libya, Sudan, and Somalia. President Moi expressed this publicly during the British foreign minister's visit in September 1988, declaring that, while Kenya was not assisting the southern Sudanese rebel movement, the Sudanese People's Liberation Army (SPLA), "it shares the concerns of the animists and Christians in south Sudan."[48] On various occasions government officials have warned Muslims not to involve foreign countries in Kenya's internal or external affairs, such as the Middle East conflict.[49] There was great concern during the period of Idi Amin's rule in Uganda, 1971–1979, about his threats against Kenya, his murder of Christian religious and political leaders, and his persecution of Christians in general. Nor was Kenya pleased about the support that Libya and other Arab countries gave to Amin's regime, which enabled him to threaten his neighbors; even Supkem issued a public statement opposing this assistance.[50] Kenya has even banned the Muslim students' union at the University of Nairobi because of its links with the ambassadors of Arab countries, who sometimes give lectures at the university.[51] The Kenyan government also expressed its indignation at the Islamic activity of extremist Arab countries during the visit to Nairobi of Taher Shweihidi, secretary-general of one of the Libyan organizations. The government spokesperson asserted that the giving of aid to a specific religious group, in this case Muslims, "could cause disquiet in other religious communities and the government opposes discrimination in public institutions."[52]

In March 1986, Kenya's foreign minister, Elijah Mwangale, also expressed opposition to Arab states' Islamic activity when he said, after returning from an Afro-Arab conference, "I made it abundantly clear that, in spite of all this talk of Afro-Arab cooperation, little has in actual fact been achieved. There is little flow of Arab capital to Africa. I also stressed that Arabs should not seek to introduce religion as part of Afro-Arab cooperation."[53]

Fears of Islamic extremism in Kenya were expressed dramatically when on 13 January 1994 the daily newspaper *The Standard* printed a full-page headline: "Terror Against Kenya: Islamic Fundamentalists to Take Over." The newspaper claimed it had received information that Sudan, with Iran's help, was planning to "turn Kenya from Dar al-Harb into Dar al-Islam" (i.e., from part of the non-Muslim world to part of the Muslim world). For this purpose Sudan was infiltrating into Kenya agents disguised as refugees to foment unrest and, with the help of fighters whom Sudan was concentrating along the Sudan-Kenya border, to overthrow the government. The Iranian embassy denied the story, which indeed sounds incredible; but it does demonstrate Kenya's concern, especially in light of the disturbances that Shaikh Khalid Balala orchestrated in Mombasa. The Islamic Peoples Conference, held in late March 1995 in Khartoum and headed by the influential Sudanese radical leader Hassan al-Tourabi, also caused disquiet in Kenya.[54]

The Christian leadership naturally does not look favorably on the Arabs' efforts to spread Islam, which are often combined with anti-Christian elements. As noted in Chapter 10, the Christian leadership opposed the coming to Kenya of foreign Muslim teachers and imams, complaining that they preach against Christianity. When Ali Mazrui criticized Kenya's Middle East policy as pro-Israeli, several Christian professors fiercely attacked him and accused him of supporting "the establishment of Arab-Islamic hegemony in East Africa."[55]

Criticism of Arab-Islamic activity also comes from Muslim leaders who oppose Arab countries' intervention in internal disputes among the Muslims, especially at election time. These leaders charge that much of the money supposedly donated for Islamic purposes finds its way into private pockets, and they demand that it be channeled through the government.[56]

Conclusion

Arab countries' Islamic activity in Kenya helps Muslims in certain ways, particularly in the sphere of education even if, as the Muslims charge, the aid given to build schools, cultural centers, and charity is insufficient. Also, the expectations the government still has of economic benefits from cooperation with Arab countries and Iran moderate its stance toward the Muslim minority, since Kenya must take into account the Muslim and Arab countries' reactions to its treatment of Muslims. On the other hand, misgivings about foreign Islamic activity felt by the authorities, Christian groups, and even some Muslims limit its political influence. Rivalries between Arab countries themselves also weaken their ability to exert influence. The Kenyan government's fears about Arab-Islamic activities were intensified by the 1992–1994 disturbances in Mombasa and later by the bombings of the U.S. embassies in Nairobi and Dar-es-Salaam (see Chapter 7).

12

The Islamic Factor in Kenya and the Middle East Conflict

Arab-Muslim activities in Kenya have been one of the main reasons for the involvement of Kenya's Muslims in the Arab-Israeli conflict. As in the case of other issues, the Muslim community was divided in its attitudes toward the Arabs and Israel. Moreover, the important role of the Middle East issue in Kenya's foreign policy sometimes became a bone of contention between the government and local Muslim leaders.

After Kenya attained independence in December 1963, Israel was one of the first countries to establish diplomatic ties and set up an embassy in Nairobi. The cornerstone was already laid a few days before independence, in the presence of future president Jomo Kenyatta and Israeli foreign minister Golda Meir, who came to Kenya especially for the ceremony. During the late colonial period, there had already been contacts between Kenyan leaders and Israel, and Israel had an honorary consul in Nairobi, Yitzhak "Izzi" Somen, who in the early 1960s also served as mayor of Nairobi and was active in Kenya's Jewish community.

Kenya's president and its Christian leaders had a special relationship with Israel, both because of their belief in the Bible and its predictions of the Jews' return to Israel and their admiration for the country's achievements. The Christian regime's concerns about the coastal and Somali Muslims also acted to bring Israel and Kenya together. Moreover, the Somali Shifta in Kenya were assisted in their subversive activities mainly by Somalia, which proclaimed the goal of Greater Somalia, that is, the annexation of those areas of Ethiopia and Kenya inhabited by Somalis. In 1974, Somalia joined the Arab League and gained support for its territorial claims from Arab countries. This chapter does not, however, focus primarily on Israel's relations with the Kenyan government, but rather on Kenyan Muslims' attitudes toward Israel and the Arab countries.

When Kenyan-Israeli diplomatic relations were first established immediately after independence in 1963, Muslims did not protest. On 21 August 1969, a fire broke out in the al-Aqsa Mosque in Jerusalem. The Muslim world reacted with outrage, vividly displayed in the Muslim conference in Rabat that year. In Kenya, several Muslim figures and organizations, including Mohamed Jehazi, who was then a member of parliament and active among the coastal Muslims, issued statements condemning Israel and accusing it of starting the fire. That same year, about forty Muslim religious leaders gathered in the al-Mazrui Mosque in Mombasa and harshly attacked Israel.[1] On the other hand, the chief qadi, Abdallah Salih al-Farsy, issued a conciliatory statement stressing that Israel should not be blamed for an act committed by an insane individual.[2]

These events reflected both the influence on the Muslims of Arab countries' activities in Kenya and the differences among the Muslims concerning relations with Israel. Arab-Islamic activity in Kenya began in the 1950s and increased after independence. Led at first by Egyptian president Jamal 'Abd al-Nasir and then by Libya, Iraq, Iran, and other countries, it negatively affected several Muslim groups' attitude toward Israel, especially in Mombasa and on the coast. On the other hand, there were circles, albeit less vociferous, that opposed involving the Arab-Israeli conflict in Kenya's foreign policy.

Since then, anti-Israeli Muslim groups have been periodically active. For example, when in 1970 Israel's ambassador to Kenya, Reuven Dafni, made a small contribution to the reconstruction of the mosque in Wajir, a Somali area, other Muslims protested. Dafni's contribution, to which the press gave much publicity, came in response to a call by Ahmad Khalif, an MP from East Wajir and assistant minister of housing. Leading those who condemned him for accepting the donation was, again, Jehazi, then MP and assistant minister of health. A number of shaikhs sided with Jehazi as did the chair of Nukem, Issa Hemed Kuria, who contended that to accept a contribution for a mosque from non-Muslims, especially Israel, which was at war with the Arabs, contravened Islam and offended the sensibilities of most of Kenya's Muslims. These leaders demanded that the ambassador's donation be returned.

This dispute now captured the headlines, and many letters to the editor, pro and con, appeared. Khalif, for his part, continued to maintain that acceptance of the donation did not go against the Qur'an, and accused Kuria of trying to drag Kenya's Muslims into the Arab-Israeli conflict. Khalif also stressed that when he made his call for contributions, neither the representatives of Arab countries nor Muslim notables in Kenya had rushed to help as had the Israeli ambassador. Kanu leaders in Wajir also supported Khalif.[3]

The issue again surfaced in October 1973 when the Yom Kippur War broke out. On 18 October, several Muslim MPs raised the matter in parliament, expressing support for the Arabs. The attorney-general opposed raising the matter and averred that if the Muslim MPs were real Kenyans, they would be careful about involving Kenya in any way in that war.[4] Thus, the government acted to block any manifestation of Muslim involvement in the Middle East conflict.

Israel, for its part, wanted to establish good relations with the Muslim community in Kenya. It emphasized that the Arab-Israeli conflict was not a conflict between Judaism and Islam. The Israeli embassy pointed out that hundreds of thousands of Arab Muslims in Israel enjoyed full religious freedom. A factor in Israel's motivation was Mombasa's importance to it as a port. Most of the port workers were Muslims, and Israel wanted to ensure that they would not harm either the passage of Israeli ships or the servicing of them. Also of concern to Israel was the fact that the Arab boycott office in Damascus monitored those Kenyan companies that did business with Israel and would send them threatening letters demanding that they break off these ties (for more on Kenyan opposition to the Arab boycott, see Chapter 11).

Muslims who supported Israel included Abdallah Mwidau, mayor of Mombasa during the 1970s and later MP, and the well-known community leader Hyder Kindy. Support for Israel also stemmed from internal political considerations in Mombasa and on the coastal strip and from competition among Muslim leaders for key positions in the community, the party, and the government. Mwidau, who as MP for the Mombasa-South constituency had rivals who sought to unseat him, was angry that these rivals received material and financial assistance from Arab countries. He criticized the Arab countries' involvement in Muslim affairs in Kenya and their anti-Israeli activities, and like Hyder Kindy he opposed in principle the mixing of religion and politics.[5]

In the 1970s, Israel encouraged the establishment of the African Muslim-Jewish Education Fund (AMJEF), whose purpose was to provide scholarships to Muslim students. In doing so, Israel sought to demonstrate that neither Israel nor Judaism was hostile to Islam, and to show the Kenyan leadership that not all of Kenya's Muslims opposed Israel that they did not form a united block concerning the Middle East conflict, and that this should be taken into account in formulating Kenya's Middle East policy. As noted earlier, the regime was somewhat sensitive to Muslim positions, especially at election time.

The AMJEF was partially sponsored by the Jewish community of Nairobi, whose approximately 300 members contributed $10,000 to the fund. The chair of the AMJEF was Hyder Kindy. The fund gave hundreds of scholarships to young Muslims and existed until 1973 when Kenya broke off diplomatic relations with Israel. Of course, Kindy's Muslim rivals did not look favorably on the setting up of the AMJEF and even accused the Israeli embassy of trying to help Kindy assume the Muslim leadership in Mombasa by means of the fund. The leaders of Nukem also opposed the fund and Kindy.[6]

Israel's need to explain itself to Kenyan Muslims also arose from the fact that in the 1960s and 1970s there sometimes appeared in the local press letters and articles attacking Israel's political and economic activities in Kenya. Some of these were submitted by Arab embassies, especially the Egyptian embassy, and some by Muslim readers. Two of the most persistent critics of Israel were Taj ad-Din Kassam, whose letters and articles appeared almost monthly for many years until the 1990s, and Salim A. Awadhan. For example, during the visit to Kenya of Israeli foreign minister Moshe Arens in 1983, Awadhan published a letter sharply censuring Israel and criticizing the Kenyan government for allowing the visit, especially since Kenya had no diplomatic ties with Israel at that time.[7] The Israeli embassy and supporters of Israel, including Muslims, responded to these letters, and the dispute over Israel and the Middle East conflict remained in the headlines.

Some Muslim groups opposed the establishment of Israeli embassies in Kenya as well as in Tanzania, and an organization calling itself the Young Muslims of East and Central Africa sent letters to these embassies, with copies to the press, demanding their closure and threatening "severe consequences" if this was not done.[8] The Organization of Muslim Students of the University of Nairobi also published articles in its journal, *Minaret,* condemning Israel and supporting the PLO and the Palestinians. Nukem, as mentioned, also worked against Israel among the Muslims, whereas the progovernment Supkem generally refrained from attacking Israel.

The bulletins published by Arab embassies devoted considerable space to anti-Israeli articles by Kenyan Muslims. Another journal that sometimes featured articles condemning Israel was *Iqra,* published by the Jamia Mosque of Nairobi—for example, "Zionism Is Racism" by Yousef Salem.[9] The journal *al-Islam* of the Islamic Foundation sometimes criticized Israel for its treatment of Muslims—and for Israel's attempts to "unite Jerusalem," obscure Islam's connection to the city, and forbid the building of mosques in it.[10] In addition, special anti-Israeli monographs were sometimes published.[11]

Although, on 1 November 1973, Kenya severed diplomatic ties with Israel and closed the Israeli embassy, the Muslim factor in Kenya did not play a part here; the action was carried out in the wake of a resolution of the Organization of African Unity (OAU). The OAU resolution, initiated by Egypt at the time of the October War, called on African countries to sever diplomatic relations with Israel. Kenya complied with the resolution out of solidarity with the other OAU members. Kenya agreed, however, that an Israeli diplomat would serve as interest officer and continue to work in the country under the auspices of a foreign embassy. In fact, relations continued as before in almost every sphere, though without formal acknowledgement, and Israeli activity in Kenya even increased during this period.[12]

Abdallah Mwidau, a supporter of Israel, managed to get elected to parliament representing the Mombasa-South constituency despite the campaign against him by his Muslim opponents led by Sharif Nassir, who was backed by Libya. In 1979, Mwidau visited the United States and conducted an information campaign among black Muslims in which he stressed Israel's contribution to African developing countries, particularly Kenya, and specifically its assistance to Muslim education in Kenya. Mwidau's rivals in Mombasa, headed by Nassir (who had close ties with President Moi), denounced this activity and called him a "Zionist agent." The Libyans published leaflets and planted articles in the newspapers that castigated him. Nassir even managed to get Mwidau dismissed from his position in an international company by "orders from above," causing Mwidau and his family severe economic hardship. In spite of all this, efforts to defeat Mwidau in the parliamentary elections repeatedly failed because of his popularity in his electoral district, and he remained in parliament until his death in 1986.[13]

Kenyan Muslims largely supported the peace agreement between Israel and Egypt signed in 1979; some, however, opposed it and maintained that Egyptian president Anwar Sadat had betrayed Islam and should be ostracized.[14]

In April 1983, while there were still no diplomatic relations between Kenya and Israel, the Israeli dance troupe Bat-Dor was invited to appear in Kenya. This prompted a stormy public debate in Kenya, particularly among the Muslims. A number of Muslim leaders joined in a protest held in Nairobi by the Libyan embassy, the PLO, and the Arab League; the Arabs even threatened that the troupe's performance would damage Kenya's relations with Arab countries. The government, which continued to maintain wide-ranging informal ties with Israel, did not give in to the pressure. As noted, Nassir, apparently on instructions from higher up, tried to placate the Muslims and reiterated the government's position that politics should not be involved in cultural matters. Moderate Muslims such as Mwidau even blasted the Arabs for trying to constrain Kenya's policies and asked the government to close the Libyan embassy. In the end, the troupe performed and was warmly received by the mainly Christian audience.[15]

On 23 December 1988, Kenya renewed diplomatic relations with Israel. As discussed in the previous chapter, Arab countries reacted angrily, but Kenya's Muslims did not criticize the move. The anti-Israeli Muslims apparently held back in light of the irrevocability of the government's decision and its angry reaction to the criticism from the Arabs, whom it warned not to dictate to Kenya.

In 1992, with the emergence of Muslim extremism headed by Shaikh Khalid Balala, attacks on Israel again combined with opposition to the government. Balala, as well as other extremist members of the Islamic Party of Kenya, accused Israel of harming the Muslims and Islam and expressed support for the PLO and Arab countries. Among other things, abusive graffiti were sprayed on the walls next to the Mombasa offices of the Israeli shipping company Zim, including even a swastika. Most of the workers in the Zim offices were Muslims, who disassociated themselves from what had been done.[16]

One of the most emphatic Muslim opponents of Israel was Kenya-born Ali Mazrui, who at the time supported the legal registration of the IPK and criticized the government for discriminating against Muslims. At the time of intense conflicts in Mombasa between the security forces and radical Muslims, he published an article berating the government for its "pro-Zionist policy," claiming that at the time of the 1976 Entebbe raid, in which Israeli hostages whose plane had been hijacked by Palestinians were freed in Uganda, Kenya had assisted Israel by permitting its planes to stop over in Nairobi for fueling and by giving medical aid to the wounded attackers, even though the Israelis had killed "hundreds of Ugandans" in the operation. Mazrui thought it appropriate to remind his readers of the explosion, perpetrated by Palestinians, that had occurred in December 1980 in the Norfolk Hotel in central Nairobi, owned by Jews; in this there was the hint of a threat to the Kenyan government. Mazrui argued that Kenya's "pro-Zionist" policy was undermining the possibility of pan-Africanism, since Arabs formed an important part of Africa's population.[17]

Another example of exploitation of Islam against Israel occurred in 1993 during a visit to Mombasa by Israel's ambassador to Kenya. At that time, the antigovernment disturbances organized by the IPK were at their peak. The ambassador met with moderate Muslim leaders and officials, including the provincial commissioner and the district commissioner, and these meetings were publicized in the press. Rashid Mzee, a Ford-Kenya MP and prominent IPK supporter (he was elected to parliament in 1992, thanks largely to the support of IPK leader Shaikh Balala), fiercely attacked the district commissioner, Ali Korane, and asked how, as a Muslim, he could receive an ambassador of Israel, "the enemy of Islam." But it seems that this was an extreme pronouncement that did not reflect the attitude of most Muslims; the anti-Israeli activities of radical IPK members did not significantly affect Israel's relations with most of the Muslim community and did not affect its relations with the government at all. The Israeli ambassador was able to meet with shaikhs and Muslim leaders without feeling any resentment against Israel. On the contrary, Muslim leaders and organizations turned to him with requests for assistance and scholarships; as a consequence, there were many Muslims among the students who completed studies on various subjects in Israel, and "on-the-spot" courses were organized in Mombasa itself or in the Northeastern Province (for example, Israel organized courses there on camel breeding in which most of the participants were Somali Muslims).

The most active anti-Israeli body in Kenya at that time was the Iranian embassy, which published anti-Israeli articles in its bulletin *The Guide*, printed in Kenya and distributed throughout East Africa. The press attaché of the Iranian embassy also published letters vilifying Israel and encouraging local extremist Muslims to do the same.[18]

My personal impression from a prolonged stay in Kenya is that the great majority of Kenyan Muslims are neither hostile toward Israel nor interested in taking sides in the Arab-Israeli conflict. Muslim leaders, such as MP Rashid Sajad, who was chairman of the Mombasa Port Authority, and Muslim business leaders sought cooperation with Israel in personnel training and in development projects such as the desalination of water for ships anchored in the port.[19] When the mayor of Nairobi, Ahmad Mwidani, and the mostly Muslim members of the town council met with the Israeli ambassador, they asked for closer cooperation, and the mayor even suggested an arrangement to "twin" the cities of Mombasa and Tel Aviv.[20] A. K. Mohamed Ali, assistant minister of labor and manpower development and MP from the mainly Muslim region of Lamu, visited the Israeli embassy in 1993 and asked for assistance in developing agriculture in the Lamu area, stressing that he did not see any problem with Israeli experts working in the area.[21]

In recent years, the Israeli government and companies have worked to develop water and agricultural projects on the coastal strip in cooperation with the Coast Development Authority headed by Professor J. A. Lugogo, a Muslim academic, who has visited Israel. Israeli experts and businesspeople in Mombasa do not encounter hostility and most of their employees are Muslims. Muslims were among the many Kenyans who sent messages of sympathy to Israel following the assassination of Prime Minister Yitzhak Rabin, and many of them signed the book of condolences at the Israeli embassy in Nairobi.

On the whole, the Islamic factor has had some influence on Kenyan-Israeli relations, but not a significant one. On the negative side, from Israel's point of view, are the following factors:

- Local Muslim groups, some of whom were supported or influenced by Arab-Islamic activity, had close ties to some of the country's leaders; and the government, especially the Ministry of Foreign Affairs, had to take their position into account, to some extent, when determining its stance in the Arab-Israeli conflict. For example, during 1993–1994 when the possibility arose of a visit by President Moi to Israel and the opening of a Kenyan embassy there, Kenya's foreign minister expressed reservations, pointing out that Kenya had to be wary of the reactions of the Arab and Muslim countries.
- Israel's standing in Kenya was somewhat damaged not only by the government's desire to maintain strong relations with Arab and Muslim countries, but also by its compliance with the OAU resolution (initiated by the OAU's Arab members) on severing relations with Israel.
- The Kenyan government sometimes turned a blind eye to the harsh attacks on Israel by Arabs and Muslims, particularly the Iranians, despite Israel's repeated requests that Kenya publicly state its objection to becoming a propaganda battlefield for the Middle East conflict.

The Islamic factor has also positively influenced, from Israel's point of view, Kenyan-Israeli relations in indirect ways:

- The Kenyan government's suspicions of certain Muslims and local Somalis who wanted to break away from Kenya, and were supported by Muslim and Arab countries, fostered closer links between Israel and Kenya, even if this factor was not always publicized.
- Fear of the spread of radical Islam in Kenya induced Kenya's leaders to cooperate with Israel and to exchange information and views on the subject (during Rabin's short visit to Kenya

in 1994, on his way from Indonesia, this was one of the main topics he and Moi discussed). Therefore, despite the reservations about a visit by Moi to Israel, he eventually did visit in January 1994, and in a speech to the Knesset he formally announced the opening of a Kenyan embassy in Israel, which occurred several months later. In 1995 Moi visited Israel twice more, once after Rabin's assassination and once for a private visit.

In conclusion, the Islamic factor has not detracted from Kenyan-Israeli relations in any decisive way; these relations have usually been friendly even after official ties were severed. Hostility has been expressed mainly by certain Muslim personalities and groups, and only to a very slight extent by leading Muslim figures in the government.

13

The Islamic Party of Kenya

On 19 May 1992, violent disturbances broke out in Mombasa, Kenya's second-largest city and its main port, where Muslims form the majority. The immediate cause of these disturbances was the arrest of seven imams and several activists of the Islamic Party of Kenya (IPK) by the security forces, who accused them of incitement against the government. Those arrested had for some time been sharply critical of the government for discriminating against the Muslims and for refusing to recognize the IPK on the grounds that no party should be based on religion. They claimed that the existing political parties were all led by Christians and that they corrupted Muslim morals. Some of the protesters even demanded the establishment of an independent Muslim state or autonomous region along the coastal strip where Muslims could live according to the shari'a.

In the wake of these arrests, the IPK organized mass demonstrations demanding the immediate release of the imams and the recognition of the IPK. During clashes between the demonstrators and the security forces, some police stations were attacked and several public buildings and government vehicles were set on fire. Stores and other property of Muslims who supported the government were also destroyed. Army reinforcements, including special elite units of the General Service Units (GSU), rushed to the scene. They dispersed the demonstrators with great force and even broke into one of the great mosques, Kwa Shibu, to pursue them, beating and shooting; several demonstrators were killed or wounded.[1]

The disturbances, during which cries of "Allah Akbar" (God is great) and "jihad" (holy war) were heard, lasted for several days. They were the beginning of a series of clashes between IPK activists and government forces that continued sporadically for nearly two years, during which there were periods of considerable tension.

Mombasa, which until then had been a quiet tourist resort and commercial center, turned into a tense and violent place.[2]

Establishment of the IPK

In January 1992, the establishment of the IPK was announced in Mombasa with great fanfare immediately after the government's acceptance of a multiparty system for the forthcoming presidential and parliamentary elections. These elections eventually took place in December 1992.

Until that time, Kenya had had a one-party system, and the president of the country was also the president of the sole party, Kanu. The initial disturbances in Mombasa and the demand to recognize the IPK occurred in an atmosphere of election campaigning and at the height of an intense political struggle between Kanu and the new opposition parties that had emerged.

The IPK was established by Muslim activists, prominent among them Omar Mwinyi, a primary school teacher, who was appointed chairman, and Abdulrahman Wandati, a madrasa teacher, who became the party's secretary. Among its leaders was also Taib Ali Taib, a lawyer, who challenged the government for refusing to recognize the IPK or to allow it to participate in the elections.[3] At this stage, the IPK's demand for recognition won wide support from Muslims, both from the coastal strip and from other parts of the country. In Mombasa especially, IPK supporters became the main political force. This was illustrated by the mass demonstrations that the party succeeded in organizing, by the people's nearly complete obedience to orders to strike and close stores and businesses, and by the many pro-IPK slogans scrawled on the walls of the city's main streets.[4]

Kanu, in fact, lost in Mombasa in the December 1992 elections because of all the charges against it; of the four parliamentary seats, Nassir won the Mombasa-Central constituency, but the other three winners were from opposition parties—two from Ford-Kenya and one from the Democratic Party. Nevertheless, in the Coast Province as a whole, where Muslims do not constitute a majority, Kanu won seventeen out of twenty seats. Nassir attributed this victory to his activities throughout the province. (In the Northeastern Province with its Somali Muslim population, Kanu won seven out of ten seats, and here too it was thanks to the vigorous campaigning of Minister Hussein Maalim Mohamed and Sharif Nassir.) In any case, the opposition parties' victory in Mombasa reflected the anger of the city's Muslims toward the ruling party, as well as the work of the IPK leaders who, in light of the government's refusal to recognize the IPK, urged its supporters to vote for opposition candidates.

This initial sweeping success of the IPK campaign also reflected more general, long-standing concerns of the Muslim minority in Kenya. Many Muslims apparently believed that the IPK was a formidable force that would eventually be able to publicize their demands and compel the government to abolish what they saw as discrimination against Muslims in all spheres of life. Many Muslims believed that, now that a multiparty system had been adopted, there was a need for a strong Islamic party that would not be afraid to warn the regime that if the present situation continued, an explosion would result. Indeed, the IPK did issue such a warning in a Public Letter its leaders sent to the attorney-general on 6 July 1993. The letter was headlined, "Mombasa—A Bosnia in the Making," and copies of it were sent to all members of parliament, to all diplomatic missions in Nairobi, and to the press.[5] The letter asserted that the security forces had acted brutally against the IPK's supporters and that the Christian regime had been oppressing the Muslim minority since independence. The letter also mentioned the "Wagalla Massacre" of February 1984, in which security forces were accused of arbitrarily killing many Somali Muslims in the Northeastern Province. The regime, the letter claimed, was doing everything possible to divide the Muslims, and to this end it had established the United Muslims of Africa (UMA), a Muslim organization whose leaders got their marching orders from the government (for the text of the letter, see Appendix 2).

Muslim Complaints Against the Regime

The discrimination the Muslims felt in the colonial era continued after independence. Their resentments reached a peak in 1992–1994, causing outbreaks of violence. Muslim complaints and demands cover many areas, some of which are discussed in the following paragraphs.

Christian Colonial Rule and Independent Kenya

Muslims stress that their religion and culture reached the coast of East Africa hundreds of years before Christianity. It was Muslims who introduced the indigenous peoples of the coast to literacy and gave rise to a glorious civilization in the Middle Ages whose remains are gradually being discovered in archeological excavations along the coast. Muslim scholars idealize the era of Muslim rule, particularly the Omani period in the eighteenth and nineteenth centuries. They disregard the discrimination practiced by the Arabs, who were the superior class, against the Swahilis and black Africans, who constituted the lower class. Why, these scholars ask, have the Muslims—whose cultural, social, and economic situation in the precolonial period was excellent—deteriorated so much? The causes, they state, are rooted in Christian colonial rule, which moved the center of government from the coast inland, and in independent Kenya, which, in their view, has humiliated the Muslim minority.[6] It is charged that some of those Muslims who fought against the colonial regime are neglected.[7]

Representation in Government and Public Institutions

Moderate and radical Muslims alike frequently claim that their representation in government and public institutions is meager. The number of Muslims in the population is usually exaggerated, some Muslims arguing that they constitute 40 percent or even more (the usual accepted figure is 20 percent of a population of 25 million; see Chapter 1). Muslims point out that during President Kenyatta's rule, there was not a single Muslim minister in the cabinet and only two or three assistant ministers. Although President Moi's cabinets include a Muslim minister and three or four assistant ministers, this is not enough considering that there are, on average, twenty-five ministers and thirty assistant ministers altogether. Few Muslims hold key positions, such as provincial and district commissioners (see Chapter 3). During the one-party system, when Kanu determined who would enter parliament, the number of Muslim parliamentarians was always small. After the 1992 multiparty elections, there were only twenty-four Muslim parliamentarians out of a total of 200, and this number included Rashid Sajad, who was appointed by Moi. In Kanu, the few key positions that are held by Muslims are mainly on the Coast and in the Northeastern Province.

There was great surprise when, on 17 February 1993, the only Muslim minister in Moi's government, Hussein Maalim Mohamed, harshly attacked the government for continuing the policy of discrimination against Muslims that dated back to the colonial period. The time had come, he declared, for Muslims to unite and demand their rights.[8] It was assumed that Mohamed was acting out of disappointment. During the elections in December 1992, he had worked hard for Kanu's victory and believed that he would receive a more substantive portfolio, but he remained in the same position of minister in the president's office (only later did he change portfolios).

Sharif Nassir, for his part, supported Mohamed's accusations; he too was apparently disappointed at remaining assistant minister after Kanu's victory, despite his tremendous work as chairman of the party's Mombasa branch (as mentioned, only after the December 1997 elections was he promoted to minister).

The Somali Issue

From independence to the present day, Muslim leaders and MPs from the Northeastern Province, regardless of party affiliation, have complained about the central government's neglect in ensuring the region's security and in allocating national resources for its development. Indeed, the province has fallen far behind the rest of the country in every domain of life. Statistics compiled in 1992 show that 70 percent of the rural people in the Wajir district have little or no access to essential services. Infant mortality rates are seven times higher than the national average. More than 87 percent of the people are illiterate.[9] It has even been claimed that the government does not consider the Somalis to be Kenyan citizens and makes it difficult for them to obtain official documents or even denies them Kenyan passports.[10] When Abdul Kader Hassan, a Somali MP, complained that the security forces had destroyed a mosque and desecrated holy books, the government reminded him that the Northeastern Province was still considered a "security zone" and that the security forces had to take all necessary measures to enforce law and order there.[11] Somali anger intensified in the 1980s when the government sent a special screening team to the Somali areas to verify who was a genuine Kenyan citizen and who was an "alien"; thousands of Somalis failed the test and were sent back to Somalia.[12] Kenya took this step because of fear and mistrust of the Somalis, sentiments that had grown since the 1960s when Kenya had to fight Somali dissidents who wanted to secede and join Somalia. After the 1982 coup attempt against President Moi, which was foiled largely because of the quick action of a loyal Somali officer, Mahmud Mohamed, there was some improvement in the Somalis' position. Mahmud Mohamed was appointed chief of staff, and his brother, Hussein Maalim Mohamed, was made a minister. In the 1990s, as a result of the civil war in Somalia and the influx of tens of thousands of Somali refugees, some of them carrying weapons, the security situation in the Northeastern Province deteriorated, and in Nairobi there was an increase in robberies and murders. Hence, Kenya again tightened its supervision of the Somalis and, again, complaints were made about discrimination and harassment. The Somalis demanded, in particular, the deletion of the word *Somali* from their identity cards and its replacement by the word *Kenyan*.[13]

Non-Somali Muslims have raised these complaints as indications of the discrimination against Kenyan Muslims in general. As mentioned, even Supkem protested the regime's indifference to the Somalis' well-being. Some of the Northeastern leaders had important posts in the establishment and in Supkem, and their complaints had a strong resonance.

In recent years, the troubled relations between the Somali sector and the government have come to the fore. Some examples will indicate the continuing role of the Somali Muslim factor in Kenya's internal affairs.

In November 1997, Mohamed Malicha Galgalo, MP from Moyale in the Northeastern Province and assistant minister for commerce and industry, announced that he was resigning from his ministerial post and leaving the Kanu Party for the opposition Ford-Kenya Party. Galgalo had constantly complained that the government did nothing to protect Moyale residents from many incidents of banditry and repeated incursions by Ethiopian forces. A few months earlier, in August, he even accused the government of colluding with the Ethiopian regime in a war of annihilation against the Boran community to which he belongs. The Ethiopian government, for its part, charged that the Borans in Kenya were providing assistance and refuge to the Oromo Liberation Front rebels, to whom they were closely related. The regime asserted that whenever its forces made incursions into Kenyan territory, they were in hot pursuit of Oromo rebels. Although the Kenyan government sent protests about the situation to the Ethiopian authorities, Moyale politicians felt these were too mild a response to the harassment and killing of Kenyan citizens and that the government was insensitive to the Borans' plight.[14]

In April 1998, the Somali Muslim minister in the cabinet, Hussein Maalim Mohamed, issued a strong protest against the security forces' brutality toward Somali citizens. In a press conference he threatened to resign from the government and from Kanu if the government did not take action against security officers whom he accused of looting, beating, torturing, and raping innocent Somali citizens. This had occurred, he said, during operations against bandits in his Dujis constituency in the Garissa district of the Northeastern Province. At the press conference, the minister was flanked by eight other Somali Muslim MPs from the Northeastern Province, among whom were Mohamed Aden Noor, assistant minister for planning and national development, Mohamed Abdi Affey, assistant minister for cooperative development, and Mohamed Mukhtar Shiddiye,

Kanu's deputy chief whip. Some of the MPs threatened to quit the ruling party unless the government took action against the security forces. The MPs also claimed that entire villages had been demolished as security personnel searched for firearms. The government reacted to these angry claims by promising to investigate the alleged abuses.[15]

In July of that year, a group of Somali MPs, headed by Minister Hussein Maalim Mohamed, held a meeting in Garissa in the Northeastern Province. The MPs blamed the government for the poor state of security, education, health, and roads. They called for the introduction of *majimboism* (federalism), which they saw as the panacea for their region's woes. Some of them even hinted at secession. The *Weekly Review* commented that the MPs' scathing attacks on the government had rekindled the regime's suspicions of a gradual resurgence of secessionist tendencies, adding that "the call for *majimboism* of the Garissa meeting may reinforce the notion that many leaders from northern Kenya do not feel that the region is an integral part of the country."[16]

The Wajir Massacre in October of that year caused a further deterioration in the situation. About 600 members of the Boran and Gabra tribes of the Northeastern Province, aided by Ethiopians of the Oromo Liberation Front, launched a brutal attack on their traditional rivals, the Degodia. According to a press statement issued by Supkem after the attack, 189 people had been massacred, 83 were missing, and dozens of others wounded. The dead included 59 women and 50 children. Also, 15,000 head of livestock, including camels, cattle, goats, and sheep, had been stolen. The statement criticized the government, asking how hundreds of armed fighters could have crossed the Kenyan-Ethiopian border without being detected by the Kenyan army, which had a garrison in the district. It also charged that no serious attempt had been made to track the missing people and livestock and pursue the raiders. The statement drew a parallel with the Wagalla Massacre of February 1984, in which 384 people "were killed in cold blood" by the Kenyan security forces. It described the government's attitude toward the continued killing of innocent people in the Northeastern Province as "pathetic and apathetic" and demanded the immediate establishment of a commission to probe the massacre.

Degodia political leaders used even harsher language against the regime. They stressed that whatever the cause of the raid—banditry or intertribal rivalry—the government had failed to protect its citizens.[17]

Thus, the situation in the Northeastern Province contributed to the discontent of Kenyan Muslims as a whole.

Discriminatory Policies in Government

According to some Muslim leaders, discriminatory policies toward Muslims are directed from above, that is, from the government. More specifically, Muslims complain that every application for a government post signed with a Muslim name, such as Mohamed, Ali, Omar, or Hassan, is generally rejected or not answered at all, whereas Christian applicants receive priority. The same is true, Muslims claim, for applications for admission to secondary schools or for identity cards or passports. Even when the passport is needed for the pilgrimage to Mecca, there are difficulties in obtaining it.[18] Kenyan policy in the area of citizenship is, Muslims complain, based on discrimination. Christians receive it automatically, by right of birth, whereas Muslims, though born in Kenya, must struggle to prove their citizenship. Muslims therefore repeatedly demand the appointment of Muslims in the immigration department.[19] As we saw earlier, even so enthusiastic a supporter of President Moi's government as Assistant Minister Sharif Nassir has often complained of discrimination against Muslims in different fields, though he did not blame this on the government but on the bureaucratic machinery.

Land Ownership

Many Muslim leaders charge that Muslims are denied land ownership, or that Christians who came from the interior ("up country") were given land on the coastal strip and obtained control of the main sources of income there. In an interview given to a Christian bulletin, Imam Ali Shee of Nairobi's Jamia Mosque said, "The government has been doubting our origin, which has gone to the extent of refusing to give us the title deeds to our land." He remarked more specifically that, despite the fact that Muslims had been living in Faza (an island north of Mombasa) for more than four centuries, they had never been provided title deeds to their lands there.[20] He further argued that if there was any group with a long history, it was the Muslim communities of the coast, and they must be given due respect as an integral part of the nation.

Muslim leaders speak of an "invasion" of "up-country" businesspeople from ethnic groups close to the ruling circles that pushed aside the indigenous coastal Muslims. These "invaders" have been given permission to build hotels, restaurants, and other profitable projects, and they get most of the income from tourism and from government and public jobs. Many of the local inhabitants are unemployed and live as squatters around Mombasa and other coastal towns.[21] In a lecture at the International Conference on Social Studies held in Nairobi in June 1994, Ali Mazrui, who is from the coast and whose family ruled it during the Omani period, asserted: "Over the years the wealth of the coast passed from coastal hands into the hands of non-coastal Kenyans with tribal connections in the central government. The coast has been colonized by non-coastal Kenyans both politically and economically." Mazrui thus called for economic decentralization.[22]

Economic Development

During the colonial period and since independence, Muslims complain, the Coast Province has been neglected and the center of government transferred from Mombasa to Nairobi. The government does not allocate the necessary funds for the coast's development. The coast's agriculture, which flourished in the precolonial period, has deteriorated.[23] Development and proper maintenance are found only around the tourist hotels along the Indian Ocean beaches. Mombasa itself is in a squalid state, without proper sewage or drainage, with buildings damaged by dampness and roads full of potholes. Visitors, indeed, immediately notice the negligence and desolation. There is a chronic water shortage and not enough is done to develop additional sources of water. Moreover, the coast's inhabitants complain, most of the income from tourism, the port, the airport, and the refineries, which together constitutes about 70 percent of Kenya's national income, goes to the treasury, whereas the local people benefit, according to their estimate, from only around 20 percent of this income.[24]

Generalized Prejudice

Muslims complain that the authorities and many Christians regard all Muslims with contempt. In a long, bitter letter by Muslim lecturers from the University of Nairobi that appeared in the *Weekly Review* in 1978, they state that Muslims on the coast have for a long time been subjected to all sorts of harassment and inconveniences. This is particularly true within the government, which, from colonial times to the present, especially on the coast, has been prejudiced against Muslims in general. The Muslims "have been branded with all the available pejorative labels and have been characterized in public rallies as an indolent and ignorant lot."

The writers attribute the diffusion of these views to missionary zealots and Christian leaders. "Even during the Maulidi reading of the Qur'an, the Christian community courted trouble by singing hymns at the top of their voices." The letter also gives special emphasis to discrimination in education.[25] Other Muslims complain about disrespect for traditional Muslim attire. They cite the incident where two Muslim MPs entered parliament in their "pilgrims' suits" and were ordered to leave the building; they ask why European attire is approved.[26] Mohamed Bakari has spoken of a "national phobia against Muslims" that could lead to serious trouble.[27]

The Media

There are also complaints that Muslims are given little time on government radio and television, where there are very few programs about Islam.[28] An article by Joe Kadhi, an editor at the popular newspaper the *Daily Nation,* focused on the media's treatment of Muslims. He complained about distorted reporting of Muslim affairs in Kenya, a practice that, he charged, was influenced by the international media, which was controlled by Christians or Jews and which portrayed the Arab and Muslim world as a dangerous hotbed of extremism. Thus, Kenyans were misled about everything pertaining to Islam.[29]

Separation of Church and State

Muslim religious leaders, politicians, and public figures who are generally moderate or even supportive of the government have harshly criticized the separation of church and state. Muslim academics also oppose this separation and maintain that the government uses it to harm Muslims, since in everything pertaining to Christians there is no separation in practice. These academics point out, for example, that President Moi misses no opportunity to demonstrate that he is a practicing Christian—for instance, every Sunday he is shown on television for several minutes praying in his church. They also claim that the purpose is to emphasize that Kenya is a Christian country (see Chapter 10).[30] Muslims charge that the authorities assist the Christians in spreading Christianity and give church leaders a freedom of action that they do not allow Muslim religious leaders. When Muslims try to disseminate their religion, they are arrested and accused of incitement. Church leaders, such as those of the National Christian Council of Kenya (NCCK), are permitted to express political opinions, whereas Muslims, on grounds of separation of church and state, are forced to hold their tongues as if "10 million Muslims did not exist."[31] Moderate Muslim critics do not demand that the whole country be run according to shariʻa law, acknowledging that this is impossible since most of the citizens are non-Muslims.

Recognition of the IPK

The demand for official recognition of the IPK was widespread among Muslims, who generally support claims of discrimination but oppose violence as proposed by Shaikh Balala. Among those who demand that the government recognize the IPK is Mazrui, who, though he spends most of his time abroad, attacks the government's treatment of Muslims in articles and lectures during his visits to Kenya. He demands that the government recognize the IPK just as it recognizes other opposition parties, arguing that the many religious parties in African countries have never destabilized the regimes (this ignores the fact that there have been religious wars in Uganda and conflicts with a religious background in other African countries, such as Nigeria and Senegal). During the clashes between the security forces and IPK supporters, Mazrui even threatened that if the government did not recognize the party, a "black intifada" would break out.[32] In his view, the Muslim community's condition has worsened since independence and Moi's government has turned the Muslims into "second-class citizens." He terms the government's treatment of Muslims "internal colonialism." Mazrui also criticizes Kenya's foreign policy and contends that Kenya is influenced by Israeli propaganda in its attitude toward the Arab and Islamic world, thus weakening Afro-Arab solidarity. Mohamed Bakari, who supported the IPK's establishment, also warned of Muslim disturbances if the discrimination continued; Imam Shee took similar positions.[33] Among MPs who thought the IPK should be recognized so that it could represent Muslim interests was Assistant Minister Mohamed Galgalo of the Northeastern Province. In an interview he reiterated, albeit moderately, the Muslim complaints.[34]

Slave Trade Issue

Mazrui, like many Muslims, complains that some Christians denigrate Muslims by claiming that they were slave traders who caused great harm to black Africans. In a long article, Mazrui contended that the Arab slave trade in East Africa was trifling when compared to the Atlantic slave trade and, furthermore, that the Arabs treated the slaves well, making them part of their families—in contrast to the whites, who used them for hard labor in plantations. In the same article, Mazrui also condemned the distortion of Islam in general and asserted that whereas when a Christian dictator did terrible things his religion was not mentioned, the fact that Idi Amin was a Muslim was always emphasized.[35]

Education

Muslims bitterly attribute their backwardness in education to the authorities. As we saw in Chapter 9, different bodies have taken steps to promote Muslim education, but most Muslims felt these were insufficient, especially compared to what the government invested in Christian schools. Muslims charge that the government does not help establish schools in Muslim areas to the extent that it does in Christian areas. In fact, contend the Muslims, independent Kenya has continued the policy of the colonial authorities, who put the educational system in the hands of Christian missionaries in order to check the dissemination of Islam.[36] Muslims who feared sending their children to these Christian schools instead sent them to Muslim teachers who taught them about Islam, but these students did not receive a well-rounded modern education that could help them in their daily lives and in obtaining government posts; hence, the Muslims became the backward sector of the society.[37] Despite these outspoken accusations, the government did not accede to Muslims' requests to set up institutes of higher education in the Coast Province. Mazrui, like other Muslim academics, pointed out that Kenya had four government universities, including the University of Moi in Eldoret, situated in the president's tribal area, and asked why the government could not found a university in the Coast Province, which was an important Islamic cultural center.[38]

* * *

Thus, the Muslims' weak position since independence, and the fact that they have not obtained government posts in proportion to their numbers in the population, to some extent reflect the policy of the predominantly Christian government, which harbors deep suspicions toward the Muslim and Somali minority. But there are other causes as well, including the divisions within the Muslim community based on personal and religious differences; the lack of a strong, accepted leadership; the long period of segregation from the rest of the population; devotion to the traditional religious system of education; and opposition to modernization and, specifically, to modern, technical education.

The dissemination of Islam in Kenya, as compared to Tanzania, was slow because of British colonial policy and the fact that the Sufi orders, such as the Qadiriya and the Shadhiliya, were not as widespread in Kenya as in Tanganyika. Furthermore, in the Omani period, Muslim trade routes passed through Tanganyika and important trade centers such as Bagamoio, Tabora, and Ujiji were founded, which also became centers for the propagation of Islam there in the colonial period and after independence.

For a long time, the widespread feelings of discrimination among Kenya's Muslims did not lead to significant outbreaks of violence. But when the formation of opposition parties was permitted for the 1992 elections and when these parties began to strongly criticize the government in different areas, the Muslims' anger over discrimination came to the fore.[39] The Muslims believed that they too had a right to establish a party that would represent their interests, especially since the leaders of the new opposition parties were Christians and it was unclear to what extent they were willing or able to deal with Muslim problems. When the IPK was founded in January 1992, most Muslims supported its legal recognition; the government's opposition to recognizing the party caused disturbances that were exploited by radical elements led by Shaikh Khalid Balala, the subject of the next chapter.

14

Islamic Extremism: The Rise and Fall of Shaikh Khalid Balala

Against the background of Muslim indignation in Kenya, a young shaikh, Khalid Balala, appeared on the scene. Balala was born in Mombasa in 1958 to a father originally from Yemen, Salim ibn Ahmad, who ran a butcher's shop. As a boy Balala studied the Qur'an and Arabic in local schools. When he was seventeen he traveled to Saudi Arabia to fulfill the Muslim duty of pilgrimage to Mecca (the Hajj), and he remained there for more than ten years studying Islam at Medina University while making a living selling religious books. He then visited various countries in Europe and Asia. In Britain he completed a course in business management, and in India he studied Islam and comparative religion. He claims he decided to combine the knowledge he had acquired of Islam and of business management in order to "sell," that is, to disseminate, the Islamic religion.[1]

Balala returned to Kenya in 1990 and was until mid-1992 an unknown street preacher in one of Mombasa's bustling market squares, Mwembe Tayari. He gradually began to attract public attention when his preachings became more and more political and critical of the government. His impressive eloquence, wide knowledge of Islam, and bold and fiery invective against the regime attracted large crowds, mainly young Muslims. Less blatant attacks by government opponents in the 1980s had led to arrests, and here was a shaikh who was not afraid and even proudly and publicly declared that he was "the only Kenyan who gives President Moi nightmares."[2] Apart from his fierce criticism of the government in general and of Moi in particular, the likes of which had not generally been heard before, Shaikh Balala expressed views that, at first, were relatively moderate:

- He demanded that Muslims be strict in observing Islamic

practices, especially daily prayers.
- He insisted on the importance of Islamic education and the setting up of Muslim schools.
- He warned that tourism corrupted the morals of Muslims, who had begun imitating foreign attire and such pursuits as going to bars and discotheques.
- He demanded that women dress modestly and keep themselves "pure."
- He repeatedly argued that Islam does not differentiate between religion and state; that politics is part of religion; that the cancellation of the ban on political parties gave the Muslims an opportunity to organize themselves and to raise their demands; and that the government should allow the IPK to operate just as it allowed other parties.[3]
- To placate the Christians, who claimed that Balala believed that shari'a law should be imposed on the whole population, Balala made it clear that the shari'a would be applied only to Muslims: "[The imposition of shari'a on the whole country] is not a priority for us but we want to show Muslims that we have our own way of solving political, economic, and social problems."[4]
- Balala's strongest criticism was directed against those Muslims who were active in the government and in the ruling party but who, he charged, only tended to their own private interests.[5]

In mid-1992, Balala joined the IPK. He immediately became its uncrowned leader and spokesman, relegating the party's founders to the sidelines. At this stage, with Balala's charisma drawing many supporters to the party, they did not complain about being upstaged. From now on Balala led the demonstrations and other antigovernment activities. Under his leadership the IPK became much more radical; his supporters, especially the youth, clashed with the security forces and exercised control through threats and violence. Balala publicly demanded that Moi's regime be toppled, accusing him of despotism and corruption.[6]

At this stage, the position of Balala and the IPK was strengthened by several factors. First, the opposition parties—especially the main one, Ford-Kenya, and its leader Oginga Odinga—supported the IPK's registration. The opposition parties hoped that by demonstrating solidarity with Balala, they would obtain, in the general elections for parliament and the presidency, the votes of Muslims who could not vote for the banned IPK.[7] Despite their party's lack of official recognition, IPK leaders also participated in the assembly of opposition parties that was held on 11–12 May 1992, seven months before the elections, and they were encouraged by the support they received. This intensified the government's anger as well as, in reaction, its measures against the IPK. The opposition parties also displayed their support for the IPK when some of their leaders took part in parades and demonstrations the IPK organized. Thus, when President Moi visited Mombasa in August 1993 to open the agricultural fair, there was a protest demonstration organized by the IPK against his visit; Rashid Mzee, professor, member of parliament and leader of Ford-Kenya, took part in this protest. Other leaders of Ford-Kenya, such as Paul Muita, first deputy party chairman and MP from the Kikuyu region, and James Orengo, a senior member of the party, attended mosques to hear Shaikh Balala's sermons in order to obtain his support. These leaders' visit to Mombasa just before the serious disturbances in September 1993 brought a strong reaction from Assistant Minister Sharif Nassir, who accused them of fanning the riots by inciting against the government.[8]

The relationship between Balala and Ford-Kenya began to change when, late in 1993, its leader, Oginga Odinga, began negotiations with the ruling Kanu Party about cooperation in development projects in the Luo areas. At the same time, Odinga started to show a more conciliatory attitude toward President Moi and relations between them improved. Angered by this closeness of Ford-Kenya to the regime, Balala announced that he was transferring his support to the second opposition party, Ford-Asili, led by Kenneth Matiba, but would continue to support Rashid Mzee because of his personal regard for him.[9] Balala even issued a joint statement with Muita, who also criticized Odinga's conciliatory stance toward the government. The statement decried all compromise with Moi's government, which it called a "dictatorial regime."[10] Later the IPK leaders demanded a separation between the presidency of the country and the presidency of Kanu, asserting that the national president should stand above all parties and not be identified with any single party.[11] In any case, despite the differences between the opposition parties, they all supported the IPK's legal recognition and took pains to forge links with its leaders.

The IPK received another shot in the arm from Ali Mazrui, who, as we have seen, supported the party's registration and identified with its complaints about discrimination against Muslims, and had even warned of disturbances and a "black intifada" if the situation did not improve.

Another factor that helped the IPK, at least indirectly, was the existence of divisions among progovernment Muslim politicians, stemming primarily from personal rivalry and competition for key posts in Kanu. Especially helpful was the strong opposition to Assistant Minister Nassir, chairman of Kanu's Mombasa branch, who had many enemies within Kanu because of his arrogant behavior and his desire to be the party's only representative and spokesman in the Coast Province.

Statements against Islam by Christian religious and political leaders at this time angered Muslims, intensified their fears, and made Balala's stance that much more persuasive. As we saw earlier, Muslims reacted fiercely when Cardinal Maurice Otunga called for a struggle against the spread of Islam in Africa. There was also much bitterness at Moi's statements about the Muslim slave trade (see Chapter 10). To further increase his popularity among Muslims, Balala sought an image as the defender of Muslim rights against discrimination by Christians. In an "open letter" to the Catholic Church, published in the press, Balala claimed that "your Church sometimes operates openly against Muslims and discriminates against them even though they are citizens of Kenya." He mentioned the incident at the Consolata Secondary School in the Meru region, from which seven Muslim girl students were expelled because they fasted during the month of Ramadan and were absent from school. He also emphasized that the Kenyan constitution proclaimed freedom of religion and that Muslims were permitted to observe their religious practices.[12]

The position of Balala and of IPK supporters was also strengthened to some extent by financial and moral support from Sudanese, other Arab, and Iranian sources. During his trips abroad, Balala visited Sudan several times.[13] Moderate Muslims in Mombasa expressed fears that Iranian involvement and support from radical Muslims would cause tensions within the Muslim community.[14] Suspicions that Iran was supporting extremist Muslims were given wide publicity when, on 13 January 1994, the *Standard* published a full-page headline: "Terror Against Kenya: Islamic Fundamentalists to Take Over" (see Chapter 11).[15]

In December 1992, the popularity of the IPK led by Shaikh Balala emerged very clearly when it succeeded, in effect, in defeating Kanu in Mombasa during the multiparty elections to parliament. Of Mombasa's four seats, Kanu won only one; the other three were won by opposition party candidates, two of whom, Rashid Mzee and Salim Mwavuno, represented Ford-Kenya, which Balala supported.

The Government's Response

The Muslim unrest and wave of violence in Mombasa surprised and concerned the authorities. For one thing, they feared that Mombasa, which was Kenya's port and an important tourist center, could be economically harmed by the disturbances. Second, the unrest stirred deep suspicions stemming from the attempts by the Muslim coastal strip to break away from Kenya at independence. Third, there was apprehension lest the unrest spread from Mombasa to other Muslim centers on the coast such as Malindi and Lamu, and to Muslim concentrations in large towns. Indeed, as we shall see, during this time in Lamu especially there were violent demonstrations against the government. Finally, the unrest in Mombasa aroused associations with the underground activity that had occurred in the Northeastern Province and the Somali Muslims' desire to secede from Kenya.[16]

The government's response to the first disturbances in May 1992 suggested that it still did not understand the true nature of militant Islam.[17] It resorted to the use of excessive force, including arrests—especially the repeated arrest of Balala, who was even charged with treason, punishable by death (later the state lifted this charge). It quickly became evident that these arrests, and the security forces' breaking into mosques in pursuit of demonstrators, only fanned the agitation and violence. Balala's arrest cast him in the role of a hero who did not fear the authorities and indeed, during his trial, preached against them harshly. The more the government tried to intimidate him, the bolder and more radical he became. His photographs and speeches filled the front pages of the newspapers,[18] especially those of the opposition.

Throughout 1992–1993 the illegal IPK controlled the streets in Mombasa, despite the security forces' actions against it. Thus, on 22 August 1992, two days before a planned visit by Moi to the city, the IPK organized a large demonstration attended by tens of thousands of Muslims—indeed the largest demonstration ever seen in Mombasa. It was led by Shaikh Abdul Rahman Khitamy, a respected Muslim leader. The demonstrators set out from the great mosque, the Sakina Mosque, passed in orderly, quiet procession through the city, and ended up at the office of the district commissioner, where they waved banners demanding the release of Balala, who was under arrest at the time. Other placards proclaimed "IPK—We shall overcome." The commissioner was handed a memorandum that he was asked to pass on to the president, which demanded that Moi immediately release Balala, apologize for a speech in which he blamed Muslims for the slave trade, recognize the IPK, and register it legally.[19] Although this demonstration was quiet compared to the events a few months earlier, it did not signal a calming of the situation.

Aside from the "stick" of force against radical Muslim elements, the regime also began to offer "carrots," showing readiness to pay more attention to moderate Muslim demands. In the past, Presidents Kenyatta and Moi had sometimes made gestures toward the Muslims to placate their feelings of discrimination and meet some of their demands, as in the case of 'Id al-Fitr. After the violence of May 1992 and the disturbances that followed, the government increased funding for Muslim institutions, and the president and his ministers more often participated in assemblies to collect money for Muslim schools. For example, the president donated 20,000 shillings at a harambe organized by Sharif Nassir and Minister Hussein Maalim Mohamed for the Muslim Academy of Kenya.[20] At these gatherings and during visits to Muslim areas, the president sometimes wore a white *koffiyah* and a *kanzu* (traditional Muslim attire), which was widely publicized in the media.[21] Further concessions were made to pilgrims to Mecca, and their foreign currency allowance was periodically increased, for which Muslim leaders who supported the regime expressed gratitude. Shaikh Mohamed Amana, for example, chairman of the Islamic Reformation of Kenya (Islahil Islamiya), thanked the government for the concessions and pointed out that in 1994, 3,500 Muslim pilgrims from Kenya were able to visit the holy places.[22] Government representatives took greater part in Muslim holiday celebrations, where they greeted the Muslim community in the name of the president and his minions. Officials also stressed that Muslims had been appointed to senior posts, especially that the chief of staff, Mahmud Mohamed, was a Somali Muslim.

An interesting example of the "carrots" approach occurred in the Muslim region of Lamu. The district commissioner, John Sala, whose harsh actions toward the inhabitants had contributed to the agitation in 1993, became more moderate, apparently on orders from above. In June 1994, he informed the Lamu inhabitants that they would receive title deeds to their land and that the government had allocated money for building roads in the regions of Lamu and Faza so as to solve the transportation problems there. He also announced that the government was ready to provide loans to entrepreneurs in the region to develop industry. The assistant minister of labor and employment, Abdul Karim Mohamed, publicly thanked the government for the attention it was devoting to Lamu, particularly the heightening of security measures (see below).[23]

In the field of higher education, President Moi acceded to Supkem's request and in January 1996 issued a presidential order granting recognition to the Mikindani College for training Muslim teachers, which entitled it to award degrees; until then, the Ministry of Education had not recognized the college's degrees. That same month, in response to a request by the Muslim leadership (and in this instance also the Christian leadership), the president announced the cancellation of the requirement to teach sex education in all schools.[24] As mentioned earlier, in response to Muslim demand, in 1994 the government banned the distribution of Salman Rushdie's *Satanic Verses*.

Along with extending the carrot as well as the stick, the government used the divide-and-conquer method. The United Muslims of Africa (UMA) was established in May 1993. Its founders were black African Muslims who supported the government, headed by Shaikh Swalih Ali; Omar Musumbuko, one of the leaders of Youth for Kanu 1992; and Emmanuel Maitha. All three were active in Kanu and had campaigned for its victory in the 1992 elections. It seems that the organization was set up with the blessing of members of the ruling elite, although the police would sometimes arrest (and later release) its activists, apparently as a way of countering the accusation that the government was behind it.[25] (For the UMA's statement of its aims, see Appendix 3.)

The UMA's main goal, openly declared, was to fight against the IPK and Shaikh Balala. The UMA demanded the cessation of the "slander" of the president and the government and of the IPK's demonstrations and incitement, which, the UMA charged, had caused division among the Muslims and the spilling of blood, contravening the commands of the Qur'an. It accused the IPK of seeking to turn Mombasa into a center of Islamic fundamentalism and sowing discord between Muslims and Christians. The UMA leaders pledged to work for Muslim unity and for an atmosphere of brotherhood between Muslims and non-Muslims. Since, in these leaders' view, the Arab countries' intervention in Muslim affairs had contributed to the unrest, they demanded the cessation of such activity, especially on the part of the rich Gulf countries. In contrast to the IPK, the UMA opposed the politicization of religion and demanded the separation of religion and politics.[26]

In its propaganda the UMA tried to portray its conflict with the IPK as a struggle between black African Muslims and Muslims of Arab descent, whom they nicknamed "brown Muslims." The UMA aimed to defend the black Muslims against the "Muslim immigrants from the Gulf countries whose purpose is to create chaos between the different Muslim communities on the continent."[27] The UMA particularly stressed that most of the IPK leaders, including Shaikh Balala, were of Arab descent and were supported by Arab countries. Balala's features are not, in fact, those of a black African; it is true that the original IPK founders, Omar Mwinyi and Abdulrahman

Wandati, were black, but with Balala's accession they were shunted aside. The UMA further accused the IPK of expelling black imams from mosques and replacing them with imams of Arab descent and threatened to boycott mosques run by Muslims of Arab descent.[28] This accusation was mostly false, but it was effective because of the historic rivalry between the two groups.[29]

The establishment of the UMA brought increased tension in Mombasa. Young UMA members disrupted IPK demonstrations by staging counterdemonstrations, and violent clashes soon erupted. During 1993–1994, the disturbances reached new levels of intensity.

On Friday, 28 May 1993, there was an almost completely observed general strike in Mombasa in response to posters distributed by the IPK. The posters warned that "all those who violate the guidelines of the IPK will be considered as enemies, and we will take appropriate steps against them because they are opposed to our way. We warn them that the IPK will catch them and set them on fire." Another poster showed a picture of MP Rashid Sajad, a close ally of President Moi, with the caption: "If you meet this man, kill him!" The timing of the strike was connected to Shaikh Balala's appearance in court to stand trial and his supporters' demand for his immediate release. The response to the call for a strike in Mombasa was startling: all transportation stopped, almost all stores closed, and the only people in the streets were groups of IPK and UMA activists who fought with each other while the police tried to maintain order.[30] Several days later, Sajad's and Sharif Nassir's cars were set on fire. Sajad was not the only one against whom a fatwa was issued; Balala also issued one against UMA leader Emmanuel Maitha, demanding that he be caught and whipped, and Maitha had to go into hiding. For this threat Balala was again arrested; the police also found and arrested Maitha for questioning and then released both of them.

In June and July 1993, the IPK-UMA clashes were fierce. IPK youth threw petrol bombs at Kanu's branch in Mombasa, and UMA members demonstrated and hurled petrol bombs at IPK leaders' houses and Balala's house (he was not at home at the time). Balala accused the government of trying to eliminate him and issued an ultimatum that if within fifteen days those who had thrown the bombs were not apprehended and punished, he himself would take extreme measures. The police arrested several young men from both camps, suspecting they were among the bomb throwers. On 8 July, the UMA held a demonstration of 5,000 people during which its leaders handed a memorandum to the provincial commissioner denying that they were to blame and demanding that measures be taken against the IPK and its leaders. In August, Nassir prepared another visit for

President Moi to Mombasa. On this occasion, Balala organized a large, peaceful demonstration of about 10,000 Muslims protesting against President Moi, the government, and the planned visit.

The unrest in Mombasa also spread to Lamu. The disturbances there began, as noted, as a protest gathering against the district commissioner, John Sala, who, according to the inhabitants, displayed contempt toward Muslims and even refused to receive a delegation sent by them to air their grievances. Their complaints concerned the lack of security on the roads, especially the road from Malindi to Lamu, where there had been many incidents of robbery and murder. The inhabitants also felt that the Lamu area was neglected and that there were no development projects there. Sala's refusal to hear these grievances, and the police order to disperse the gathering, ignited severe rioting in early September 1993. Rioters shouted pro-IPK slogans; homes of government supporters and government property were set on fire and in some cases destroyed, including the law courts, the tax offices, and Kanu's offices in Lamu. Shaikh Balala and the other IPK leaders immediately exploited the situation, praising the protesters for their courage and urging them to keep protesting until they achieved their objectives.[31]

The Lamu disturbances intensified government fears that the trouble would spread to other areas, partly because they had erupted simultaneously with serious renewed agitation in Mombasa after Moi's visit there. Early in September, Balala called for a "national strike" to be held on 20 September to protest the government's "brutal policy," and on that day Mombasa as well as Malindi turned into ghost towns. Many residents, however, stayed in their homes so as not to be injured in the clashes between IPK supporters and the security forces, not out of solidarity with the IPK. In Mombasa, petrol bombs were thrown at the Kanu office and at the central police station; the clashes involved injuries and deaths, especially in the city's old quarter, the IPK's stronghold. In Malindi, too, there were confrontations with the security forces.[32]

During 1992–1993, the IPK was at the height of its power and constituted a serious concern to the regime. Moderate Muslims and even some Christian groups joined the demand for registration of the IPK. In a long article in *The Standard* on 30 May 1993, "More Caution over Booming Unrest," the Christian journalist Dominic Odipo argued that the IPK's success in the strike two days earlier in Mombasa proved that it constituted a substantial force and therefore should be legally registered; failure to do so would only increase its popularity and effectiveness. Odipo pointed out that even the trade union umbrella organization, COTU, which had declared a general strike in

1992, had not had such success. He warned that if the government continued to oppose the IPK's registration, the result would be chaos in Kenya that could well worsen. In the opposition newspaper *Society*, in an article on 4 October 1993 "Coast Polarized," Christian journalist Mwangi Chege also expressed fear that the disturbances would snowball if the government did not agree to register the IPK. He attributed the disturbances to discrimination against the Muslims and criticized the security forces' brutality.

There was also criticism of the government, mainly from opposition sources such as MP and Ford-Kenya leader Rashid Mzee, for supporting the UMA and its activities.[33] But even progovernment Muslim leaders viewed the UMA's emergence with concern. Supkem, which was critical of the IPK, came out against the UMA's activities, contending that they had contributed to the bloodshed; Supkem apparently regarded the UMA as a rival Muslim organization. Another Muslim organization, the Kenya Koran Teachers' Union, accused the UMA of fostering division and racism because it attacked imams who were not black, averring that "after all, in the mosque you do not pray to the imam but to Allah" and that Islam opposed discrimination on the basis of color or race.[34] Sharif Nassir, for his part, fearing that his rivals for Muslim leadership on the coast (such as Rashid Sajad) stood behind the UMA, attacked the organization's leadership.[35] Interestingly, even the only Muslim minister in the government, Hussein Maalim Mohamed, expressed unease about the UMA and its violence.[36] This criticism again manifested the divisions and competition for leadership within the Muslim community.

The government, for its part, saw to it that within the framework of its anti-IPK activities there were statements against the IPK by progovernment Muslims, and it did this first and foremost via Supkem. Against the background of Balala's arrest in July 1992 and the demonstrations protesting it, Supkem organized a large Muslim delegation of religious leaders, businesspeople, and public figures who met with President Moi and expressed their reservations about the IPK and Balala, assuring the president of their loyalty. This meeting took place despite the IPK's threats that members of the delegation would be punished.[37] Later the government organized gatherings of Muslim MPs and other public figures that censured Balala and his party. On 20 June 1994, in a large Muslim assembly at Wajir in the Northeastern Province, MP Ahmad Khalif voiced support for the government and condemned the IPK.[38] During the entire period of demonstrations and disturbances, the chief qadi issued pronouncements opposing the violence perpetrated by Balala and his supporters—which sowed division among the Muslims—and stressing that Moi's government preserved freedom of religion and hence deserved gratitude.[39]

Division in the IPK and the Fall of Shaikh Balala

By acting against the IPK, the government aimed at limiting the party's influence. Ultimately, however, what seriously damaged the party and Shaikh Balala's position was a split within the IPK itself. Some of the party's founders began to question the extremism of Balala's actions, including his threats against government leaders and his constant calls for demonstrations that caused harm to the residents of Mombasa and led to deaths and injuries. Among other things, he announced that he had under his authority ten suicide bombers who were ready to carry out whatever he ordered, and he declared several days later that he had managed to recruit a total of fifty-five potential suicide bombers.[40] Nor did the IPK founders look favorably on his issuing fatwa edicts against people, such as Sharif Nassir, Emmanuel Maitha, and Rashid Sajad.[41] Furthermore, in late 1993 and the first half of 1994, Balala intensified his personal attacks on President Moi and his provocation of the security forces, which led to further deaths and injuries. In one violent incident in March 1994 between the security forces and young IPK radicals, petrol bombs were thrown at government institutions. In this instance, the disturbances spread into Bondeni, the old quarter of Mombasa, and several young men were injured. These young radicals even nicknamed themselves the Islamic Jihad Organization and printed posters vowing to take measures against the government.[42]

In May, several IPK leaders decided to organize a procession to mark the second anniversary of the May 1992 disturbances and, the deaths of IPK leaders whom they called *shahids* (martyrs). The district commissioner warned them not to hold the demonstration; they held it nonetheless, although this time only about 200 participated; the security forces shot several demonstrators with rubber bullets and again there were injuries.[43] In mid-1994, another group emerged that opposed the IPK. Composed of Muslim and Christian supporters of the government, it called itself the Coast Protection. Led by Nyonga Wa Makemba and the UMA activist Emmanuel Maitha, this group threatened to disrupt every demonstration that the IPK organized. It also acted against members of opposition parties who supported the IPK's activities. Thus, when one of the leaders of Ford-Kenya, Raila Odinga (son of the party's founder Oginga Odinga), announced in May 1994 his intention to visit the Coast Province, the Coast Protection Group accused him of inciting the coastal residents against the government and warned him that he would be endangering himself if he came.[44] Odinga indeed changed his mind and did not visit Mombasa.

The IPK founders concluded that Balala's violent militancy was provoking harsh reactions by the government and by progovernment organizations and damaging the economy of the Coast Province, especially Mombasa. They began to criticize Balala publicly, charging, among other things, that he had not been elected leader of the party and had in fact "hijacked" it—and that he used the party as his own private domain, acting arbitrarily without consulting the IPK founders. Balala, they noted, would boast that without him the IPK would disintegrate.[45] He deviated, they claimed, from the founders' original aims of representing Muslim demands by legal means and establishing a democratic society influenced by Islamic principles; instead, Balala had undermined both the law and democracy. They accused him of being hungry for publicity, more interested in capturing headlines than in the welfare of Muslims, and even of embezzling money donated to the party and using it for his own private needs. They questioned how the shaikh, who not long before had been a poor preacher in the streets of Mombasa, was now the owner of numerous houses and cars.[46] Some of his opponents within the IPK warned that the radicalism of some of his teachings and actions went beyond the acceptable—for instance, his order to apprehend Muslim women who walked about Mombasa after sunset and publicly flog them (for criticism of Balala by an IPK supporter, see Appendix 4).[47]

In June 1994, the IPK leaders decided to expel Balala from the party, and that September they even supported a fatwa issued against him by the UMA, according to which anyone who encountered him was required to kill him for harming Islamic values by his incitement to violence. The IPK leaders had joined in the fatwa, they explained, because Balala had become a "threat to the Muslim community."[48]

Immediately after his expulsion from the IPK, Balala decided to form a new party called the Islamic Salvation Front, modeled on the militant Islamic party in Algeria. But this was a desperate move that did not bring him any supporters. In August 1994, in Europe, Balala gave an interview to the BBC in which he boasted that he had under his command a well-trained and well-equipped private army of several hundred young Muslims, whose purpose was to launch "Phase 2" of the struggle, aimed at destroying Moi's regime.[49] Several Muslim religious leaders who were critical of the government, including

Shaikh Ali Shee, now came out publicly against Balala, contending that the Muslim community had never authorized him to be its spokesperson and that he had violated the Qur'an's commands to seek peace and damaged the good name of all Muslims by his warlike words and deeds.[50]

Late in 1994, Balala left Kenya for an extended trip to Europe and Asia to garner support for his party, during which he continued his sharp attacks against his country's government and president. In April 1995, while in Germany, he requested a passport extension at the Kenyan embassy in Bonn and was informed that, according to instructions received from Nairobi, his passport had been canceled and he was forbidden to return to Kenya. The government claimed that Balala also had Yemenite citizenship and could go to Yemen; moreover, the holding of dual nationality was prohibited under Kenyan law. From exile, Balala sued the government in court for the return of his passport.[51] He even declared that he was resolved to return to Kenya with or without a passport and boasted that he intended to run for president in the 1997 elections. He gave himself the titles "Shaikh General Balala" and "Simba (Lion) Balala," indicating mental imbalance. He even expressed support for Richard Leakey, who had announced the formation of a new opposition party called Safina, and promised he would soon send $2 million to support its activities. When Safina's establishment was also prohibited by the government, Balala regarded the party as a fellow sufferer. President Moi, for his part, exploited Balala's declaration and criticized the ostensible contacts between Safina and the IPK.[52] It is absolutely clear, however, that Leakey had no interest whatever in connections with Balala.

In September 1995, during preparations for the holiday of the Maulidi, marking the birth of the Prophet, Balala issued a statement from abroad threatening that he would, through his agents, turn the festivities into antigovernment demonstrations.[53] Moi again responded, assuring the Muslims that the security forces would protect them from any attempted disturbances. During the festival, reinforcements were sent to Mombasa to ensure order, and the processions went ahead quietly. Balala's absence from Kenya greatly weakened his supporters and the radical Muslim groups. The IPK, for its part, declined drastically in influence and its activities almost ceased. Occasionally opposition groups tried to raise the question of the revocation of Balala's passport. For example, in December 1995, Rashid Mzee, deputy chairman of Ford-Kenya, introduced the issue in parliament and demanded that Balala's passport be restored to him; the minister of state in the president's office responded by reiterating that Balala had illegally held dual nationality and was not entitled to

Kenyan nationality.[54]

By the end of 1995, Shaikh Balala and the IPK had already faded from the headlines and not much was written or heard about them. Balala's fall had been as swift as his rise.

In 1997, the subject of Balala reemerged in a short episode when, seeking to infiltrate into Kenya, he managed to get on a flight from Germany, his place of exile, to the Nairobi airport. Immigration officials who recognized him called the security forces; they put him on a German plane and returned him to Germany. The date of his arrival was in fact known to some opposition leaders, including the Ford-Asili leader Kenneth Matiba, and they tried to prevent him from returning to Germany by blocking the German plane with their bodies but were removed by the security forces. At the same time, opposition groups were organizing demonstrations to demand a change in the constitution before the 1997 elections, and it seems that some of the opposition leaders wanted Balala's assistance in their endeavors.[55]

Then, on 2 July, the Kenyan government made a surprise announcement canceling the ban on Balala's return to Kenya, and he returned on 12 July. This unexpected move on the eve of the 1997 elections, amid intensifying conflict between the authorities and opposition groups, apparently stemmed from several factors: Balala had taken legal action against the government, and the Supreme Court ruled that he must be allowed to return to Kenya and raised doubts about the cancellation of his passport; Kenya wanted to demonstrate that it was a law-abiding country; the government assessed that Balala's position had weakened and he would only have a divisive effect on the Muslim opposition groups; and his family promised, apparently with his consent, that he would refrain from violence.

On his return, Balala continued to criticize the government but more moderately, and he also criticized the opposition, claiming that it did not reflect the views of the majority. On one occasion, when he began to denigrate the government in front of journalists, his mother, Fatima Sadik bint Salim, warned: "I shall stitch his mouth up unless he tones it down."[56] Nevertheless, Balala could not always restrain himself. On the eve of the 1997 general elections, Balala was one of the opposition speakers at the Uhuru park rally. He declared that he intended to disrupt the polls because they had been rigged by Kanu. The government, as a precaution, had Balala arrested in Mombasa shortly before the voting began.[57]

In any case, it seems that for the time being the shaikh does not enjoy the sort of fame and publicity he once did and does not pose a threat to the regime.

15

Similarities and Differences in the Political Status of Muslims in Kenya, Uganda, and Tanzania

Islam in East Africa—especially in Kenya, Uganda, and Tanzania—has displayed in its development both similarities and differences.

In all three countries, Islam was initially disseminated by teachers and religious leaders who came from Hadramaut and from the Comoro Islands. It was, therefore, mainly Sunni-Shafi'i Islam, and the number of Shiites was small—most of them Indians and Pakistanis such as the Ithna'ashriya and Ismailis. Therefore, especially along the coast of Kenya and Tanzania where the Swahilis form a significant percentage, there are many similarities—the Maulidi celebrations, saint worship, and the prevalence of Sufi orders. In Tanzania, the widespread Qadiriya order was particularly with many African Muslims holding high positions in its hierarchy, played an important role in the diffusion of Islam. In Kenya, the Sayids and the Sharifs, immigrants from Hadramaut who were related to the Prophet, disseminated the Alwiya order, which was less prominent among black African Muslims. In Uganda, the Sufi order of the Shadiliya played an important role.

In Tanganyika, there was more involvement of Muslims in political organizations that struggled for independence. Muslims, among them leaders of the Qadiriya Sufi order, were active in the 1950s in the Tanganyika African Association, a political party that later changed its name to Tanganyika African National Union, or Tanu. In Kenya and Uganda where their number was smaller, Muslims did not play a similar prominent role in the independence movements.

All three countries, on gaining independence, proclaimed in their constitutions the freedom of religion and worship, but they also declared the separation of religion and state, and in this regard they considered themselves "secular" states. They opposed the formation of parties based on religion, whether Muslim or Christian. At the same time, all three governments helped establish Muslim umbrella organizations that were not, in theory, political but by means of which the government could supervise Islamic activity. In Kenya, this organization was Supkem; in Tanzania, it was the Higher Council of Muslims in Tanzania (Bakwata, an acronym of Baraza Kuu Waislamu Watanzania). During Milton Obote's rule (1962–1971) in Uganda—where there have been many revolutionary changes in government since independence—a progovernment Muslim organization was formed: the National Association for the Advancement of Muslims (NAAM). After Idi Amin's coup in 1971, this organization was replaced by the Uganda Muslim Supreme Council (UMSC). President Yoweri Museveni, who seized power in 1986, has so far stayed out of Muslim disputes and has not set up any Muslim umbrella organization.

In all three countries, Islamic law is imposed by shari'a courts headed by qadis, mainly in personal and religious matters such as marriage, divorce, inheritance, and waqf affairs. At the head of the hierarchy is the chief qadi; in Uganda he is also called the mufti.

Muslim communities in East Africa are marked by divisions based on ethnicity and religion. Ethnic divisions are primarily between Arabs on the one hand (together with Swahilis, who wish to be regarded as Arabs), and black African Muslims from Bantu ethnic groups on the other. The former group regards itself as superior partly because, in the precolonial period, it ruled the coast. In all three countries, the colonial regime sharpened the traditional social inequality by granting more rights and administrative status to those of Arab descent, whom they saw as more developed than the Africans. In Kenya this division was recently manifested in the conflict between the IPK and the UMA. A similar polarization exists in Tanzania between the prestigious elite of the 'ulamaa, who mostly originated in Hadramaut, and the followers of the Qadiriya Sufi order, whose leaders are black African Muslims. In Uganda, these differences play less of a role because of the very small number of Arabs and their distance from the coast.

The rift between Arab and African Muslims substantiates the thesis that Islam did not necessarily succeed in overcoming the racial divisions that had existed before the European colonial period; in fact, it sometimes only deepened them. In Zanzibar, all of whose inhabitants are Muslims, a serious outbreak of violence by Africans against Arabs occurred in January 1964, when the Omani sultanate was abolished. Compared to Kenya, however, the Arabs in Tanzania were more willing at independence to accept African rule, and there was no secessionist movement as there was on the Kenyan coast.

Moreover, in all three countries there are similar religious disputes, such as those among the Sunnis over determining the dates for the start and end of the Ramadan fast. There are also differences of opinion concerning the use of drums during prayers. The disagreement as to whether the afternoon prayer (zuhr) should be added to the Friday prayer (jum'a) exists in all three countries, but it is particularly intense in Uganda and Tanzania.[1] In all three, the ethnic, religious, and personal differences among the Muslims have weakened their status.

In Uganda, the divisions within the Muslim leadership have in recent years been much more severe than in Kenya or Tanzania. The support that competing Arab countries, such as Saudi Arabia and Libya, have given to one side or the other has intensified rivalries that are based mainly on personal competition for leadership. Within the UMSC, for example, the Saudi favorite, Shaikh Ahmad Mukasa, and Libya's protégé Shaikh Ibrahim Saad Luwemba have continuously struggled for the post of chief qadi. In September 1993, during the celebrations in Kampala of the thirty-first anniversary of Uganda's independence, when the head of the ceremony called on the Muslim leader to recite a blessing, two shaikhs walked up to the stage, quarreled, and caused great embarrassment to all present.[2] As noted, Museveni, unlike his predecessors, has avoided intervening in religious disputes among the Muslims—or among the Christians for that matter. When in February 1998 Museveni appointed a Muslim, Major General Abubaker Jeje Odongo, as chief of staff to replace Major General Munyisha Muntu (a Christian and member of Museveni's own Ankole tribe), Museveni was seeking to demonstrate his policy of promoting the best individuals available without regard to ethnic or religious affiliation.[3]

In all three countries, Muslims feel that they are discriminated against vis-à-vis Christians. They indeed lag behind in modern secular education, which is mostly in the hands of Christians, whereas Muslims have concentrated on Qur'an and religious studies in the traditional system of chuo and madrasas. Although in all three countries progressive Muslim circles have tried to introduce modern, technical education into Muslim schools, government jobs are filled almost entirely by graduates of Christian and state schools.

In all three countries, Muslims complain that Christians treat them as foreigners and as Arabs and not as local citizens. A striking illustration of this occurred in Uganda as early as the colonial period, when Captain MacDonald, who regarded Baganda converts to Islam as Arabs, suggested they leave the country and emigrate to Tanganyika. In Kenya, as we have seen, Muslims with Arab names complain about difficulties in obtaining identity cards and passports. In all three countries, feelings of discrimination fueled the activities of radical Islamic groups.

The political awakening of Muslims throughout East Africa was a response to the process of democratization in African countries in general, to the transfer of rule to the black majority in South Africa, and to the growing pressures for the introduction of a multiparty system in Kenya, Uganda, and Tanzania. Both Kenya and Tanzania had a one-party government: Kanu in Kenya and Tanu in Tanzania (Tanu changed its name to Chama Cha Mapinduzi, CCM, the Revolutionary Party); Uganda then had many parties but later did away with parties altogether. In Tanzania, where the percentage of Muslims is higher, some groups tried in 1957 to set up an Islamic political organization as a pressure group, known as the All Muslim National Union of Tanganyika (AMNUT), but it ceased to operate in 1963.

In multiparty elections held in Kenya in 1992 and in Tanzania in 1995, the ruling party won again. In Uganda President Museveni held nonparty elections in 1996 for the parliament and presidency, which he won. In Museveni's view, his no-party system is better suited to the traditions and conditions of Africa.

All three governments harbor suspicions about Muslim political groups. In Kenya, the government mistrusts Muslim politicians from the coastal strip and from the Northeastern Province. In Tanzania, there are apprehensions about Muslim groups in Zanzibar that fought against union with Tanganyika, most of which belong to the main opposition party, the Civic United Front (CUF), whose stronghold is on the island of Pemba and which is led by Seid Shariff Hamed. In the 1995 general elections in Zanzibar, the CUF lost by a small margin to the ruling CCM, and CUF leaders claimed that the results were falsified.

As for Islamic extremism, the appearance of militant groups is a common phenomenon throughout East Africa. It is, first and foremost, a symptom of the backwardness of Muslims in the economic, social, and political spheres and their strong sense of being discriminated against. Muslim frustration, desperation, and indignation have been exploited by local religious and political leaders who were inspired by the triumph of the Islamic revolutions in Iran and Sudan and by the activities of militant Muslim groups in the Middle East that preach that the only remedy for the Muslims' distress is the return to fundamentalist Islam. The more extremist among these groups go further, believing that the redemption of the Muslims can come only by violent means to achieve the expansion of Dar al-Islam at the expense of Dar al-Harb.

In Tanzania, the phenomenon was illustrated when in April 1993 extremist Muslims staged demonstrations over the sale of pork and destroyed several Christian butcher shops; they also attacked bars that sold alcoholic drinks. Shaikh Yahya Hussein, leader of a radical Muslim group called the Council for the Promotion of the Qur'an in Tanzania (Balcuta), was arrested along with about forty of his followers. He was accused of distributing cassettes that called on Tanzanian Muslims to overthrow the regime and to establish a Muslim state on the basis of the shari'a. President Ali Hassan Mwinyi, himself a Muslim, issued a strong warning stressing that his government was resolved to eradicate every sign of religious extremism.[4]

Again, in February and April 1998, an Islamic militant group known as Khidmat Da'wat Islamiyya (the Service for Islamic Propagation) incited demonstrations during prayers in Mwembechai Mosque in Dar-es-Salaam. In the subsequent riots they torched tires and damaged dozens of vehicles, shouting anti-Christian slogans and complaints about discrimination against Muslims, with warnings that Islam was in danger. In clashes with the police, several protesters were shot dead, others were injured, and more than 100 were arrested. The government accused the group's leaders of inciting hatred against other religions.

During the police investigation, claims were heard that foreigners living in the country were behind the violence; suspicions focused on Saudi Arabia, Iran, Libya, and Sudan. The Iranian ambassador denied any complicity in the riots.[5] As for Sudan, in recent years Sudanese nationals living in Tanzania have been accused of actively agitating in the Morogoro district and in Dar-es-Salaam, and a number of Sudanese teachers have even been expelled. On 25 April 1998, during a time of religious tension, Prime Minister Frederick Samaye reiterated the government's intention to deal firmly with actions that endangered security and warned against using religion to disturb the peace in Tanzania. One wonders whether this atmosphere of religious violence had any effect on the instigators of the bombing of the U.S. embassy in Dar-es-Salaam in August that same year. In that case too, foreign Muslim nationals, as well as local Muslims, were among the suspects.

In Uganda, radical Islam was manifested by the emergence of the Tabligh group (from the Arabic *tabligh al-shari'a al-Islamiyya*, which means the propagation of Islamic law). This group called for imposing the shari'a on the country. In a clash between Tabligh members and security forces in 1991, a number of policemen and civilians were killed and others were severely injured; subsequently, the government outlawed the organization and banned its journal *Shariaat*.

As in Kenya, there was also an attempt to establish an Islamic party—the Islamic Revolutionary Party of Uganda, which was illegally created in April 1993. In September 1997, two of its leaders were arrested and tried for treason in Kampala. Like every political party in Uganda during those years, its activities were meager compared with those of the IPK.[6]

The Ugandan government fears the infiltration of radical Islamic ideas from Sudan, with which Uganda has always had a tense relationship. Interestingly enough, today the radical religious opposition comes from a Christian group called the Lord's Resistance Army (LRA), which is supported by Sudan and demands that rule in Uganda be based on the Ten Commandments. Most members belong to the northern Acholi ethnic group. Their struggle against the regime of President Museveni, who is from a southern Bantu ethnic group, is clearly connected with the intertribal conflict.

Another subversive group, which has stepped up its activities against Museveni's regime since 1996, calls itself the Allied Democratic Forces (ADF) and operates mainly in the west of the country. It has killed dozens of soldiers and citizens, and thousands of residents have had to flee their homes. Museveni reiterates that the ADF is composed mainly of radical Muslims connected to Tabligh and that they receive assistance from Sudan.[7]

In each of the three countries, especially Kenya, the government suspected that Muslim foreigners used local Muslim extremists to bomb the U.S. embassies. In Nairobi and Dar-es-Salaam, the instigators succeeded in carrying out their design on 7 August 1998; in Kampala they failed.

Arab states conduct Islamic activities in all three countries, aimed at spreading Islam and working against Israel. In Tanzania, apprehension about Sudan's Islamic activities was manifested in 1993 when President Mwinyi expelled three Sudanese teachers after the Muslim riots over the issue of the sale of pork. In the wake of the 1998 religious violence, the government suspected that some Muslim countries were involved. Iran has active embassies in all three countries. Recently Iran's operations through its embassy in Nairobi have increased significantly. In Uganda and Kenya, on the other hand, there are Muslims groups that oppose the Arabization of Islam and the injection into religion of the Middle East issue by Arab countries and their local supporters. They point out that the Arab-Israeli conflict is not a conflict between Judaism and Islam.

Concerning the Arab-Israeli conflict, all three countries support the establishment of a Palestinian state and back pro-Arab resolutions in international forums, especially the Organization of Unity and the UN.

All three countries severed and then restored diplomatic relations with Israel. Idi Amin's Uganda was one of the first of the thirty African countries to cut off relations, doing so before the October War. The Muslim factor was one of the main causes of Amin's shift toward the Arab states; he hoped that Muslim countries, especially Libya, would support his regime financially, politically, and militarily. Thus, in the joint Ugandan-Libyan communiqué issued in Tripoli on 13 February 1972, both Amin and Qadhafi undertook to base their respective revolutions on Islamic ideals.[8] It was a month later that Amin severed diplomatic relations with Israel. In Kenya and Tanzania, in contrast to Uganda, the Muslim factor—that is, external or internal Muslim pressure—did not play any role in the rupture of relations. Tanzania and Kenya severed diplomatic relations with Israel immediately after the October War (Tanzania on 19 October 1973, Kenya on 1 November 1973), mainly because of the OAU resolution and out of solidarity with Egypt.

Kenya was the first of the three to resume these relations, on 23 December 1988; next was Uganda on 26 July 1994, then Tanzania on 24 February 1995. The latter two restored ties in response to the Israeli-PLO and Israeli-Jordanian peace accords. It is notable that Tanzania resumed relations with Israel during Mwinyi's presidency. The Islamic factor and the Arab countries' activities did not prevent the three countries' resumption of ties with Israel. Kenya always had good relations with Israel and, as noted earlier, even after formal relations were cut off, practical cooperation continued as before. With the restoration of formal relations in 1988, President Moi demonstrated his country's friendly attitude toward Israel with his visits there in 1993 and 1995. Of the three countries, only Kenya has a resident ambassador in Israel.

Even though it has the smallest percentage of Muslims, Uganda is the only one of the three countries that is a member of the Organization of the Islamic Conference (OIC), which is mainly a political-governmental organization; in Kenya, the subject has not even arisen. Uganda joined the OIC during the rule of Amin, who received assistance from Arab countries, especially Libya. President Museveni, a Christian, apparently kept Uganda in the OIC for practical reasons, despite his opposition to mixing religion and politics and his fears of radical Islam. Museveni hoped to receive grants and loans for development from the Islamic Development Bank, which was established by the OIC and was one of the most active of the financial institutions in Muslim countries. The bank's headquarters are in Jiddah, and only members of the OIC can apply to it for financial assistance. As for Tanzania, when it was announced in 1992 that Zanzibar had joined the OIC, there was an uproar in the Tanzanian parliament and media and Zanzibar was forced to retract.

In Kenya, despite tensions, there have been no violent conflicts between Muslims and Christians, although because of repeated provocations from both sides and the increasing influence of radical Islamic circles from outside and inside, this might happen. In Tanzania clashes broke out in 1993–1994, when Muslim militants attacked butcher shops and bars and the security forces had to intervene and arrest the organizers of the riots. There have also been provocative bomb threats against Christians and against evangelical rallies, heightening concern about Muslim-Christian relations in Tanzania. In June 1997 in Zanzibar, a Catholic church was destroyed in an explosion after a misunderstanding between Muslims and Christians in the predominantly Muslim island.[9] In Uganda, however, there is a legacy of bloody battles between Christians and Muslims that occurred in the late nineteenth century, and religion has been a significant political factor. After independence, Christians were harshly persecuted under Amin (1971–1979), dealing a severe blow to their religious and political leadership. President Museveni, who seized power in 1986, proclaimed the state's nonintervention in religious matters and refrained from supporting one of the rival Muslim organizations and from getting involved in the religious disputes between Muslims and Christians; instead, Museveni urged the two sides to peacefully resolve their differences. Meanwhile, the Christian churches as well have suffered rivalries and rifts, and with both the Muslim and Christian communities busy with their internal disputes, dialogue between the two has been impossible.

So far, each of the three countries has had some success in containing the spread of militant Islam and in conciliating its Muslim population. In Kenya, the conflict between radical Muslims and the government was prolonged and bitter, much more violent than in Tanzania or Uganda. Even so, efforts have been made since independence to conciliate the Muslims. Thus, in all three countries, 'Id al-Fitr is a national holiday, Muslims supervise the slaughtering in public abattoirs, and a number of Muslims are given posts in the government and in public institutions (though Muslims claim that this is insufficient). In Kenya, there was no Muslim minister during Kenyatta's presidency, but Moi now has two Muslim ministers in his cabinet. In Uganda, after the 1996 elections, Museveni appointed five Muslim ministers. In Tanzania, where the percentage of Muslims is larger, more of them have occupied key positions. The presidency has seemingly passed in rotation: Julius Nyerere, a Christian, was succeeded by the Muslim Ali Hassan Mwinyi, who served until 1996, completing two terms; he was followed by another Christian, Benjamin Mkapa. The Muslim president of Zanzibar also acts as deputy president of Tanzania. In the 1995 elections, a Muslim candidate, Jakaya Kikwete, competed for the presidency but lost. However, Mkapa took pains to conciliate the Muslims, and fourteen Muslim ministers serve in his government compared to nineteen Christians; and Kikwete has been appointed foreign minister. In Kenya, unlike in neighboring Uganda, Tanzania, and Malawi, there has never been a Muslim president, but certain Muslim groups claim that the time has come. There were in fact suggestions that Ali Mazrui run for president in the 1997 elections.[10]

In all three countries, the emergence of radical, political Islam was also influenced by divisions within the Muslim community itself. Extremist groups arose partly in protest against the official Muslim establishments, which cooperated with the respective governments and did their bidding. In Kenya, the IPK and its supporters censured Supkem; in Uganda, Tabligh opposed the UMSC; in Tanzania, Balcuta and other Islamic groups took a stance against Bakwata. In all three countries, however, the radical groups were themselves weakened by rifts, caused largely by personal rivalries. In Kenya, as we have seen, the IPK founders, Omar Mwinyi and Abdulrahman Wandati, expelled Shaikh Balala from the leadership because of his dictatorial style and violent extremism, also accusing him of embezzlement. In Uganda, Tabligh split into two: on one side was Jamil Mukulu, a radical whom other members accused of embezzlement and who like Balala was arrested and later went abroad; Mukulu's rival was the more moderate Shaikh Sulaiman Kakuto, who opposed violence and whose main concern was the dissemination of Islam by peaceful means.[11]

Thus, despite the historical, political, and religious differences between the three countries, there are also similarities in the position of the Muslims and their relationship with the state.

16

Conclusion

The Muslim riots that broke out in Mombasa in 1992–1994 were primarily a manifestation of Muslims' long-standing grievance that the mainly Christian government discriminates against them economically and politically. The prolonged clashes between Muslims and the security forces dominated the headlines and provoked heated debates in parliament between Muslim and non-Muslim MPs. Yet the surge of Muslim violence, which caused deaths and injuries as well as massive damage to business and property, intensified the government's deep-rooted suspicion of the Muslim minority. These suspicions are periodically revived also by suggestions from some Muslim radicals to create a "Muslim jimbo" in the Coast Province. Later, the twin bombings of the U.S. embassies in Nairobi and Dar-es-Salaam on 7 August 1998, in which the main suspects were Muslims (both foreigner and local) again raised the issue of the Muslims in Kenya.

Kenya's 5 million Muslims form a significant minority. In the pre-colonial era, Muslims ruled Kenya's coastal strip and Tanganyika from their center in Zanzibar. But during the colonial era and after independence, their political standing deteriorated, leading to deep frustration. At present, the Muslims' influence is felt primarily during election campaigns for the political parties or for the parliament and presidency, when the regime tries to recruit their support. At such times, the authorities tend to show greater readiness to comply with Muslims' requests, such as declaring 'Id al-Fitr a national public holiday and giving them other benefits and privileges.

The Muslims are made more influential by their large number—20 percent of the population—and by being concentrated in strategically and economically important areas as well as in urban centers.

Kenya's Muslims also receive financial and moral support from the Arab-Muslim world. The Muslims project unity and strength, albeit very seldom, when they feel their religion has been vilified by Christians or other local or foreign persons. Such unity was conspicuous in their reaction to Cardinal Otunga's statements against Islam; in their objection to the marketing of Salman Rushdie's book *The Satanic Verses*, a demand the government had to accede to; in their furious reaction to the letter published in *The Standard* supporting Rushdie (see Chapter 5), which forced the editor to publicly apologize; and, recently, in their vehement protests against the banning of the Muslim NGOs following the U.S. embassy bombings, which led to conciliatory steps by the government.

On the other hand, the Muslims' weaknesses stem from religious and political cleavages and ongoing personal rivalries. Also, the historical division between black African Muslims and Muslims of Arab origin, which persists, makes it harder for them to unite. Above all, the position of Muslims in Kenya is weakened by the regime's misgivings about their loyalty, which are rooted in past efforts by coastal and Somali Muslims to secede from independent Kenya.

The Somali Muslims of the Northeastern Province repeatedly accuse the government of neglecting their security and development and of discriminating against them in the provision of schools and social services. Recently, their anger was again aroused by what they call the Wagalla Massacre of 1994 and the Wajir Massacre of 1998. Somali religious and political leaders—and even Somali MPs, members of the ruling Kanu Party—often direct accusations at the government. Somali complaints are often accompanied by threats to secede or to leave Kanu, and this only augments the government's mistrust.

Muslim economic hardships and increasing unemployment among youth, particularly in the urban centers of the coast, were among the reasons for the establishment in Mombasa of the Islamic Party of Kenya on the eve of the first multiparty elections of December 1992. Muslim leaders complained that all the other parties were headed by Christians who were indifferent to the plight of Muslims. Only a Muslim party, they stressed, would genuinely attempt to promote Muslim interests. Initially, the IPK was enthusiastically received by wide circles of Muslims, including academics and public figures, and exerted significant influence in the Muslim community. The government's refusal to register the IPK on the grounds that it was a religious political party, violating the principle of separation of religion and politics, seemed to most Muslims a mere pretext. They asserted that the government itself did not adhere to that principle; on the contrary, it emphasized, implicitly and explicitly, the centrality of Christianity to Kenyan society. In practice, Muslims claimed, there was no separation between religion and state but instead an effort by the state to control religion and use it to further its own interests.

Muslims' continued resentments against the government set the stage for the emergence of Islamic extremism headed by Shaikh Khalid Balala. At first Balala seemed moderate, but gradually his attacks against the government became more audacious. He became popular among the coastal Muslims and was considered a hero, the first who had the courage to sharply criticize the government, in contrast to Supkem and other Muslim leaders who were regarded as government stooges. The 1992–1994 disturbances worried the regime, especially when they became violent and disrupted peace and order in the main centers of the coastal strip. Eventually, the government took control of the situation and crushed Shaikh Balala and his militant followers, using carrot-and-stick and divide-and-conquer methods.

Several points emerge from the episode of Shaikh Balala and the IPK:

- Muslim extremism in Kenya is first and foremost the outcome of a difficult economic situation and a sense of being the victims of discrimination.
- The timing of the outbreak of the disturbances was connected to the introduction of the multiparty system and the government's refusal to register the IPK.
- Muslim militancy in Kenya was also influenced by radical Muslim movements in Egypt, Sudan, and North Africa and by the Iranian Islamic revolution. In the neighboring Horn of Africa as well, recent years have seen a significant expansion in the activities of Muslim groups. Prominent among them is the Islamic Ittihad, whose aim is to establish an Islamic republic that would include all Muslims in the Horn of Africa and Kenya. The Ittihad, which operates mainly against Ethiopia in the Ogaden region, apparently receives assistance from Sudan, Iran, and extremist groups in Saudi Arabia.[1]
- The vast majority of the Muslims who supported the establishment of the IPK rejected Balala's violent extremism, and this was one of the reasons for his fall.
- The government later tried to address some of the Muslims' grievances, but the basic factors that caused Muslims to feel discriminated against remained, and Muslims still level complaints against the government, albeit without the violence seen in 1992–1994.

The aftermath of the bombings of the U.S. embassies again highlighted the problematic relations between the Muslims and the government. The government, for its part, suspected Muslim involvement;

the Muslims felt unfairly singled out, especially in the episode of the banning of Muslim NGOs.

There are similarities in the development of Islam and in the position and role of the Muslims in Kenya, Tanzania, and Uganda. These reflect similar ways in which Islam was disseminated in East Africa, including the influence of teachers from Hadramaut; effects of the Omani rule on the coast of Kenya and Tanganyika and of the British rule in the three territories; and Arab-Islamic religious and political influences.

Notwithstanding many similarities, no united Sunni Muslim organization has emerged in East Africa, both because the respective governments would not allow it and because of differences between the three countries. These include Uganda's greater distance from the Islamic centers on the coast and in Arabia; German rule in Tanganyika until World War I, with its different approaches to Islam and the Muslims; and the distinct political systems in the three countries since independence.

It is likely that Islam as a religion will further expand and gain strength in Kenya as well as in Tanzania and Uganda. In its nonextremist form, it may assume a greater political role in light of the progress Muslims are making in the field of education and the increasing numbers of Muslim intellectuals, journalists, and politicians (though these numbers are still smaller than their percentage in the population).

The Kenyan government, like the Tanzanian and Ugandan governments, had the upper hand in subduing the militant Muslims, and they do not seem to pose a threat to stability. Nevertheless, the prolonged struggle against government policies has fostered Muslim solidarity and self-consciousness even among nonobservant Muslims. The Kenyan government needs to be more understanding and responsive to Muslim grievances, especially those that are justified, and to provide Muslims with equal opportunities and make greater efforts to integrate them into government and public life. Above all, the government must help them to advance the education of their youth. This would make it harder for Muslim extremists, from within and from outside, to incite the Muslim community against the government.

Is there a possibility of a revival of Islamic extremism in Kenya since Shaikh Balala? As in the wake of the U.S. embassy bombings, Muslim demonstrations may erupt when Muslims believe the government has seriously harmed their image and interests. Nevertheless, the majority of Muslims are moderate, tolerant, and pragmatic and know that it is impossible to turn Kenya into an Islamic state based on the shariʿa. This was evident when, as mentioned in Chapter 6, the proposal of appointing a khalif was immediately rejected.

The record shows that present-day militant Muslims in sub-Saharan Africa, both in the East and the West, have not succeeded in establishing Islamic states based on the shariʿa as they interpret it. In West Africa—even in countries where Muslims form 80–90 percent of the population and the president is a Muslim, such as Senegal, or where they constitute a very significant percentage, such as Nigeria, the largest Muslim community in black Africa (in Nigeria alone Muslims number about 50 million)—the governments have taken very firm measures against any manifestations of Islamic militancy. Most countries in sub-Saharan Africa insist on the separation of religion and state, and oppose the establishment of Muslim political parties. In sub-Saharan Africa, then, Muslim militants do not seem to have fertile ground on which to spread their extremism.

Appendix 1

Declaration by a Person Being Converted to Islam

IN THE NAME OF ALLAH, THE BENEFICENT, THE MERCIFUL	Kwa jina la Mwenye-ezi Mngu, mwingi wa rehma, mwenye kurehemu
All praise be upon ALLAH and Peace and Blessings be upon his last PROPHET, MUHAMMAD BIN ABDILLAH, and also to his relatives, colleagues and each and every of their followers up to the Day of Judgement - AMIN.	Swifa njema zote ni zenye kumthubutukiya Mwenye-ezi-Mngu, na rehma na amani zimfikiliye Mtume wake, wa mwisho, Muhammad Bin Abdilah, ziwafike na ali zake, na swahbaa zake, na kulla mwenye kufuatiya wao mpaka siku ya malipo :- AMIN.
MAALIM SAID BIN AHMED	**MAALIM SAID BIN AHMED**
(This is a Declaration for a person converted to Muslim Religion)	(Hii ni Shahada ya alo ingia katika Dini ya Islam)
The bearer has voluntary and wholeheartedly consented and has announced in his own tongue that there is no one who can be truly worshipped except ALLAH, who has neither wife nor child.	Huyu amekubali kwa movowake, ametamka kwa ulimi wake, yakuwa hakika hapana mola apasae kuabudiwa kwa hakki, illa Mwenye-ezi-Mngu ambaye hana mke wala kijana.
And has further, wholeheartedly consented and announced in his own tongue that MOHAMED is the follower of ALLAH and is also the Phophet of ALLAH.	Na amekubali kwa moyo wake, ametamka kwa ulimi wake, yakuwa Muhammad ni mja wa Mwenye-ezi-Mngu na ni Mtume wa Mwenye-ez-Mngu.
This Declaration has been announced in my presence :-	Ametamka Mashahada haya mbele zangu :-
MAALIM SAID BIN AHMED	**MAALIM SAID BIN AHMED**
His/Her Name	Jina lake ....
His/Her Nationality	Kabila yake ....
His/Her Religion	Dini yake ....
His/Her Name in Muslim	Jina lake Katika Uislam ....
His/Her Religion	Dini yake ....
His/Her Age	Umri wake ....
His/Her Place of Domicile	Mji wake ....
His/Her Profession	Kazi yake ....
His/Her Signature	Sahihi yake ....
Place of conversion	Mji aliyo Silimu : ....
Date	Tarehe : ....

Appendix 2

An Open Letter from the Islamic Party of Kenya to the Attorney General

IN THE NAME OF GOD THE BENEFICENT, THE MERCIFUL.

THE ISLAMIC PARTY OF KENYA

An open letter to Hon. Amos Wako, Attorney General of the Republic of Kenya.

6th July, 1993

Dear Sir,

RE: MOMBASA—A BOSNIA IN THE MAKING

I am writing this letter to raise a warning of an ominous cloud looming over Mombasa and Muslims in particular, of impending clashes similar to the one going on in Bosnia against Muslims. I have given reasonings of how we came to the conclusion and can supply names and details to the police if required.

Our investigations have revealed that it is KANU youthwingers who are behind the recent petrol bomb attacks in Mombasa, the culmination of a plot by the KANU government to divide Muslims along ethnic lines thereby creating fertile ground for Molo like clashes.

This plot was kicked off by the formation of bogus Islamic organisations (UMKE, UMA) by the Mombasa district youth for KANU "92" Chairman Mr. Mohamed Omar Masumbuko followed immediately by claims by the losing KANU Parliamentary candidate for Kisauni constituency Mr. Emmanuel Maitha that he was training an army in the bush to kill Arab Muslims. Mr. Maitha was immediately backed by inflammatory utterances by members of Mr. Masumbuko's group calculated to drive a wedge among Muslims of different ethnic backgrounds. It is a well known fact that dividing Kenyans has been KANU's stock in trade ever since the start of multi parties.

Mr. Masumbuko and KANU youthwingers have since gone about recruiting youth by giving them money and informing them that they will be sent for military training in order to kill IPK supporters. We have learnt of this through some youths who are our supporters and were unknowingly approached. Further, on Friday 28th May, the day of the IPK called strike in Mombasa, members of the press photographed a large number of these youths, who had been recruited by Mr. Masumbuko's organisation, at Mama Ngina Drive under the direction of police reservists and stating openly that they intended to kill IPK supporters. Mr. Masumbuko himself stated the same during an interview with the BBC on 21st June.

Proof of high level connivance and support for Mr. Masumbuko and his organisation was when they were licensed to hold a public rally on Saturday 19th June, despite the fact they are not registered and were accorded security by the state, similar to the President's himself. Further, after the meeting it was reported in the press that police battled IPK supporters who stoned a bus after the rally. The truth of the matter is that KANU youthwingers stoned the bus and police used it as a pretext to enter Bondeni and Makadara and beat up anyone in a Muslim dress.

Ever since the formation of IPK early last year the Government has adopted an overly heavy-handed manner in dealing with us and our supporters, as we were perceived to be a threat to KANU in Muslim-dominated areas which are thought to be KANU strongholds especially in the Coast and NorthEastern Kenya.

As a result, Muslim preachers were stopped from preaching in Mombasa, followed by the storming of the Kwa Shibu Mosque where G.S.U. fired bullets in the mosque and beat up worshippers, an act that sparked off widespread anger among Muslims, after which police shot dead three people in the disturbances that followed. From then on our supporters have suffered all manner of violations of their constitutional and human rights including being fired upon by the police at the slightest reason, being forcibly prevented by the police from attending court cases concerning us and targetting by the police in the course of their routine patrols of anyone wearing Muslim dress for harassment and intimidation. All this has led to a feeling of being persecuted by our supporters with some of them fleeing to London as refugees. The UNHCR can confirm this fact.

Now we have learnt that KANU has set up camps at Nguu Tatu in Bamburi and Watamu near Malindi for their Moran Warriors who will unleash terror on supporters of IPK in order to cow them into submission.

All this is just the latest of 30 years of KANU oppression of Muslims in Kenya, and to massacre Muslims is not new to them, as memories of the Wagalla Masssacre and other atrocities still being perpetrated against our brothers in NorthEastern province by the security forces are still fresh in our minds. However, this will not deter us from continuing our struggle for our right to be treated equally like any other Kenyan.

We are in the process of documenting all human rights abuses perpetrated against our supporters and compiling a list of all those who have been victim of police brutality with a view to take legal action against the state.

ABUBAKR A.M. AWAGH
INTERIM ORGANISING SECRETARY.

P.O. BOX 334
MOMBASA

cc: The Provincial Commissioner, Coast Province, P.O. Box 90424, MOMBASA
The Police Commissioner, P.O. Box 30083, NAIROBI
Mohamed Fakih, Advocate, MOMBASA
Taib A. Taib, Advocate, MOMBASA
Professor Rashid Mzee MP, for circulation to all members of parliament.
All Human Rights Organisations, KENYA
Members of the Press Corps.
All Diplomatic Missions in Kenya

Appendix 3

Objectives of the United Muslims of Africa

THE STANDARD, Tuesday, May 25, 1993.

UNITED MUSLIMS OF AFRICA (UMA)
P.O. BOX 12170 HEADQUARTERS MOMBASA.

OBJECTIVES

UMA is against IPK which has been constantly engaging in abuse to the head of state and leaders affiliated to other political parties, for this is against Islamic teachings.
Qur'an is against hooliganism and thuggery agitated by the leaders of IPK.
UMA is ready to defend the integrity of Africans from this disease that has been inflicted to the continent of Africa by rich particular Gulf states to create harvoc between various denominations of Africa.
UMA is here not to engage into any confrontation with anybody but warns all Muslims who have been letting loose their sons and daughters to engage in riots and destroying of property for we are here to clean the once respected religion of Islam.
We are opposed to the Islamic Party of Kenya for the following reasons:
— At the time of the installation of Islam in the pagan Arabia, Prophet Mohammad (S.A.W.) did not form a political party to fight the Muslim rights in Mecca.
— Islam is to submit oneself into doing the will of God (SWT) but not to commit oneself into hooliganism, violence, burning of property and encouraging the youth in meditation and hallucination to disrupt peace.
— No consultation on the modalities of fronting the Muslim rights within the Muslims and the government was ever made from the various Islamic denominations eg. Sunni and Shias, of which have the right of integration under the banner of Islam.
— Exploitation of Islam by selfish and fanatics for their own personal gains as evidently displayed by a few people in our society for Islam is not for a cheap place. Like a Social Hall but its for God and nobody else.
— UMA harbours no political ambitions neither their support to politicians to further their personal gains but there to develop a foundation to help promote the living standards to all who are African and accept Africa with its realities.
— UMA is going to help and assist those people who fell victims of the hooliganism brought about by the IPK.
— UMA is for all Muslims and should not be seen to be dividing Muslims on racial lines.
— UMA wants all Muslims and non-Muslims to be brothers and sisters as they have always been before the formations of divisive groupings. There should be respect among them all to promote Islamic and African brotherhood.

**WE WISH ALL THE KENYANS AND AFRICANS AT LARGE
A HAPPY IDD-UL-HAJJ.**

SECRETARY-GENERAL
   MAUR ABDALLAH BWANAMAKE
DIRECTOR OF OPERATIONS
   MZEE SAID KAMRANI
Treasurer
   MUNYI HAMIS BAKAULI

Appendix 4

"Principles of Democratic Leadership"

By Khelef A. Khalifa, an Islamic Party of Kenya Supporter

Until recently, the Islamic Party of Kenya (IPK) appeared to be a strong and united movement with every potential of growing into a formidable opposition grouping of national stature. President Daniel arap Moi's regime had come to fear its militancy and its sense of purpose and determination, and nationally it had come to acquire the reputation of being the most principled political force. Even some of the harshest critics of the IPK among Muslims had to acknowledge that the movement had precipitated a new political equation in the country.

Today, however, IPK is at a crossroads between the path of disintegration and that of consolidation. Its enemies and detractors, led by the Kanu regime, are busy conspiring to ensure its destruction. Where they have failed to combat it from the outside, they have sought every possible crack and weakness within the movement to plant poisonous seeds of divisiveness. The United Muslims of Africa (Uma) is just one of the more recent manifestations of this conspiracy to kill the IPK.

The people who can prevent the IPK from being dragged down the perilous path of disintegration are IPK supporters themselves, especially those who have played an active role in its operations. It is in this spirit that I decided to offer this candid critique of the movement, for a movement that proceeds without periodic and honest reflection on its strengths and weaknesses is an easy victim of the machinations of its enemies.

Opinion piece published in *The Weekly Review* (defunct), Nairobi, 17 September 1993.

One of the most critical problems facing the IPK today is the style of leadership. And since, in the minds of many people, the leadership of the IPK is synonymous with the name of Sheikh Khalid Balala, this problem is best personified by him. The IPK was born in the heat of the democratic struggle in Kenya with the explicit aim of representing the democratic interests and aspirations of Muslims and contributing to the creation of a democratic society inspired by Islamic principles. But a democratic movement and a democratic society cannot emerge out of the undemocratic practices of their leaders. It can only come about from a leadership that is democratic both in its sentiments and its behaviour.

The principles that form the basis of a democratic leadership include:

Participation

One major test of a democratic leadership is the extent to which it allows its followers to participate in decision making. Despots believe that they are the only ones who hold any views and opinions, and who have the voice to articulate them, and instead of serving as enlightened leaders who stand to benefit from reasoning with others, they end up acting like authoritarian commanders of military regiments. This is Balala's style of leadership. The thousands of Muslims who form the backbone of the movement and who have sacrificed their lives and security for the cause of the movement have suddenly become inconsequential to him. Indeed, every time Balala is called upon to reason collectively with others in the IPK, his blind arrogance and sheer disdain for the democratic principle of participation and consultation are clear.

Balala personifies the "*mukipenda musipende*" (whether you like it or not) syndrome. And the collective good of the community has been sacrificed at the altar of individualism and egocentrism. Hitting the newspaper headlines has become more important for Balala that careful and consultative planning of major substantive issues that affect the political, social and economic welfare of the community.

The end result of this lack of participatory style of leadership is that decisions in the IPK have come to be based on individual whims rather than on collective planning. As a result, the IPK's activities have been haphazard. Furthermore, in his craving to appear in newspaper columns as the only voice of the IPK, Balala has alienated those once closest to him, committed people whom he could have reasoned with for the collective good of the community. By alienating other

IPK leaders and activists, Balala is personally largely responsible for making its leadership uncoordinated and fragmented.

Balala feels terribly insecure working with independent-minded and intellectually resourceful people.

The IPK does not have such immense resources, and depends entirely on the goodwill and commitment of its supporters to get things done. In a sense, this has been its greatest strength. But precisely because of this, its survival depends on involvement of people at various levels in the decision making process. In the final analysis, therefore, a leadership that does not submit itself to collective thinking will make the movement intellectually bankrupt. Ultimately the movement will choke to death under the weight of its own ignorance.

Openness

A democratic leadership, on the other hand, must be open to criticism from others. But Balala not only treats nonconformist opinions of others with complete contempt, but is quick to excommunicate anyone who so much as differs with him.

This tendency betrays an uncertainty about the correctness of his own position and an insecurity about the source of his leadership. A person who is secure about his role as a leader and confident of the support of the people has no cause to fear dissent or criticism. A person who takes a position on issues through honest reflection in pursuit of truth and justice does not fear to be proven wrong.

Transparency

Transparency in leadership implies a situation where the followers have direct access to information about what the leaders are doing, about the basis of leadership decisions and actions, and about what is actually going on within the movement at every point. Without this kind of information, the people cannot even begin to participate effectively in the decision-making and in determining their own destiny.

But lack of transparency is precisely what Balala thrives on as a way of maintaining an authoritarian hold on the movement. He considers the movement his private property and its affairs as privileged and personal information. By controlling and personalising information he is thus able to combine truths and untruths, substance and trivia, to mystify his leadership and manipulate the people. Because the leadership is not transparent, it can continue to feed the people with more and more lies in an attempt to create a false image of itself. And when people are kept ignorant they can become mere pawns in the designs of their leaders and easy victims of their machinations. In terms of information control, Balala is second only to Suheli, a staunch Shia Ithnaashari and Khalid's closest aide. Through a well calculated design of misinformation Suheli was able to set some of the IPK's most committed activists against each other and distance them from Balala. This was part of a grand conspiracy to undermine the IPK's radicalism and militancy and reduce it to a mere welfare organisation. And rather than work closely with well-meaning and committed people, Balala chose to submit himself to the control of this conspiratorial Suheli.

Anyone who is familiar with Suheli's language knows that a letter that Balala sent to the Bohra Maulana Burhanuddin was actually written by Suheli. Why should any IPK leader or activist suddenly sing praises to a leader who, on the evidence of some members of his own community, is known to be corrupt? Why should the IPK embrace a Muslim leader who fraternises with the discredited regime of President Moi and who, throughout his stay in Kenya, had nothing to say about the plight of Muslims in this country and their just struggle? What exactly was the motive for writing such a letter?

It is the same Suheli who, through his family connections with the organisers of the Ithnaashari Muharram procession last month, arranged for Balala's participation in the procession and positioned him directly behind nominated MP, Mr. Rashid Sajjad. Ironically, even a staunch Shia like Sheikh Abdillahi Nassir had never been known to join the Muharram procession. But here was a leading IPK activist who had repeatedly expressed anti-Shia sentiments participating in the most dramatic Shia event. What then lay behind this move, which was designed by Suheli? Balala's supporters have us believe that it was intended to woo the Shia community to support the IPK. But this is the kind of misinformation that can only be propagated by a non-transparent leadership. Those who have worked tirelessly to extend the IPK network of community relations know that the Shia community does not need to be won over; many of its members have always been strong supporters of the IPK. The truth of the matter, then, is that Khalid's participation in the procession was engineered by Suheli exclusively to safeguard Sajjad, a mortal enemy of the IPK, against a possible attack by its militant youth.

A leadership that insists on maintaining a privileged monopoly of information is both undemocratic and unIslamic.

We should not be expected to accept and support a position only because Balala espouses it. We should accept it only on the strength of the information and evidence before us and our understanding of the circumstances of the matter.

Accountability

A democratic leadership must also be accountable to the people. At the political level this means that it must act responsibly, bearing in mind the public interest of its Muslim followers, and must take the initiative to seek the mandate of the people and explain its actions to them. At the economic level it means laying all financial information open to public scrutiny, and justifying all financial matters connected with the movement.

But, again, Balala completely lacks this democratic sense of accountability. He can write a letter in praise of Maulana Burhanuddin, and another to His Highness Saud Al Faisal bin Abdul Aziz, opposing the appointment of Mr. Said Hemed as ambassador to Saudi Arabia, without feeling the need to explain his actions to the people. He can enter into talks with the notorious pro-imperialist International Republican Institute of America and seek to work with anti-Islamist western governments without consultation or explanation (see The People, July 25–31, 1993). He can make all sorts of exaggerated claims on behalf of the IPK without providing us with any supportive evidence or information.

Balala has also introduced a dangerous money culture into the IPK. He has supposedly established a Baitu-I-Maal whose income and expenditure only he knows. While the Baitu-I-Maal was established by Balala and the funds may come through him, they are ultimately intended for the benefit of the Muslim community at large. In fact the monies are raised in the name of the IPK and the Muslim community. Every Muslim, therefore, has a right to be informed about and decide on the affairs of the Baitu-I-Maal. But if total lack of accountability is so prevalent in the IPK, on what basis can we begin asking Muslim organisations like Nukem to account for its finances? What we require of others we must first do.

When individuals, organisations and governments donate funds to support certain projects or causes, some of them may have a hidden agenda that may be in conflict with the interests of the recipients. The decision to accept or not to accept contributions from a specific individual or body should not be made by an individual, but should be a collective one made by a representative committee that has deliberated the pros and cons of all contributions. Otherwise how can we know that the IPK is not subject to the kind of scandal that has hit

Ford Kenya, in which party chairman Mr. Oginga Odinga entered into a private and silent deal with Mr. Kamlesh Pattni of the notorious Goldenberg enterprise?

The same applies to expenditure. There are many key members of mosque committees who devote a lot of their time to propagating the ideals of the IPK, to raise our Islamic awareness and consciousness and mobilise us around specific issues. Yet these selfless workers have not received a single cent from the Baitu-I-Maal to facilitate their work. Instead Balala goes around dishing out thousands of shillings to football clubs. He even promised matatu touts a million shillings for their support of the IPK strike of May 28 when, in fact, he does not have the faintest idea of what actually went into organising that mass action.

In my discussions with various people I came across several respectable community leaders who said that they had personally been asked by Balala to supply him with a list of names of the needy who can benefit from the resources of the Baitu-I-Maal. But these lists were ignored and he proceeded to offer support only to individuals of his choice. As it turned out, some of these people selected by Balala for driving and computer training, for example, are known Kanu and Uma supporters and activists. His individualism and lack of respect for the principle of accountability, therefore, have ended up discrediting and undermining community elders and IPK functionaries in the eyes of their own people.

The Baitu-I-Maal has become Balala's new source of buying support and controlling people. The money is not put into projects that will benefit the needy in a sustainable way. Rather it is dished out to individuals as a personal favour to get them to feel indebted to Balala. These are precisely the tactics of President Moi and the Sajjads and, unfortunately, these seem to be the degenerate footsteps that Balala has chosen to follow.

Conclusion

Leaders are built by the people and not vice versa. Without a committed following that shares their sentiments and vision and that is willing to sacrifice and bear the consequences of its actions, leaders are doomed to oblivion. It is the people who provide leaders with their legitimacy. But some leaders often forget this fact. They quickly and foolishly come to believe that they as individuals and not the people are the "dynamos" of the movement. Instead of seeing themselves as part and products of the people, they place themselves above the people.

Eventually, drunk with their ego, arrogance and self-righteousness, they come to see themselves as indispensable to the movement.

Balala came into the picture when the nation in general, and Mombasa in particular, was bubbling with the democratic spirit. His words, uttered with courage and boldness, struck a chord in people's hearts precisely because the majority of the people were ripe and ready for the struggle that lay ahead. When he got into trouble with the law, people responded spontaneously to demand his release all in the more general cause of justice, democracy and liberty.

Yet, typical of leaders who lack democratic sentiments, Balala mistook this support for his personal fame. And increasingly he began to see himself as the IPK's indispensable owner. But, just as leaders are created by the people, no leader is indispensable. All major and successful mass activities that promoted a sense of unity among the Muslims and instilled fear in the Kanu government took place when Balala was absent. From major demonstrations to civil strikes, from electoral campaigns to militant activism, IPK supporters responded to issues of justice and liberty without the prompting of Balala or any other leaders for that matter. Indeed, the strike of May 28 took place when virtually all the IPK leaders in Mombasa were either in police custody or had gone underground. So, let none of us live under the illusion that his leadership is indispensable to the movement.

If we play blind to a style of leadership that is undemocratic, and a leadership that is egocentric, authoritarian and intolerant, we shall be sowing the seeds of our destruction. The way out is to begin thinking of developing a more democratic leadership style. We must think of ways of establishing small but representative committees and councils to participate in formulating policies and making decisions that affect the affairs of the IPK and Muslims in general. Representative committees are one form of participation by the people. We must encourage dialogue, tolerance and accommodation, and open channels of communication that will allow us to provide constant feedback to the leadership. There is also need for a regular IPK organ through which the leadership can provide information to the community and explain its actions and decisions to the people. In short, we need to democratise our style of leadership. Only in this way can we hope to consolidate the IPK and protest it from being derailed by internal forces and external enemies.

May Allah guide us in this constructive Jihad. Amin.

Appendix 5

Excerpts from "Imam Khomeini and Other Scholars on Muslim Unity"

a) Muslims all over the world must unite in order to prevail over their enemies and confront their oppressors. Arabs, Turks, Persians and other Muslims should establish "a great community called the Islamic Ummah in the world and, due to their great numbers, no one will be able to dominate the Islamic centres and governments. The superpowers and their subservient lackeys in the Islamic countries are planning to divide the Muslim people and want to sever the brotherhood among Muslims which God, the Most High, has ordained for them. . . . Also, they have sought to bring about enmity between the Muslim people which is totally against the path decreed by islam and the Noble Quran." If the Muslims come together and achieve unity, "problems like that of Quds (Jerusalem), Afghanistan or the other Muslim countries will not arise."

b) Since the vast majority of Muslims in Kenya are Sunnis, while the Iranians are Shiites, the article emphasizes Khomeini's call for understanding between Shia and Sunna: Sunnis and Shiites are brothers, Khomeini stresses. They should "join each other and walk towards one destination. . . . The great satanic powers do not want the good of Muslim and Islam. . . . I extend the hand of brotherhood to all the committed Muslims of the world, I ask them to look upon Shiites as their brothers and, with this action of theirs, thwart the ominous plans of the foreigners. . . . I hope that, with the endeavours of the most learned among the scholars, all the lands of the Sunni and Shiite brothers will join and remove themselves from these disagree-

---

These excerpts are taken from an article published in the *Guide*, the bulletin of the Iranian embassy in Nairobi, vol. 7, no. 1, January 1994, pp. 11–12.

ments which the corrupt and the corruptors want to create among us and each warn the people in his own region."

c) Condemnation of Israel is prominent in the sayings of Khomeini which are cited in the article: for example: "God willing, all Muslims will become brothers. . . . And this germ of corruption, Israel, will be driven out from al-Aqsa mosque and our Islamic country, Palestine. God willing, we will all go to Quds and perform the prayer of unity there. . . . If all the people of Islam were to each spill a jar of water upon the soil of Israel, it would destroy Israel."

Appendix 6

A Letter from Muslim Lecturers at the University of Nairobi

Discrimination Against Muslims

SIR—We should like to register our support for the sentiments (*The Weekly Review*, February 13, 1978) expressed by the Hon. Sharif Nassir over the rampant practice of discriminating against Muslims.

As educationalists, we find it extremely repulsive for a public servant, and an educationist at that, who condones discrimination based on colour or creed. For a time now, local administrators have cowed the people at the Coast into silence and, in the same vein, arrogated to themselves the function of discriminating against Kenyans of either Arab or Islamic background. What is even more shocking is that the same administrators, in their hypocrisy, tongue in cheek, have been at the fore-front of demoralising Muslims by constantly harping on them that they should avail themselves of educational opportunities. They have been branded with all the available pejorative labels and have been characterised in public rallies as an indolent and ignorant lot.

We wish to differ from this kind of stereo-type image which has given the Coast provincial education officer his raison d'etre for discriminating against Muslims.

Muslims at the Coast have for a long time been subjected to all sorts of harassment and inconveniences. This is particularly true within government, from the colonial times to the present, especially at the Coast, have been prejudiced against Muslims in general.

It is not difficult to see why during the colonial times the Muslims were viewed as the pariahs of society. Both the government and the missionaries established all over the country were de facto Christian.

The Weekly Review (defunct), Nairobi, 27 February 1978.

Apart from carving their spheres of influence in various tribal areas, the missionaries were unanimous in their suspicion and hatred for Muslims. They made sure that, in their crusading spirit, their primary objective was to make life difficult for Muslims wherever they were. It is all too obvious that the present cadre of administrators have unconsciously or unwittingly perpetuated the ominous practice of discriminating against Kenya nationals who do not share their creed.

Because western education in Kenya came invariably with the missionaries, the Muslim population was destined to be discriminated against or at best be admitted to Christian institutions at the cost of de-Islamising them. Sensing the political climate at the time, the Muslims were left with only one option, and that was to boycott those institutions calculated to undermine their culture and religion. Therefore, the history of Muslim education in Kenya was always been one of continual struggle between the Christian administrator-cum-educationist and the Muslim parent.

Way back in the 1930s, Muslims had their first encounter with missionary zealots and their arrogance when they were shown open defiance. Researching on the development of education at the Coast, Abdulhamid Bagha observed that "on many occasions angry feeling about this had been voiced by the people, but the government did not act; moreover, the Christian community courted trouble by singing hymns at the top of their voices during the Maulidi reading of the Kor'an." It was, therefore, not surprising that the bulk of the population, which was Muslim, did not evince any interest in mission education.

One would think that the modern educational administrator would be one who has stripped himself of missionary prejudice and would treat the rest of those in his charge impartially. It is unfortunate, as the Hon. Sharif Nassir observed in his letter, that there are still remnants of those missionary zealots in the garb of educationalists.

The present Coast provincial education officer is indeed an administrator whose mentality is reminiscent of Nineteenth Century missionaries. It is also obvious that he is intoxicated by his own prejudice against Kenyan Muslims in general who, we have reason to believe, he knows very little about. He has come out in the open by sending circulars intended to implement his prejudices. His victims have not only been Arabs, but also Africans with Muslim names who for generations before the coming of Christianity have espoused the Islamic religion.

He is, it is unfortunate for us to say, also not conversant with the simple discipline of public relations. If he is convinced of his mission against the Muslims, why does he not resign from his present job where he is expected to exercise extreme impartiality and join some American or European crusading Christian mission? We are sure his services would be most welcome.

M. Bakari
Dr. A.M. Shatry
Dr. R.M. Mzee
Dr. A. El-Busaidy
University of Nairobi

Notes

(Newspapers and periodicals for which location is not mentioned here or in the Bibliography are published in Kenya.)

Introduction

1. Arye Oded, *Islam in Uganda: Islamization through a Centralized State in Pre-Colonial Africa* (New York and Jerusalem, 1974).
2. Daniel H. Levine, "Religion and Politics in Comparative and Historical Perspective," *Comparative Politics* 19, 1 (1986): 95–122.
3. Terence Ranger, "Religious Movements and Politics in Sub-Saharan Africa," *African Studies Review* 29, 2 (June 1986): 1–69.
4. J. Spencer Trimingham, *Islam in East Africa* (Oxford, 1964), p. vi.
5. J. Spencer Trimingham, *Islam in East Africa* (Edinburgh, 1962), p. 8.
6. Holger Bernt Hansen and Michael Twaddle, eds., *Religion and Politics in East Africa* (London, 1995).
7. Mohamed Bakari and Yahya Saad, eds., *Islam in Kenya*, Proceedings of the National Seminar on Contemporary Islam in Kenya (Nairobi, 1995), pp. xi, xii.
8. Cited in Levine, "Religion and Politics in Comparative and Historical Perspective," p. 111.
9. Victor C. Ferkiss, "Religion and Politics in Independent African States: A Prolegomenon," in J. Butler and A.P. Castangna, eds., *Transition in African Politics* (New York, 1967), pp. 27, 28.
10. Ibid., p. 28.
11. Levine, "Religion and Politics in Comparative and Historical Perspective," p. 99.
12. Cited in Levine, ibid., p. 113.
13. Ferkiss, "Religion and Politics in Independent African States," p. 25.

Chapter 1: A Profile of the Muslim Community in Kenya

1. The number has also been estimated at 8 percent (François Constantin, "Loi de l'Islam contre loi d'état: Petite chronique d'un été kenyan,"

Islam et Sociétés au Sud du Sahara 3 [1989]: 62–66, relying on the censuses of 1962 and 1979); 6–8 percent, which seems too low (Donal B. Cruise O'Brien, "Coping with the Christians: The Muslim Predicament in Kenya," in Holger Bernt Hansen and Michael Twaddle, eds., *Religion and Politics in East Africa* [London, 1995]); and 6 percent (D. B. Barret, ed., *World Christian Encyclopedia* [London, 1982], pp. 432–437). Recent government statistics do not cite religious affiliation.

2. *Sunday Nation*, 24 April 1994.

3. *Daily Nation*, 5 April 1994. A Muslim researcher, Ali Kettani ("Muslim East Africa: An Overview," *Journal of Muslim Minority Affairs* 4, 1–2 [1982]: 104–119), estimates that Muslims constitute 30 percent; Mohamed Bakari of the Department of Religious Studies, University of Nairobi, stated in an interview (29 April 1994) that Muslims constitute 40 percent.

4. Barret (*World Christian Encyclopedia*) claims that Christians constitute 73 percent; Constantine ("Loi de l'Islam") cites 45 percent, asserting that the followers of traditional religions are "very numerous."

5. J. Spencer Trimingham, *Islam in East Africa* (Oxford, 1964), p. 153.

6. On the culture and religion of the Swahilis, see Hyder Kindy, *Life and Politics in Mombasa* (Nairobi, 1972); Ahmed Salim, *The Swahili-Speaking Peoples of Kenya's Coast 1895–1965* (Nairobi, 1973).

7. Richard Weeks, ed., *Muslim People: A World Ethnographic Survey* (Westport, Conn., 1984), pp. 732–736.

8. Carol Eastman, "Who Are the Waswahili?" *Africa* 41 (1971): 228–236. In the 1989 census, only 14,000 defined themselves as Swahilis and 55,000 as Bajun (northern Swahilis). Because of the lack of an accepted definition of a Swahili, it is difficult to give their exact number (Republic of Kenya, *Kenya Population Census*, 1989, vol. 1, pp. 2–6).

9. Kindy, *Life and Politics*, p. 47; Salim, *Swahili-Speaking Peoples*, pp. 9–10.

10. Kindy, ibid.

11. J. Spencer Trimingham, *Islam in East Africa* (Oxford, 1964), p. 81; Arye Oded, *Islam in Uganda* (New York and Jerusalem, 1974) pp. 310–312.

12. Salim, *Swahili-Speaking Peoples*, p. 10.

13. Shaheen Ayubi and Sakina Mohyuddin, "Muslims in Kenya: An Overview," *Journal of Muslim Minority Affairs* 15, 1–2 (January/July 1994): 147. According to the 1989 census, 42,000 defined themselves as Arabs.

14. Salim, *Swahili-Speaking Peoples*, p. 10.

15. Kindy, *Life and Politics*, in many places in the book.

16. Weeks, *Muslim People*, p. 700. In the 1989 census, 45,000 defined themselves as Somalis; 80,164 as Boran; 27,444 as Hawiyah; and 139,000 as Ogaden.

17. For example, the visit of the mayor of Nairobi on the eve of the March 1989 municipal elections and his promise to build a mosque, a cultural center, and so on. The Somalis unanimously appointed him a Somali Elder (*The Standard*, 12 March 1989).

18. According to the 1989 census, Asians numbered 89,000.

19. J. Schacht and R. Brunschvig, "Notes on Islam in East Africa," *Studia Islamica* 23 (1965): 91–136.

20. Ayubi and Mohyuddin, "Muslims in Kenya," pp. 150, 154.

21. *East African Standard*, 16 February 1971, p. 20.

22. *Kenya Times*, 29 June 1993.

23. *The Standard*, 5 October 1977. On the work of the Aga Khan Foundation in Kenya and elsewhere, see the organization's publication, *Programme, Interests and Current Projects* (1987).

24. Mohamed Bakari and Yahya Saad, eds., *Islam in Kenya,* Proceedings of the National Seminar on Contemporary Islam in Kenya (Nairobi, 1995), p. 65.
25. Ayubi and Mohyuddin, "Muslims in Kenya," p. 154.
26. *Nurul Islam,* August 1980, p. 3.
27. *Voice of Africa,* 24 July 1980.
28. *Daily Nation,* 14 March 1979.
29. W. Hutley, "Mohammedanism in Central Africa and Its Influence," unpublished report, London Missionary Society Archives, 1881.

Chapter 2: Muslim Organizations

1. Donal B. Cruise O'Brien, "Coping with the Christians: The Muslim Predicament in Kenya," in Holger Bernt Hansen and Michael Twaddle, eds., *Religion and Politics in East Africa* (London, 1995), p. 205.
2. *Daily Nation,* 26 May 1994.
3. Farouk Muslim, "The Supreme Council of Muslims," *Nairobi Times,* 27 November 1977, p. 12. See also the wide-ranging article on the council in *The Standard,* 13 January 1979.
4. For example, the speech of Kassim Mwamazandi reported in the *Daily Nation,* 7 April 1980; the speech of Supkem's secretary, Mohamed Amana, in BBC, *Summary of World Broadcasts,* B11, B12, May 1987.
5. Such as the chief qadi's call during the Supkem conference, *The Standard,* 11 June 1979.
6. *The Standard,* 13 January 1979.
7. See, for example, the advertisement published by Supkem offering scholarships in engineering and medicine, which were donated by the Islamic Development Bank, *Daily Nation,* 2 December 1982. There was also information about scholarships for Muslims in *The Standard,* 13 January 1979, and the *Daily Nation,* 7 April 1980.
8. *Nairobi Times,* 27 November 1977, p. 12.
9. *Sunday Standard,* 3 March 1996; Mohamed Bakari and Yahya Saad, eds., *Islam in Kenya,* Proceedings of the National Seminar on Contemporary Islam in Kenya (Nairobi, 1995), p. 239.
10. *The Standard,* 13 January 1996; Bakari and Saad, *Islam in Kenya,* p. 225.
11. *Sunday Standard,* 3 March 1996.
12. *Weekly Review,* 6 November 1998.
13. *Kenya Times,* 17 December 1993.
14. *Nairobi Times,* 2 December 1979; *Daily Nation,* 27 September 1994.
15. *Taifa Leo* (Swahili newspaper), 12 May 1994.
16. *Daily Nation,* 28 September 1994.
17. *al-Islam,* March-April 1978.

Chapter 3: Muslims in the Establishment

1. For example, in 1968, out of fifty ministers and assistant ministers, there were only two Muslim assistant ministers, Shaikh S. H. Balala and Mohamed Jehazi. The appointment of a large number of assistant ministers is

meant to give some representation to various ethnic groups and religions; assistant ministers usually have no significant influence.
2. *Weekly Review*, 8 January 1999.
3. *Daily Nation*, 12 May 1973.

Chapter 4: The Political Importance of the Muslims

1. *East African Standard* and *Daily Nation*, 8 September 1971.
2. *Gazette Notice*, no. 190, 10 September 1971.
3. *East African Standard*, 19 October 1971.
4. Hyder Kindy, *Life and Politics in Mombasa* (Nairobi, 1972), p. 127.
5. *Sunday Nation*, 5 November 1978.
6. *The Standard*, 1 November 1979.
7. Ibid., 17 May 1980.
8. *Daily Nation*, 9 July 1973.
9. *East African Standard*, 5 November 1979.
10. *Daily Nation*, 20 July 1983.
11. *Sunday Nation*, 8 June 1980.
12. *Daily Nation*, 20 July 1983.
13. *East African Standard*, 10 February 1976.
14. *Daily Nation*, 5 December 1979.
15. Ibid., 30 September 1978.
16. N. K. Maina, "Muslim Education in Kenya with Special Reference to the Madrasa System in Nairobi," master's thesis, Kenyatta University, 1993, p. 167.
17. *Daily Nation*, 19 January 1991.
18. Ibid.
19. Ibid., 5, 6 March 1993.
20. Ibid., 19 November 1992.
21. *Weekly Review*, 21 September 1979, p. 11 (the bridge was built by the Israeli company Solel Boneh as a donation, at Ngmba's request).
22. *Daily Nation*, 2 April 1979.
23. Ibid., 30 July 1976.
24. Ibid., 27 July 1976.
25. *The Standard*, 11 September 1978.
26. Ibid., 16 December 1978; 13 January 1979.

Chapter 5: Religious Leadership and Muslim Solidarity

1. See, for example, the process of appointing two additional qadis, *Daily Nation*, 14 October 1977.
2. *East African Standard*, 15 March 1996.
3. *Daily Nation*, 30 January 1982.
4. Ibid., 9 March 1982.
5. See similar declarations, *Daily Nation*, 23 July 1982.
6. *Daily Nation*, 23 July 1982; *The Standard*, 13 August 1994.
7. On the festivities in Lamu, see, for example, *Daily Nation*, 22 August 1995. In the 1994 celebrations, there were 15,000 participants, including

Muslims from the Comoros, Tanzania, Uganda, Zaire, Rwanda, and Great Britain (*The Standard*, 2 September 1994).

8. See the article on the Lamu festivities by B. B. Sharma in the *Weekly Review*, 4 March 1979, p. 1; also see the article in *Coast Week*, 9–15 February 1979, p. 5.

9. *The Standard*, 1 June 1994.

10. Ibid., 22 July 1994.

11. Ibid., 24 July 1994.

12. For example, the gathering organized by Shaikh Mohamed Saalim Balala, assistant minister of finance, to collect money for the foundation of a technical college for Muslim students at which the ambassadors of Egypt and Pakistan were present (*Daily Nation*, 14 February 1971); in July 1983, Ahmed Abdallah, deputy-governor of the Central Bank of Kenya, organized a harambe at which 646,000 shillings were raised for the building of a mosque in Garissa (*Daily Nation*, 26 July 1983). Gatherings of this sort occur from time to time.

13. Appendix 1 presents an example of a page on which a convert to Islam has signed, which I received from Shaikh Khamis after I interviewed him on 5 September 1979.

14. *Daily Nation*, 23 May 1994.

Chapter 6: Religious, Political, and Personal Divisions

1. For example, the proclamation of Shaikh Mohamed Saalim Balala, assistant minister of finance, and his warning about divisiveness, *Daily Nation*, 12 May 1973.

2. Such as the statements of Ahmad Khalif, assistant minister of technology and secretary-general of Supkem, *Sunday Standard*, 3 March 1996.

3. *Daily Nation*, 18 November 1971. See also the dispute about this in the *East African Standard*, 7 October, 19 October, 8 November 1971.

4. *Daily Nation*, 14 March 1994; *Weekly Review*, 18 March 1994. On Shee's views, see *The Guide*, January 1994, p. 21.

5. *Economic Review*, 4–10 March 1996, p. 39.

6. *Daily Nation*, 13 October 1994. Hyder's words gave rise to anger and criticism from some members of Supkem, and afterward she denied what had been published under her name and said that she supported the government and the chief qadi, *Kenya Times*, 15 October 1994.

7. *Daily Nation*, 15 August 1994.

8. *East African Standard*, 22 February 1996.

9. Ibid., 26 February 1996.

10. Ibid., 29 February 1996; *Daily Nation*, 29 February 1996.

11. *Sunday Standard*, 3 March 1996.

12. *Sunday Nation*, 3 March 1996.

13. *East African Standard*, 2 March, 15 March 1996.

14. *The People*, 31 May–6 June 1996.

15. According to the government publication *Directory of Diplomatic Corps*, May 1993, p. 4.

16. *Sunday Nation*, 3 March 1996.

17. Ibid., 29 February 1996.

18. *East African Standard,* 24 July 1995; *Economic Review,* 4–10 March 1996, p. 36.
19. *Economic Review,* 4–10 March 1996, p. 39.
20. *Weekly Review,* 12 January 1996, pp. 12–13. The assertion that the number of worshipers grew during Imam Shee's tenure is true; I can attest to this myself having visited the mosque several times on Fridays.
21. *Weekly Review,* 12 January 1996, pp. 12–13.
22. *Kenya Times,* 18 May 1996.
23. Susan Beckerleg, "'Brown Sugar' or Friday Prayer: Youth Choices and Community Building in Coastal Kenya," *African Affairs 94* (1995): 31.
24. Arye Oded, *Islam in Uganda* (New York and Jerusalem, 1974), pp. 310–311.
25. See, for example, the article in *al-Islam,* April 1978, p. 3.
26. Ahmed Salim, *The Swahili-Speaking Peoples of Kenya's Coast 1895–1965* (Nairobi, 19073), pp. 159–168.
27. Published in Nairobi in 1978.
28. For some articles on these subjects, see *The Standard,* 14 February 1979, 8 June 1980; *Daily Nation,* 30 January 1980, 13 February 1980; *Sunday Standard,* 18 May 1980.
29. *Daily Nation,* 8 November 1977. Juma Boy participated in one of the courses given in Israel in the 1970s and, on his return, was active in sending young Muslims to Israel for training, especially in the areas of agriculture and cooperatives.
30. *Kenya Times,* 13 January 1996.
31. Mohamed Bakari and Yahya Saad, eds., *Islam in Kenya,* Proceedings of the National Seminar on Contemporary Islam in Kenya (Nairobi, 1995), p. 231.
32. *Daily Nation,* 27–28 September 1994.
33. Ibid., 28 September 1994.
34. Ibid., 13 August 1994.
35. Ibid., 16 October 1981.
36. On the dispute about this, see *The Standard* and *Daily Nation,* 20 February 1979.
37. On this issue, see Beckerleg, "'Brown Sugar' or Friday Prayer."
38. *Sunday Nation,* 24 April 1994; Bakari and Saad, *Islam in Kenya,* p. 225.
39. Bakari and Saad, ibid., pp. 168–193.
40. Carol Eastman, "Who Are the Waswahili?" *Africa* 41 (1971): 228–236.
41. A. H. Hardinge, *A Diplomatist in East Africa* (London, 1928).
42. Salim, *Swahili-Speaking Peoples,* pp. 75–76.
43. Kindy, *Life and Politics,* p. 32.
44. Ibid., p. 69.
45. Ibid., p. xi.
46. Anne Kubai, "The Early Muslim Communities of Nairobi," *Islam et Sociétés au Sud du Sahara* 6 (December 1992): 34–44.
47. Kindy, *Life and Politics,* p. xiv.
48. Ibid., p. 188.
49. A. B. K. Kasozi, "Christian-Muslim Inputs into Public Policy Formation in Kenya, Tanzania and Uganda," in Holger Bernt Hansen and Michael Twaddle, eds., *Religion and Politics in East Africa* (London, 1995), p. 235. On the question of the future of the coastal strip, see the British report, "The Kenya Coastal Strip," Comm. 1585, HMSO, December 1961.

50. *The Standard,* 12 October, 29 October 1977.
51. *Kenya Times,* 12 May 1994, 1 June 1994.
52. *Sunday Times,* 3 July 1994.
53. Interview with Tsuma, Nairobi, 10 February 1993.
54. Bakari and Saad, *Islam in Kenya,* p. 185.
55. Ibid., p. 188.
56. See, for example, the proclamations and the calls to follow Moi ("Nyayo"), *Daily Nation,* 11 July 1983.
57. *Nairobi Times* and *Daily Nation,* 13 May 1979.
58. Interview with Abdallah Mwidau, Nairobi, 5 May 1980; *Nairobi Times,* 2 December 1979.
59. *The Standard,* 20 May 1980.
60. *Daily Nation,* 24 July 1980.
61. Ibid., 30 September 1981, in an article titled "I'm Moi's Friend Again."
62. There are extensive articles on the conflict between Nassir and Hamed, including speculations that President Moi himself got sick and tired of Nassir's involvement and therefore brought Hamed back from Saudi Arabia to take his place (something that seems unlikely to me). See *Weekly Review,* 9 February 1996, pp. 12–13; 16 February 1996, pp. 17–18.
63. On the conflict between Nassir and Rashid Sajad, see "Tension Reigns in Mombasa," *Weekly Review,* 4 June 1993, pp. 13–14. See also *Sunday Nation,* 12 March 1995; *Kenya Times,* 14 March 1995.

Chapter 7: Muslims and the State

1. See the opposition journal *Law* 24 (September 1990): 29.
2. Ibid.
3. *Daily Nation,* 28 September 1988.
4. *Law* 28 (1990): 8.
5. *Daily Nation* and *Kenya Times,* 15 July 1988.
6. *Weekly Review,* 29 March 1985.
7. Ibid., 26 April 1996.
8. Ibid., 1 May 1992, pp. 10–12.
9. *Weekly Review,* 30 January 1998, p. 7.
10. *Daily Nation,* 30 September 1988.
11. *Law* 39 (1991): 15.
12. Associated Press, 5 October 1988; *Kenya Times,* 14 October 1988.
13. *The Guardian* (London), 1–2 July 1988.
14. Associated Press, 16 March 1988.
15. *Kenya Times,* 6 March 1995.
16. Daniel arap Moi, *Kenya African Nationalism* (London, 1986), p. 24.
17. Associated Press, 26 April 1988.
18. *Daily Nation,* 26 June 1979.
19. Mohamed Bakari and Yahya Saad, eds., *Islam in Kenya* (Nairobi, 1995), p. 238.
20. Interview with Professor Bakari, Nairobi, July 1994; ibid., p. 226.
21. *Daily Nation,* 23 April 1994; *Sunday Nation,* 24 April 1994.
22. Interview in *Sunday Nation,* 15 May 1994, p. 14.

23. "Kenya: Report of the Northern Frontier District Commission," December 1962.
24. *Sunday Nation,* 9 January 1994.
25. *Daily Nation,* 7 November 1980.
26. Interview with J. Omari, activist in Muslim organizations, Nairobi, 15 October 1980.
27. *Le Monde,* 19 November 1989, p. 7.
28. On the subject of the 1987 riots, see *The Standard,* 6, 7, 9 November 1987; *Sunday Nation,* 1, 8 November 1987; *Daily Nation,* 2, 9 November 1987.
29. *International Herald Tribune,* 26, 27 September 1998.
30. Ibid., 9, 10 January 1999.
31. *The Times,* 14 August 1998, citing *Jane's Foreign Report.*
32. Ibid., 13 August 1998.
33. Ibid.
34. *Weekly Review,* 18 September 1998.
35. Ibid., 8 September 1998.
36. BBC, *Focus on Africa,* 4 November 1997.
37. *Weekly Review,* 2 October 1998.
38. Ibid., 9 October 1998.
39. Ibid.
40. Ibid., 12 February 1999.

Chapter 8: Muslims and the Law

1. Kasozi, "Christian-Muslim Inputs," p. 235.
2. Ibid., pp. 236, 239.
3. *Daily Nation,* 3 September 1981.
4. Ibid., 5 September 1981. On Muslim opposition in Lamu, see ibid., 28 July 1981.
5. Ibid., 5 September 1981.
6. Ibid., 8 September 1981.
7. Ibid., 29 August 1981.
8. Ibid., 4 September 1981.
9. Ibid., 10, 11 September 1981 (some letters to the editor on the subject).
10. Ibid., 4 September 1981.
11. *Sunday Nation,* 6 September 1981.
12. *Daily Nation,* 7, 16 September 1981.
13. Ibid., 3 September 1981.
14. Ibid., 12 October 1981.
15. Ibid., 3 September 1981.
16. *The Standard,* 22 April 1994.

Chapter 9: Muslims and Education

1. Hyder Kindy (*Life and Politics in Mombasa* [Nairobi, 1972]) and Ahmed Salim (*The Swahili-Speaking Peoples of Kenya's Coast 1895–1965* [Nairobi, 1973]) deal in various places with colonial policy toward the education of Muslims in Kenya.

2. See the article by Mohamed Quraishy, who served as Supkem's director of education, "History of Islamic Religious Education in Kenya," *Nurul Islam* (May 1980): 9, 10, 14.
3. Kindy, *Life and Politics,* p. 119.
4. J. Spencer Trimingham, *Islam in East Africa* (Oxford, 1964), p. 171.
5. Ibid.
6. "Mombasa Institute of Muslim Education, Review of Progress, 1948–1958."
7. "Mombasa Coast: The Politics of Institutes," *Weekly Review,* 7 April 1978.
8. Quraishi, "History of Islamic Religious Education."
9. Donal B. Cruise O'Brien, "Coping with the Christians," in Holger Bernt Hansen and Michael Twaddle, eds., *Religion and Politics in East Africa* (London, 1995), p. 206. In April 1994, MEWA organized one of the largest conferences to discuss problems of Muslim education in general, and those of Kenyan Muslims in particular.
10. *East African Standard,* 27 October 1971.
11. Farouk Muslim, "The Supreme Council of Muslims," *Nairobi Times,* 27 November 1977, p. 12.
12. Quraishi, "History of Islamic Religious Education."
13. Kindy (*Life and Politics*) warns of the dangers of restriction to a narrow Qur'anic education. In "Muslims Lagging Behind in Education" (*Sunday Nation,* 21 July 1976, p. 8), Zafer Kahn asked how it could be that Islam, which reached the East African coast hundreds of years before Christianity, lagged behind it; he attributed this to the traditional madrasa system of learning, which closed the gates of modern science to young Muslims. See also the similar views of Juma Muhamed in *The Standard,* 30 November 1978; in a speech delivered to the residents of Mombasa, Bashir Mchangamwe, responsible for education in Mombasa, also stressed that Islam did not prohibit secular education along with religious education.
14. *Daily Nation,* 13 October 1994.
15. See the booklet about the fund's activities, "The Aga Khan Foundation Programme," 1987.
16. See, for example, the article about the rehabilitation of the mosque in Machakos, *al-Islam,* March–April 1978.
17. *East African Standard,* 8 February 1978.
18. *Daily Nation,* 17 March 1981.
19. Ibid., 18 May 1983.
20. Ibid.
21. *Sunday Nation* and *East African Standard,* 11 July 1993.
22. *Coast Week,* 16–24 February 1979, p. 14.

Chapter 10: Muslim-Christian Relations

1. Ahmed Salim, *The Swahili-Speaking Peoples of Kenya's Coast 1895–1965* (Nairobi, 1973), p. 165.
2. Ibid., p. 166.
3. Interview with Kinoti, Nairobi, 22 June 1994. On the Christian missionaries using the educational system to disseminate Christianity, see the letters by Muslim lecturers in the *Weekly Review,* 27 February 1978.

4. Donal B. Cruise O'Brien, "Coping with the Christians," in Holger Bernt Hansen and Michael Twaddle, eds., *Religion and Politics in East Africa* (London, 1995), p. 208; *Society*, 29 June 1992, p. 11.
5. *African Events*, July 1992, cited in O'Brien, ibid., pp. 214, 215.
6. Danield arap Moi, *Kenya African Nationalism* (London, 1986), p. 24.
7. The contentions of Assistant Minister Sharif Nassir in an article in the *Weekly Review*, 13 February 1978.
8. Matano, *Daily Nation*, 8 September 1981.
9. *Sunday Nation*, 1, 8 November 1987; *Le Monde*, 19 November 1987.
10. *Society*, 13 September 1993.
11. *Daily Nation*, 17 July 1993.
12. O'Brien, "Coping with the Christians," p. 208.
13. *al-Nur* (Egypt), 5 February 1986.
14. Reuters, 18, 20 September 1995.
15. Ibid.
16. O'Brien, "Coping with the Christians," p. 212.
17. This is an essay about a Christian who converted to Islam in the sixteenth century and claimed that Jesus himself asserted that he was not the messiah but a prophet who had come to proclaim the advent of the real messiah, Muhammad. O'Brien ("Coping with the Christians," p. 211) says that he found copies of this publication with Muslims and in Mombasa schools in an English translation, which was used to preach for conversion to Islam (*da'wa*).
18. *The Standard*, 6 October 1987.
19. *JPR News Analyses and Reports*, 30 June 1993, pp. 1–2.
20. Nairobi Deanery, Priests and Laiety, "Circular," 1993.
21. *Sunday Nation*, 12 September 1993; 22 May 1994.
22. Jeff Mbura's article in *JPR* (see note 19) describes this incident. See also the *Daily Nation* and *The Standard*, 13 January 1993.
23. *Daily Nation* and *The Standard*, 14 January 1993. In these issues there are also many letters to the editor and reactions from Muslims.
24. *Daily Nation* and *The Standard*, 13 January 1993; see also Mbura's article in *JPR* (note 19).
25. *Daily Nation*, 29 August 1994.
26. *Kenya Times*, 30 August 1994.
27. *Daily Nation*, 26 April 1994.
28. *JPR*, 30 June 1995, p. 5.
29. See, for example, his statement after the 1987 riots (*Daily Nation*, 2 November 1987).
30. Associated Press, 15 September 1995.
31. See Sharif Nassir's speech to graduates of the madrasa in Mombasa, *East African Standard*, 7 January 1987; also also his reaction to Cardinal Otunga's statements, *The Standard*, 14 January 1993.
32. Reuters, 18 September 1995.
33. *Daily Nation*, 14 July 1983.
34. *Weekly Review*, 29 August 1997, p. 13; Associated Press, 16 August 1997.

Chapter 11: Arab-Islamic Activities

1. Jamal 'Abd al-Nasir, *Egypt's Liberation: The Philosophy of Revolution* (Washington, D.C., 1955), p. 112.

2. Ismael Tareq, "Religion and UAR African Policy," *Journal of Modern African Studies* 6, 1 (1968): 49–57, citing *al-Aharam*, 27 December 1953.

3. For details of Arab-Islamic activities in Africa, see Arye Oded, "The Promotion of Islamic Activities by Arab Countries in Africa: Contemporary Trends," *Asian and African Studies* 21, 3 (November 1987): 281–304.

4. Arye Oded, *Africa and the Middle East Conflict* (Boulder, 1987), p. 121.

5. Because of Abdallah Mwidau's opposition to the Islamic political activity of Arab countries in general, and their operations against Israel in particular, he was attacked by Libya in declarations and articles (interview with Abdallah Mwidau, Mombasa, 15 September 1980).

6. See, for example, article in *The Standard,* 8 August 1984.

7. *Daily Nation,* 9 September 1983.

8. *Kenya Times,* 19 November 1987; *Daily Nation,* 27 May 1988.

9. *The Standard,* 22 March 1992.

10. Arab missions working in Kenya in 1993 were: Algeria, Djibouti, Egypt, Iraq, Kuwait, Lebanon, Saudi Arabia, Sudan, Tunisia, United Arab Emirates, Yemen, as well as Iran (Ministry of Foreign Affairs, *Dictionary of Diplomatic Corps* [Nairobi, May 1993]).

11. The bank gives grants and loans only to countries that are members of the Organization of the Islamic Conference (OIC). Since Kenya is not a member, the bank extends grants to Supkem and not to the government. See, for example, the notice in the press about the bank's granting of loans, *Kenya Times,* 21 April 1995.

12. See Oded, "Promotion of Islamic Activities."

13. On Egypt's suspicions of Iranian activities and on its activities against Iran, see the article in the newspaper *al-Usbu' al-'Arabi* (Lebanon), 13 July 1988.

14. *Daily Nation,* 15 August 1994.

15. *Kenya Times,* 28 April 1984.

16. Interview with Faraj Dumila, Nairobi, 10 July 1980.

17. Report on the Machakos Institute of Higher Islamic Studies, *Kenya Muslims* 2, 1 (November 1970): 12–14.

18. Syllabus for Islamic Institutions and Schools in East Africa, 1974.

19. *Daily Nation,* 26 June 1994.

20. In connection with Iran's activities against the West, see, for example, the statements of the Iranian ambassador to Kenya, Hamid Moeyyer, at the ceremony distributing certificates to forty graduates of the course in Arabic at the Iranian Cultural Centre, in which he warned against Western domination and Western culture (*Kenya Times,* 26 April 1994). Also at the women's congress held by the Iranian embassy in November 1994, Iran's representatives denounced Western permissiveness, which, they said, was harming morals and leading to the spread of AIDS (*Daily Nation,* 8 December 1994).

21. *West Africa,* 19–25 July 1993, p. 127.

22. David Menashri, ed., *Islamic Fundamentalism: A Challenge to Regional Stability* (Tel Aviv, 1993), p. 26. (Hebrew)

23. Radio Teheran, as reported by the BBC, *Summary of World Broadcasts,* ME/8448/A, 22 December 1986, pp. 3–4.

24. Mohammad Mohaddesin, *Islamic Fundamentalism: The New Global Threat* (Washington, D.C., 1993), p. 39.

25. Iranian News Agency (IRNA), Khartoum, 15 June 1994.

26. *Weekly Review,* 7 April 1995, p. 30.

27. *Kenya Times*, 2 December 1994.
28. See, for example, the special supplement published in the government newspaper *Kenya Times*, 11 February 1993, in which the article "Islamic Revolution That Was a Victory over All Darkness" was spread over two pages.
29. *Kenya Times*, 30 May 1994.
30. Ibid., 8 June 1994.
31. Like the anti-Christian sentence "They lie before idols in the church," in the article in *The Guide*, 1 January 1994, p. 3.
32. *West Africa*, 13–19 February 1995, p. 23.
33. Iranian News Agency (IRNA), 10 November 1992. Iran's interest in sub-Saharan Africa is reflected by its many embassies there. In 1998 Iran had twenty-one embassies in Africa, located in: Burkina Faso, Chad, Democratic Republic of the Congo, Ethiopia, Gabon, Gambia, Ghana, Guinea, Kenya, Madagascar, Mali, Mozambique, Namibia, Niger, Nigeria, Sierra Leone, Somalia, South Africa, Sudan, Tanzania, and Zimbabwe.

The following twelve sub-Saharan African countries had embassies in Teheran: Democratic Republic of the Congo, Ethiopia, Gambia, Ghana, Guinea, Kenya, Mauritania, Mozambique, Namibia, Nigeria, Somalia, and South Africa (compiled from *Africa South of the Sahara*, London, 1999, and *Teheran Times*, 22 November 1998).

34. Interview with Hisham Mwidau, 30 March 1992; interview with Shaikh Khamis, 12 September 1992; interview with Mohamed Warsama, 11 October 1992.
35. *Daily Nation* and *East African Standard*, 29 February 1996.
36. In an interview with Haj Nashir of Nakuru (15 December 1994), he said that the Iranians, through Asian Shiites in Nakuru, had contributed toward the building of the local mosque.
37. *Daily Nation*, 8 April 1994; *East African Standard*, 7 June 1994.
38. *Africa Research Bulletin*, 1–30 September 1996, p. 12411.
39. *The Standard*, 20 June 1994.
40. *Sunday Nation*, 19 June 1994.
41. *Kenya Times*, 21 June 1994.
42. *Kenya Times*, 21 June 1994; *The Standard*, 22 June 1994.
43. For example, the statements of the acting Iranian foreign minister, Ali Mohammad Bisharati, during his visit to Kenya in May 1987 (*Kenya Times*, 15 May 1989). Outside of Kenya, apparently, Iran is not so careful about declaring its ambitions. In "The Agony of Muslims in Kenya," a May 1984 editorial in the Iranian newspaper *Imam*, published in London, there was harsh criticism of Kenya's treatment of its Muslim minority (according to *The Standard*, 20 August 1984). At that time, however, relations between the two countries were not as good as they later became.
44. Iranian News Agency (IRNA), 9 October 1997.
45. In a conversation with David Perkins (Jerusalem, 22 April 1996), lecturer at the University of Nairobi, he mentioned that in the village of Ruruta in the Kikuyu region, there was much Iranian activity, especially among young Muslims, and that recently the Iranians had contributed 800,000 shillings toward the building of the local mosque. This had aroused the suspicions of the veteran leadership and of local residents, most of whom were Sunnis. Since all of the mosque's trustees were Shiites, the Muslims, in 1997, turned to the courts to change the trustees' composition. The court ruled that their composition should be decided by elections in the area held by the chief qadi.

46. Meanwhile, the trade gap is greatly in favor of the Iranians. In 1992, Kenya bought oil worth $30 million and sold tea worth half a million (figures from the Kenyan Chamber of Trade and Industry).

47. According to Hisham Mwidau in an interview in Mombasa (30 March 1992), the Iranian embassy provided funds to several Muslims, including opposition leaders. There is information that the Iranian embassy in Nairobi maintains contacts with the Zanzibar opposition party, the Civic United Front (CUF), and that on the eve of the 1995 elections in Zanzibar, members of the opposition visited Nairobi and met with Iranian embassy officials. Iran had an interest in a CUF victory because its leaders favored dissolving the union with Dar es-Salaam and giving the island a stronger Islamic character. The Kenyan government, on the other hand, feared that the strengthening of the CUF would encourage Muslims in Kenya's coastal strip to revive the idea of the coast's annexation by Zanzibar.

48. Reuters, as reported by the BBC, *Summary of World Broadcasts*, ME/7654, 25 May 1988.

49. As Kenya's attorney-general declared in parliament on 18 October 1973, at the time of the October War, *Daily Nation*, 19 October 1973.

50. *Daily Nation*, 30 July 1976.

51. Interview with J. Omar, 15 October 1980.

52. *Daily Nation*, 9 September 1983.

53. *West Africa*, 11 March 1986, p. 454.

54. *Weekly Review*, 7 April 1995, p. 30.

55. *Sunday Nation*, 31 October 1993. An interesting letter to the editor was published in the opposition paper *Society* on 4 October 1993, criticizing Ali Mazrui and his support for the IPK and calling him "an agent of Islamic fundamentalism."

56. Such as the article by the journalist Joe Kadhi in the *Daily Nation*, 13 May 1979.

Chapter 12:
The Islamic Factor in Kenya and the Middle East Conflict

1. *Daily Nation*, 25 August 1969.

2. Ibid., 26 August 1969.

3. On this incident, see the *Daily Nation*, 9 December 1970; *East African Standard*, 23 December 1970; letter of the second secretary at the Israeli embassy in Kenya, Avi Pazner, to the Israeli Foreign Ministry, 24 December 1970; and the ambassador's letter to the Israeli Foreign Ministry, 7 January 1971.

4. *Daily Nation*, 19 October 1973.

5. Hyder Kindy (*Life and Politics in Mombasa* [Nairobi, 1972]) deals with this issue in several places.

6. Pazner's letter to the Israeli Foreign Ministry, 21 July 1971; Nukem's objection to the press announcement, signed by Nukem's general secretary, Issa Hemed Kuria, *Daily Nation*, 17 July 1971.

7. *Kenya Times*, 12 September 1983.

8. A copy of the 26 June 1972 letter is in my possession. Excerpts appeared in the *Jerusalem Post*, 26 July 1971.

9. *Iqra* 26 (September 1993): 29.

10. For example, the article "The Arab and Islamic Character of Jerusalem," *al-Islam* 1, 4–5 (December 1977): 36–37; and in the March–April 1978 issue, p. 6.

11. Such as the anti-Israeli *Israel: The Jewish State in Palestine* by Abdallah Khalid (Nairobi, 1976).

12. I served as Israeli interest officer in Nairobi from 1978 to 1981, operating as an ambassador in every regard apart from external, formal aspects.

13. Information on Mwidau's conflicts with his rivals is from interviews I conducted with him from 1977 to 1981.

14. Such as the letter to the editor by Said Salem of Mombasa, "Sadat Left Islam," *Daily Nation,* 19 September 1981.

15. On this episode, see *Kenya Times,* 30 April, 13 May 1983; *Al-Hamishmar* (Israel), 19 May 1983.

16. Interview with Shimon Aroch, director of Zim office in Mombasa, 19 August 1993. I was a witness to these events.

17. *Sunday Nation,* 24 October 1993, p. 4.

18. For example, the letter to the editor by the press attaché of the Iranian embassy, "Israel Does Not Advocate Peace," *Daily Nation,* 25 December 1992, and the Israeli embassy's response, "Iran Is a Global Threat to Peace," *Daily Nation,* 2 January 1993.

19. Interview with Rashid Sajad, Mombasa, 26 May 1994.

20. The mayor's letter to Ambassador Arye Oded, 8 July 1994.

21. Interview with the assistant minister at the Israeli embassy in Nairobi, 5 June 1994.

Chapter 13: The Islamic Party of Kenya

1. See the detailed description of the riots in Mombasa in the *Daily Nation,* 20, 21 May 1992; see also the opposition journal *Society,* 29 June 1992, pp. 8–9.

2. See the investigation into several violent episodes in Mombasa during this period in the *Sunday Nation,* 1 November 1992; *The Standard,* 30 May 1993; *Weekly Review,* 7, 20 September 1993.

3. *Sunday Times,* 24 April 1994.

4. On the widespread support for the IPK, see articles in *Drum,* 23 October 1993; *Sunday Times,* 24 April 1994.

5. A copy of the letter was also sent to me, at the time serving as Israeli ambassador to Kenya.

6. See, for example, Zafar Khan, "Muslims Lagging Behind in Education," *Sunday Nation,* 21 November 1976; also Mohamed Quraishi, "History of Islamic Religious Education in Kenya," *Nurul Islam* (May 1980).

7. See the article (*East African Standard,* 20 January 1978) on the part played by Haji Abdulla Tairara, who, according to the writer, greatly assisted the freedom fighter Harry Thuku and was arrested by the British. The writer requested that a road in Mombasa be named after him.

8. *Daily Nation,* 18 February 1993.

9. BBC bulletin *Focus on Africa,* November 1998.

10. See, for example, the statements of the member of parliament for the Moyale area, Osman Aruru, and of Ahmed Ahmed of Garrisa, *East African Standard,* 12 September 1973.

11. *Daily Nation,* 7 November 1980.
12. *JPR,* 30 June 1993, p. 6.
13. *Daily Nation,* 8 June 1992.
14. *Weekly Review,* 28 November 1997, pp. 6, 7.
15. *Weekly Review,* 10 April 1998, p. 12.
16. *Weekly Review,* 31 July 1998, p. 15.
17. *Weekly Review,* 6 November 1998; *Africa Research Bulletin (ARB),* 1–31 October 1998, p. 3303.
18. *East African Standard,* 12 September 1973; *Society,* 29 June 1992; interview with Hassan Mohamed Mwinyi, Mombasa IPK activist, 5 January 1994.
19. This request was raised again at a meeting of a delegation of moderate Muslim leaders with President Moi on 20 February 1995, *Daily Nation,* 21 February 1995.
20. Interview in *JPR,* 30 June 1993, p. 6.
21. Interview with the prominent business leader Jafer Mohamed, Nairobi, 6 June 1994, in which he listed some of the Muslims' complaints; *JPR,* 30 June 1993, p. 6.
22. *Daily Nation,* 2 July 1994.
23. On the Lamu residents' complaints about the island's economic deterioration compared to the situation before the colonial period, when agriculture and shipbuilding were important sources of income, see *The Standard,* 14 February 1979. The island's inhabitants also complain about the lack of roads and development projects.
24. Interview with Jafer Mohamed, 6 June 1994, and with local shaikhs. In recent years, the government has done more; it established the Coast Development Authority, whose task was to rehabilitate agriculture and to develop the region and its sources of water. The head of the authority is a Muslim professor, J. A. Lugogo.
25. Letter to the editor in the *Weekly Review,* 27 February 1978, p. 2, signed by Mohamed Bakari, A. M. Shatry, R. M. Mzee, and A. El-Busaidy.
26. *Daily Nation,* 10 January 1977.
27. *JPR,* 30 June 1993, p. 6.
28. Hassan Mwakimako's lecture at the seminar in Mombasa, *Sunday Nation,* 24 April 1994.
29. Mohamed Bakari, "The Coverage of Islamic News for Kenyans," in Mohamed Bakari and Yahya Saad, eds., *Islam in Kenya* (Nairobi, 1995), pp. 108–194.
30. *Sunday Nation,* 24 April 1996, quoting the words of Hassan Mwakimako in his lecture at the Muslim Seminar in Mombasa. One Sunday the television station did not follow its usual practice of broadcasting the president's participation in church prayers, sparking rumors that he was mortally ill.
31. Hassan Mwakimako mentioned these claims in his lecture at the MEWA congress in April 1994 (*Sunday Nation,* 24 April 1994). This is also the view of other academics and politicians, such as Mohamed Bakari and MP Mohamed Galgalo (*JPR,* 30 June 1993, pp. 3–4).
32. See, for example, Ali Mazrui, "Mombasa Riots: The Folly Behind the Time Bomb," *Sunday Nation,* 1 November 1992; also the criticism of the regime in *JPR,* 30 June 1993.
33. *JPR,* 30 June 1993, p. 6. IPK leaders made a similar claim in a letter they sent to Kenya's attorney-general on 6 July 1993 (see Appendix 6).
34. *Sunday Nation,* 15 May 1994, p. 14.

35. Ibid., 30 January 1994, pp. 10–11.
36. Quraishi, "History of Islamic Religious Education."
37. Hyder Kindy, *Life and Politics in Mombasa* (Nairobi, 1972), p. 119.
38. *JPR*, 30 June 1993, p. 6; the author's interviews with Mohamed Bakari, Nairobi, 29 April 1994; Hassan Mwakimako, Nairobi, 11 May 1994; Ali Ahmad (considered a moderate Muslim), Mombasa, 10 May 1994.
39. All the complaints about discrimination against Muslims were aired at length in the MEWA seminar in Mombasa in April 1994. Six videocassettes containing the lectures given at the seminar are in my possession.

Chapter 14: Islamic Extremism: The Rise and Fall of Shaikh Khalid Balala

1. *Weekly Review*, 17 September 1993, p. 3; *The Standard*, 14 July 1993.
2. "Islamic Party of Kenya: Changing the Face of Coastal Politics," *Drum*, October 1993, pp. 6–8, 17.
3. Interview of Raphael Kahaso with Shaikh Balala, "We Are Going to Win," *The Standard*, 28 October 1993.
4. *The Standard*, 28 October 1993.
5. *Daily Nation*, 5 November 1992.
6. *The Standard*, 28 October 1993.
7. *Weekly Review*, 17 September 1993, p. 8.
8. Ibid.
9. *The Standard*, 28 October 1993.
10. *Weekly Review*, 24 September 1993.
11. *Daily Nation*, 3 June 1994.
12. *Taifa Leo*, 4 March 1993, p. 9.
13. Evidence presented to the U.S. Congress by researcher Khaled Durna, 6 April 1995.
14. Among those who, in interviews, expressed fears of Iranian involvement were Hisham Mwidau (Mombasa, 30 March 1992); Shaikh Khamis Ahmad Said (Mombasa, 12 September 1992); the Muslim journalist Muhamed Warsamah (Nairobi, 11 October 1992).
15. On moderate Muslims' opposition to Iranian involvement in Muslim affairs in Kenya, see the many letters to the editor in *The Standard*, 2 October 1994. On the support of radical Muslims, including Sudanese, for the IPK, see *Drum*, October 1993, pp. 6–8, 17.
16. On attempts at separation before independence and on the Kenyan government's apprehensions, see Hyder Kindy, *Life and Politics in Mombasa* (Nairobi, 1972).
17. Serving at the time as Israel's ambassador to Kenya, I was present at discussions on this matter with government representatives.
18. For example, *Sunday Nation*, 22 May 1994.
19. *JPR*, 30 June 1993.
20. *The Standard*, 11 July 1993.
21. For example, the *Kenya Times*, 1 September 1993, printed a large photograph of President Moi in Muslim attire during his visit to the Muslim region of Lamu.
22. *Taifa Leo*, 12 May 1994; *Daily Nation*, 24 March 1994.

23. *Daily Nation,* 3 June 1994.
24. *Weekly Review,* 12 January 1996, pp. 17–18.
25. On the view that Kanu leaders established the UMA, see the Christian journal *JPR,* 30 November 1993, p. 6. The Muslim journalist Mohamed Warsamah expressed the same opinion in an interview on 13 January 1993. See also "Tension Reigns in Mombasa," *Weekly Review,* 4 June 1993, pp. 13–14; *Weekly Review,* 17 September 1993.
26. On the organization and its aims, a large announcement was published signed by its founders, *The Standard* (25 May 1993); see Appendix 3. See also Mustafa Idd, "Coast Muslims Face Big Split," *Kenya Times,* 14 July 1993.
27. *Weekly Review,* 17 September 1993.
28. *Kenya Times,* 8 July 1993.
29. *The Standard,* 25 May 1993, reports on the disagreements over the appointment of imams to mosques. Kindy (*Life and Politics*) deals at length with the background to the controversies between Arabs and black African Muslims.
30. *Sunday Standard,* 30 May 1993; *Weekly Review,* 4 June 1993, pp. 13–14.
31. *Weekly Review,* 17 September 1993, pp. 3–9.
32. On the simultaneous riots in Mombasa, Lamu and Malindi, see *Weekly Review,* 17, 24 September 1993.
33. *Weekly Review,* 17 September 1993.
34. *Kenya Times,* 8 July 1993.
35. *Weekly Review,* 17 September 1993.
36. *The Standard,* 11 July 1993.
37. Donal O'Brien, "Coping with the Christians," in Holger Bernt Hansen and Michael Twaddle, eds., *Religion and Politics in East Africa* (London: 1995), p. 214.
38. *Kenya Times,* 22 June 1994.
39. *The Standard,* 18 July 1995.
40. *Weekly Review,* 4 June 1993, pp. 13–14.
41. *Daily Nation,* 17 May 1993.
42. Ibid., 5 March 1994.
43. Ibid., 25 May 1994; *Sunday Times,* 29 May 1994.
44. *The Standard,* 26 May 1994.
45. *Sunday Times,* 24 April 1994.
46. For a detailed summation of the complaints against Shaikh Balala, see the article by one of the IPK leaders, Khalef A. Khalifa, "Principles of Democratic Leadership," *Weekly Review,* 17 September 1993, pp. 10–12. (See Appendix 4.)
47. *Kenya Times,* 8 July 1993.
48. Ibid., 5–6 September 1994.
49. *Daily Nation,* 5 September 1994.
50. *Kenya Times,* 23 December 1994.
51. *East African Standard,* 1, 24 July 1995; *Daily Nation,* 18 August 1995.
52. *East African Standard,* 1, 7 July 1995.
53. *Kenya Times,* 5 September 1995.
54. *Daily Nation,* 13 December 1995; *Kenya Times,* 14 December 1995. In the matter of Shaikh Balala's citizenship, the Yemeni embassy in Nairobi came to his assistance by declaring, in June 1997, that Balala was not a citizen of Yemen. The ambassador explained that, although Khalid Balala's

father was a Yemenite, Balala himself had never received Yemenite citizenship and had never even visited Yemen (*Weekly Review*), 13 June 1997, p. 11.
    55. *Weekly Review,* 13 June 1997, p. 11.
    56. Reuters, 16 July 1997.
    57. *Africa Research Bulletin (ARB)*, December 1997, p. 12920.

Chapter 15: Similarities and Differences Between the Political Status of Muslims in Kenya, Uganda, and Tanzania

    1. Arye Oded, *Islam in Uganda* (New York and Jerusalem, 1974), pp. 310–311.
    2. "Sheikhs Fight at Kololo," *New Vision,* 10 October 1993.
    3. *New African,* March 1998.
    4. *Kenya Times,* 16 April 1993; *Daily Nation,* 21 April 1993.
    5. *Africa Research Bulletin (ARB),* 1–30 April 1998, p. 13089.
    6. "Muslims Form Party," *New Vision* (Kampala), 1 May 1993; *New Vision,* 19 September 1997.
    7. Associated Press, 23 June 1997, 4–6 September 1997; Reuters, 28 June 1997.
    8. *Uganda News,* 15 February 1972.
    9. All African News Agency, 17 August 1998.
    10. *The People* (opposition paper), 23–29 February 1996, pp. 1–2.
    11. *New Vision,* 27 November 1996.

Chapter 16: Conclusion

    1. *International Herald Tribune,* 11 November 1992; *Washington Post,* 5 January 1994. On the Islamic Ittihad's activities in Ethiopia and their battles against the Ethiopian army on the Somali-Ethiopian border in August and December 1996, see Reuters, from Mogadishu, 24 December 1996; Associated Press, from Mogadishu, 21, 26 December 1996, 5 January 1997.

Bibliography

Archives and Unpublished Material

Kenya National Archives, Nairobi
Makerere University Library, Africana
University of Nairobi, Archives of Department of Religious Studies
Private archive of letters, interviews, and manuscripts collected in East Africa, in the author's possession

* * *

Bagha, Abdulhamid. "The History of Secondary Education on the Kenya Coast." Master's thesis, University of Nairobi, 1978.
Bagha, Abdulhamid. "Development of Secondary School Education in the Mombasa and Kilifi Districts of Kenya: A Comparative Analysis 1964–1978." Ph.D. diss., University of Nairobi, 1981.
Hutley, W. "Mohammedanism in Central Africa and Its Influence." Unpublished report, London Missionary Society Archives, 1881.
Maina, N. K. "Muslim Education in Kenya with Special Reference to the Madrasa System in Nairobi." Master's thesis, Kenyatta University, 1993.
Makokba, J. "The Politics of Nationalism in the Northeastern Province of Kenya." Master's thesis, University of Nairobi, 1979.

Kenyan Newspapers and Periodicals

Africa Events
Daily Nation and *Sunday Nation*
East Africa Journal
East Africa Law Journal
The East African (weekly)
East African Standard
Economic Review
al-Islam (quarterly journal of the Islamic Foundation)

JPR: News Analyses and Reports (published by the National Council of Churches of Kenya)
Kenya Times (Kanu's daily)
Law (an opposition magazine)
Maendeleo (a monthly religious publication of the Supreme Council of Kenya Muslims; formerly *Nurul Islam*)
Mapenzi ya Mungu (magazine of the Ahmadiyya Muslim Mission, published in Nairobi)
Milestone (newspaper of the Islamic Party of Kenya)
Mombasa Times
Muslim
The People (an opposition weekly)
Society (an opposition magazine)
The Standard and *Sunday Standard*
Taifa Leo (a Kiswahili daily)
Weekly Review

Books and Articles

'Abd al-Nasir, Jamal. *Egypt's Liberation: The Philosophy of Revolution.* Washington, D.C., 1955.
Abu Lughod, Ibrahim. "The Islamic Factor in African Politics." *Orbis* 8, 2 (1964): 425–444.
Alexandre, Pierre. "L'Islam en Afrique Orientale." *Sociétés Africaines, Monde Arabe et Culture Islamique* 1(1981): 103–110.
Amiji, Hatim. "Religion in Afro-Arab Relations." *UNESCO Studies* 7 (Paris, 1984): 101–124.
Anderson, J. N. D. "Comments with Reference to the Muslim Community." *East African Law Journal* 5 (1969): 5–20.
Argyle, W. J. "The Migration of Indian Muslims to East and South Africa: Some Preliminary Comparisons." *Collection Purusartha* 9 (1986): 135–147.
Ayubi, Shaheen, and Sakina Mohyuddin. "Muslims in Kenya: An Overview." *Journal of Muslim Minority Affairs* 15, 1–2 (January, July 1994): 144–156.
Azevedo, Mario, and Gwendolyn Porter. "The Minority Status of Islam in East Africa: A Historico-sociological Perspective." *Journal of Muslim Minority Affairs* 12, 2 (1991): 482–498.
Bakari, Mohamed. *The New Ulamaa in Kenya.* Nairobi, 1990.
———. "What Ails the Muslims?" *African Events*(June 1992).
Bakari, Mohamed, and Yahya Saad, eds. *Islam in Kenya.* Proceedings of the National Seminar on Contemporary Islam in Kenya. Nairobi, 1995.
Barret, D. B., ed. *World Christian Encyclopedia.* London, 1982.
Beckerleg, Susan. "'Brown Sugar' or Friday Prayer: Youth Choices and Community Building in Coastal Kenya." *African Affairs* 94 (1995): 23–38.
Brenner, Louis, ed. *Muslim Identity and Social Change in Sub-Saharan Africa.* London, 1993.
Bunger, R. L. *Islamization Among the Upper Pokomo.* Syracuse, 1980.
Castango, A. A. "The Somali-Kenyan Controversy: Implications for the Future." *Journal of Modern African Studies* 2, 2 (July 1964):165–188.
Constantin, Francois. *Les Communautés musulmanes d'Afrique Orientale.* Pau, 1983.

———. "Loi de l'Islam contre loi l'etat: Petite chronique d'un été kenyan." *Islam et Societes au Sud du Sahara* 3 (1989).
———. "Social Stratification of the Swahili Coast." *Africa* 2, 2 (1989).
Cooper, Frederick. "Islam and Cultural Hegemony: The Ideology of Slave-owners on the East African Coast." In Lovejoy, Paul, ed. *The Ideology of Slavery in Africa.* London, 1981.
Dawisha, Adeed. *Islam in Foreign Policy.* Cambridge, 1983.
Doi, A. R. "The Political Role of Islam in West Africa." *Islamic Quarterly* 12, 4 (1968): 235–242.
Drysdale, J. *The Somali Dispute.* London, 1964.
Dumila, F. *Mombasa KANU on the Move.* Mombasa, n.d.
Duran, Khalid. "The Threat of Islamic Extremism in Africa." Paper submitted to U.S. Congress, 6 April 1995.
Eastman, Carol. "Who Are the Waswahili?" *Africa* 41 (1971): 228–236.
Elmasri, F. H. "Sheikh al-Amin bin Ali al-Mazrui and the Islamic Intellectual Tradition in East Africa." *Journal of Muslim Minority Affairs* 8, 2 (1987): 229–238.
Esposito, John. *Islam and Politics.* Syracuse, 1984.
Etienne, Bruno. *L'Islamism Radical.* Paris, 1987.
al-Farsy, A. S. *Tarehe ya Imam Shafi na Wanavyuoni Wakubwa wa Mashariki ya Afrika* [The History of Imam Shafi and the Great Learned People of East Africa]. Zanzibar, 1945. (Swahili)
Ferkiss, Victor C. "Religion and Politics in Independent African States: A Prolegomenon." In Butler, J. and A. P. Castangna, eds. *Transition in African Politics.* New York, 1967, pp. 1–38.
Gertzel, C. *The Politics of Independent Kenya.* Nairobi, 1970.
Ghai, Y. P., and J. McAuslan. *Public Law and Political Change in Kenya: A Study of Legal Framework of Government from Colonial Times to the Present.* London, 1970.
Hansen, Holger Bernt, and Michael Twaddle, eds. *Religion and Politics in East Africa.* London, 1995.
Hardinge, A. H. *A Diplomatist in East Africa.* London, 1928.
Hecht, E. D. "Harar and Lamu: A Comparison of Two East African Muslim Societies." *Transafrican Journal of History* (1987).
Holway, J. D. "The Religious Composition of the Population of the Coast Province of Kenya." *Journal of Religion in Africa* 3, 3 (1970): 228–239.
Jahadhmy, Ali Ahmed. "A Note on Arab Schooling and Arab Role in East Africa." *African Affairs* 51 (1952): 150–152.
Kagabo, José. "L'Islam en Afrique Orientale: Notes des recherches." *Cahiers d'Études Africaines* 27, 3–4 (1987): 411–417.
Kakole, Omari. "The Islamic Factor in African-Arab Relations." *Third World Quarterly* 6, 3 (1984): 687–702.
Kasozi, A. B. K. "Christian-Muslim Inputs into Public Policy Formation in Kenya, Tanzania and Uganda." In Hansen, Holger Bernt and Michael Twaddle, eds. *Religion and Politics in East Africa.* London, 1995.
Kassam, F. M. "Notes and Comments on the Report of the Commission on the Law of Succession." *East African Law Journal* 12 (1969): 221–245.
Kenny, Joseph. "Sharia and Christianity in Nigeria: Islam and a 'Secular' State." *Journal of Religion in Africa* 26, 4 (1996): 339–364.
Kenya, Republic of. *Kenya Population Census.* Nairobi, 1979, 1989.
Kerekes, T. "Islam and Nationalism in Africa." In Kerekes, T., ed. *The Arab Middle East and Muslim Africa.* London, 1961, pp. 63–84.

Kettani, Ali. "Muslim East Africa: An Overview." *Journal of Muslim Minority Affairs* 4, 1–2 (1982): 104–119.
Kindy, Hyder. *Life and Politics in Mombasa.* Nairobi, 1972.
King, Noel. *Christian and Muslim in Africa.* New York, 1971.
Kokole, Omari. "The 'Nubians' of East Africa: Muslim Club or African 'Tribe'? The View from Within." *Journal of Muslim Minority Affairs* 6, 2 (1985): 420–448.
Kubai, Anne. "The Early Muslim Communities of Nairobi." *Islam et Sociétés au Sud du Sahara* 6 (December 1992): 34–44.
Lansdale, John. "The Emerging Pattern of Church and State Cooperation in Kenya." In Fashole-Luke, E., ed. *Christianity in Independent Africa.* London, 1978, pp. 267–284.
Levine, Daniel H. "Religion and Politics in Comparative and Historical Perspective." *Comparative Politics* 19, 1 (1986): 95–122.
Lienhardt, Peter. "The Mosque-College of Lamu and Its Social Background." *Tanganyika Notes and Records* 53 (1959).
Matheson, Alastair. "Kenya Expels Three Preachers: Riot Stirs Fears of Islamic Extremism." *The Times*, 11 November 1987, p. 9.
Mazrui, Ali. "Islam, Political Leadership and Economic Radicalism in Africa." *Comparative Studies in Society and History* 9 (1967): 274–279.
———. "Speaking Out for Muslims." *Weekly Review* (Kenya), 26 February 1993, pp. 8–10.
———. *Swahili State and Society: The Political Economy of an African Language.* Nairobi, 1995.
———. "The Unfinished Islamic Agenda: Reflection After Elections." *Sunday Nation* (Kenya), 14 February 1993, pp. 11–12.
Menashri, David, ed. *Islamic Fundamentalism: A Challenge to Regional Stability.* Tel Aviv, 1993. (Hebrew)
Mohaddesin, Mohammad. *Islamic Fundamentalism: The New Global Threat.* Washington, D.C., 1993.
Moi, Daniel arap. *Kenya African Nationalism.* London, 1986.
Nairobi Deanery Priests and Laity. *The Catholic-Muslim Relationship: A Call for Better Understanding of One Another.* Nairobi, 1993.
Nimtz, August H. *Islam and Politics in East Africa.* Minneapolis, 1980.
Nurse, Derek, and Thomas Spear. *The Swahili: Reconstructing the History and Language of an African Society 800–1500.* Philadelphia, 1985.
Nyang, Sulayman. "Islam and Politics in West Africa." *Issue* 13 (1984): 20–25.
Nzibo, Yusuf. "Islamization in the Interior of Kenya: A General Overview." In Bakari, M. and Yahya Saad, eds. *Islam in Kenya.* Nairobi, 1995, pp. 40–52.
O'Brien, Donal B. Cruise. "Coping with the Christians: The Muslim Predicament in Kenya." In Hansen, Holger Bernt and Michael Twaddle, eds. *Religion and Politics in East Africa.* London, 1995.
Oded, Arye. *Africa and the Middle East Conflict.* Boulder, 1987.
———. "Islamic Extremism in Kenya: The Rise and Fall of Sheikh Khalid Balala." *Journal of Religion in Africa* 26, 4 (1996): 406–415.
———. *Islam in Uganda: Islamization Through a Centralized State in Pre-Colonial Africa.* New York and Jerusalem, 1974.
———. "The Promotion of Islamic Activities by Arab Countries in Africa: Contemporary Trends." *Asian and African Studies* 21, 3 (November 1987): 281–304.
Ojwang, J. B. "Polygamy as a Legal and Social Institution in Kenya." *East African Law Journal* 10, 1 (1974): 63–91.

Pénard, Jean-Claude. "'Sauti ya Bilal,' ou les transformations de l'Islam Shiite missionnaire en Afrique Orientale." *Islam et Sociétés au Sud du Sahara* 2 (1988): 17–33.
Pouwels Randall, L. "Sheikh al-Amin B. Ali Mazrui and Islamic Modernism in East Africa 1875–1947." *International Journal of Middle Eastern Studies* 13 (1981): 329–345.
Quraishi, Mohamed A. *Islam.* Nairobi, 1987.
———. "History of Islamic Religious Education in Kenya," *Nurul Islam* (May 1980).
Ranger, Terence. "Religious Movements and Politics in Sub-Saharan Africa." *African Studies Review* 29, 2 (June 1986): 1–69.
Ritchie, J. H. "Islam in Politics: East Africa." *Muslim World* 56 (1966): 296–303.
Rothchild, D. *Racial Bargaining in Kenya: A Study of Minorities and Decolonialisation.* London, 1973.
Salim, Ahmed. "Early Arab-Swahili Political Protest in Colonial Kenya." In Ogot, B. A., ed. *Politics and Nationalism in Colonial Kenya.* Nairobi, 1972, pp. 71–84.
———. "The Movement of 'Mwambao' or Coast Autonomy in Kenya 1956–1963." In Ogot, B. A., ed. *Hadith,* vol. 2. Nairobi, 1973.
———. *The Swahili-Speaking Peoples of Kenya's Coast 1895–1965.* Nairobi, 1973.
Schacht, J., and R. Brunschvig. "Notes on Islam in East Africa." *Studia Islamica* 23 (1965): 91–136.
Sergeant, R. B. and V. C. Griffiths. "Report by the Fact-Finding Mission to Study Muslim Education in East Africa." Nairobi, 1958.
Sicard, S. Von. "Christians and Muslims in East Africa." *African Theology Journal* 7, 2 (1978): 53–67.
Stern, R. "Factional Politics and Central Control in Mombasa 1960–1969." *Canadian Journal of African Studies* 4, 1 (1970): 33–56.
Strobel, Margaret. "Mombasa Society." In Ogot, B. A., ed. *History and Social Change in East Africa.* Nairobi, 1976, pp. 207–232.
Tareq, Ismael. "Religion and UAR African Policy." *Journal of Modern African Studies* 6, 1 (1968): 49–57.
Trimingham, J. Spencer. *Islam in East Africa.* Edinburgh, 1962.
———. *Islam in East Africa.* Oxford, 1964.
———. *Islam and the Integration of Society.* London, 1961.
Watt, M.W. "The Political Relevance of Islam in East Africa."*International Affairs* 42 (1966): 36–44.
Weeks, Richard, ed. *Muslim People: A World Ethnographic Survey.* Westport, Conn., 1984.
Westerland, David. *From Socialism to Islam: Notes on Islam as a Political Factor in Contemporary Africa.* Uppsala, 1982.
Yahya, Saad. *The Social Needs of Muslims in Kenya.* Nairobi, 1988.
el-Zein, Abdul. *The Sacred Meadows.* Boston, 1976.

Index

Abdallah, Ahmad, 23, 32, 98
Abdulaziz, M. H., 99
Abdulghfar al-Busaidi, 85
Abdulkarim, 18
Abdul Karim Mohamed, 154
Abdullah, Fidahussein, 18, 32
Aden, Mohamed Shaikh, 23
Affey, Mohamed Abdi, 140
al-Afgani, 55
Afghanistan, 82
African Muslim-Jewish Education Fund (AMJEF), 66, 127–128
African Muslims, 15, 19, 60–67, 155, 164. *See also* Muslims; Swahilis
Afro-Arab Association, 62
Afro-Asian Youth League, 62
Aga Khan, 16, 96
Aga Khan Foundation, 17–18, 99
Ahmadiya sect, 18–19, 42
Ali, A. K. Mohamed, 131
Ali, Shaikh Salih, 155
Allied Democratic Forces (ADF), 168
All Muslim National Union of Tanganyika (AMNUT), 166
Alwiya order, 163
Amana, Mohamed, 56–57, 90
Amana, Shaikh Mohamed, 26, 154
Ambassadors' Association of Muslim Countries, 113
Amin, Ali Shaikh, 22, 100
Amin, Idi, 26, 38–39, 102, 122, 169–170

Amin al-Hinawi, Shaikh Ali, 22, 108
al-Amin al-Mazrui, Shaikh, 55, 59, 115
Anglican Church. *See* Church of the Province of Kenya
animal slaughter, 36, 170
Ansaar Muslim Youth, 97
al-Aqsa Mosque, 126
Arab countries, 108, 113, 123; aid to Kenyan leaders, 30, 69; aid to Muslim organizations, 22, 26, 81, 111, 152; and education, 23, 98, 99–100; involvement in Muslim affairs, 29, 70, 155; and Israel, 127; propagation of Islam, 8, 106, 132–133, 168; and Uganda, 165
Arab League, 23, 113, 125, 129
Arab Muslims, 60–67, 164; discrimination by, 14, 19, 69–70, 138; history in East Africa, 1–4, 12–14. *See also* Muslims
Arens, Moshe, 128
Aringo, Peter Oloo, 76
Aruru, Osman, 29
Association for Closer Links Between Muslim Sects, 52
Association for Reforms in Islam (*Islahil Islamiya*), 26, 56, 154
Association for the Study of the Qur'an, 99
Avenire (journal), 107
Awadhan, Salim A., 19, 128
al-Azhar, Shaikh, 105

Badamana, Muhammad Salum, 59, 67
Badawi, Said Ali, 59
Badawi, Shaikh Sharif Ahmad, 81
al-Badr, Muhmad Said Yusuf, 50
Badru Kakungulu, 47
Bakari, Mohamed, 5–6, 27, 78, 144, 145; on education, 56, 58–59, 99, 103
Baladia Muslim Mission, 66
Balala, Najib, 87
Balala, Shaikh Khalid, 11; fall of, 159–162; and Ford-Kenya, 66, 120, 131; and Islamic extremism, 7, 130, 145, 175; as leader of IPK, 150–153, 155–157, 158; as street preacher, 149–150
Balala, Shaikh Mohamed Salim, 21, 29, 31, 65, 114
bans: on media, 76, 112, 167; of Muslim NGOs, 26–27, 83–86, 174, 176; of students' union, 81, 122
Barre, Mohamed Siad, 80
Basadiq, Q. S., 89
al-Bashir, Omar Hassan, 116
Bawazir, Mohamed, 34
Bilal Muslim Mission, 17
Bin Ahmad, Sherif Abdul Rahman, 61
Bin Alwi, Sharif Habib Swalih, 43
Bin Laden, Usamah, 82–83
Bint Salim, Fatima Sadik, 162
Bohra sect, 17–18, 140, 141
Boy, Boy Juma, 31
Boy, Juma, 31, 56, 66, 70
British East Africa Association, 60
Buganda, 3, 4, 47
Burhani Foundation, 18
Bushnell, Prudence, 82

"Call to End the Violence," 75
Catholic Church, 11, 105, 170; criticism of state, 73, 75, 76; opposition of Islam, 22, 37, 107–108, 152, 174
Central Bank of Kenya, 23, 32, 98
Central Organization of Trade Unions (COTU), 31, 56, 70, 157
Chama Cha Mapinduzi (CCM), 166
Chege, Mwangi, 158
Chief qadi, 61, 77, 158, 164; criticism of, 53, 58; government appointment of, 41–42, 50, 51; Muslim selection of, 25, 50, 53, 56–57; and Ramadan timing, 48–53; role of, 26, 41–42, 50–52, 64, 90
Christianity: African history of, 2, 4, 5, 9; propagation of, 22, 76, 95, 101–104, 109, 144; in Uganda, 4, 168
"Christian-Muslim Relations: Let's Have Better Understanding," 109
Christians, 11, 40, 81, 93; control of education, 37, 55, 95, 102, 146; control of state, 8, 21–22, 79, 103, 137–138, 144, 146, 173–174; criticism of state, 74–76; and Islam, 123, 152; Muslim relations, 86–87, 104–110, 112, 117–118
Church Missionary Society, 5
Church of the Province of Kenya (CPK), 74–75, 76, 106, 109, 110
Civic United Front (CUF), 166
civil disobedience, 75
Coastal League, 64
Coastal Peoples Party, 63
coastal strip (Sayyidieh), 11, 85, 111; separatism in, 63–65, 79, 135, 153; social divisions in, 4, 60, 61, 64, 67, 89–90; and state, 81, 142–143, 166
Coast Development Authority, 132
"Coast Polarized," 158
Coast Protection Group, 159–160
Coast Province, 11, 21–22, 39–40, 67, 77; economics, 143, 160; separatism in, 63, 87, 173; and universities, 120, 146
Commission of Inquiry, 90, 109
Committee to Mark Five Years Since the Death of Khomeini, 120
Conference on Population and Development, 57
Constitution, 74, 75, 89, 90; demand for reforms, 86–87, 110
corruption, 24, 53, 75
Council for the Promotion of the Qur'an in Tanzania (Balcuta), 167
coup attempts, 30, 71, 80, 139
Criminal Investigation Department (CID), 82, 84

Dafni, Reuven, 126
Daily Nation (newspaper), 39, 91, 92, 144
Dar al-Iftah, 67
Darani, Ali Mohamed Ali, 91
Dar-es-Salaam, 82, 167, 168
Democratic Party, 136
discrimination: against African ethnic groups, 66–67; against African Muslims, 19, 53–54, 62, 155; by Arab Muslims, 14, 19, 69–70, 138; by Christians, 101, 108, 143–144, 165–166; in education, 95, 97, 100, 146; by government against Muslims, 32–33, 73, 78, 80, 137–146, 151; and Islamic extremism, 116, 158, 167, 175; against Muslims, 22, 40, 65, 116. *See also* ethnicity
drug use, 105
Dumila, Faraj, 55–56

East Africa Muslim Welfare Society (EAMWS), 16 96
East African Islamic Conference, 111
East African Order in Council, 89
East African Times (newspaper), 18
East Africa Protectorate, 60
education, 62, 103; Christian control of, 37, 101, 102, 165; Israeli aid to, 127, 129; Muslim attire in schools, 37, 104; and Muslims, 26, 36–37, 95–100, 139, 154–155; nationalization of schools, 36–37, 97; support for, 23–24, 70, 146, 154; for women, 23, 55, 59, 100. *See also* harambe
education, Islamic, 26, 44, 146, 150, 165; aid from Arab countries, 111, 113–114, 120, 123; *chuo* (primary school), 14, 95, 97; *madrasa* (high school), 14, 95, 97; Shiite aid to, 16, 17; traditional *vs.* modern, 55–59, 95, 98, 99, 105
Educational Delegations to the Middle East, 114
Egypt, 65, 100, 104–105, 111–113, 129, 169
elections, 9, 15, 74–77, 90; of 1992, 152, 166; courting Muslims in, 38, 40; irregularities in, 52, 74, 76
Entebbe raid, 130
Etemesi, John, 84
Ethiopia, 140, 141
ethnicity: African tribespeople, 74, 79, 141; Bantu ethnic group, 1–2, 164, 168; distribution, 1–4, 11–15; ethnic divisions, 19, 60–67, 76, 155, 164, 168; ethnic violence, 75, 113, 140, 141; Giryama ethnic group, 21, 45, 67; Kikuyu, 17, 62, 74, 75, 76, 77, 100; Miji groups, 12–13, 67, 71

Fadhul, Abdallah Mohamed, 83
family planning, 57, 110
al-Farsy, Shaikh Abdallah Saleh, 126; as chief qadi, 33, 42, 49, 55; criticism of, 59, 92
Faruki, Shaikh Ali, 38
fatwa edicts, 159, 160
Faza, 142, 154
Federal Bureau of Investigation (FBI), 82, 83, 84
Ferkiss, Victor C., 6, 8
"Focus on Christian-Muslim Relations in Kenya: Rising Tension as Fundamentalism Sets In," 106
Ford-Asili, 52, 151, 162
Ford-Kenya, 38, 140
Ford-Kenya Party: and IPK, 136, 150–152; and Mzee, 66, 120, 131
foreign currency, 40, 43, 77, 154
Forum on Islam (television program), 35
freedoms: of assembly, 74, 75; of expression, 8, 78; of religion, 64, 73, 76, 91, 152, 159, 163; of speech, 42, 74, 75

Galgalo, Mohamed Malicha, 78, 140, 145
Garissa district, 140–141
Gating, Reverend, 109
Gilani, Hassan, 16
Gilseman, Michael, 6, 7
Gitary, Bishop David, 74, 75
"Gospel of Barnabas, The," 105
Great Britain, 13, 48; colonial rule,

4, 8, 60–64, 79; law under, 89–90
Greater Somalia, 79, 125
Guide (newsletter), 117, 131

Hadramaut Arabs, 2, 14, 95, 163, 164; origin of shaikhs, 59; propagation of Islam from, 12
Haji, Yossuf, 32
hajj. See Mecca, pilgrimage to
Halali Suna, 57
Hamed, Said, 31, 70–71, 81
Hamed, Seid Shariff, 166
Hanafi school, 15
Hansen, Holger Bernt, 5
al-Haramain Foundation, 84
harambe, 35, 36, 38, 44, 100, 154
Harding, Arthur, 60–61
Hassan, Abdul Kader, 80, 139
Hatib, Ahmad, 118
Help African People, 84
holidays, religious, 33–37, 154. *See also* 'Id al- Fitr; Maulidi; Ramadan fast
human rights, 7, 64, 73, 74, 102
Hussein, Saddam, 115
Hussein, Shaikh Yahya, 167
Hyder, Fatma, 25, 50, 99, 117
Hyder, Mohammed, 99

Ibadiya sect, 2, 13, 19
Ibn Ahmad, Salim, 149
Ibn Ibad, 19
Ibrahim bin 'Abd al-'Aziz al-Ibrahim Foundation, 84
'Id al-Adha, 34
'Id al-Fitr, 35, 37, 45, 110, 114, 117, 154; as national holiday, 34, 42–43, 48–52, 57, 77, 170, 173
'Id al-Hajj, 34, 35, 48, 52
identity cards, 36, 140
"Imam Khomeini as I Know Him, The," 117
imams (religious teachers), 14, 15
Imams and Preachers Council of Kenya, 85
Imperial British East Africa Company (IBEA), 60
"In Defense of Islam," 26
inheritance, 22, 57, 61, 89–93, 103
Inland Church, 76

Inooro (newsletter), 76
Institute of Islamic Teaching, 27
International Conference on Social Studies, 143
International Islamic Relief Organization, 84
Inter-Party Parliamentary Group (IPPG), 75
"intifada, black," 145, 151
Iqra (journal), 128
Iran, 17, 100, 121, 167; activities in Kenya, 7, 67, 113, 115–122, 123; embassies of, 52–53, 117–118, 120, 131, 168; and Islamic extremism, 8, 83, 107, 115, 123, 152, 175
Iranian Cultural Council, 119
Iranian Medical Center, 121
Iraq, 17, 67, 113–115, 117
"Is Kenya Culture on the Move?" 55
Islahil Islamiya (Association for Reform in Islam), 26, 56, 154
Islam, 17, 18, 53, 79, 158; conversions, 17–18, 45, 53, 106; politicization of, 8, 106, 111, 149, 150; propagation by Muslim organizations, 27, 44–45, 81, 84–85, 167; propagation by sects, 17, 18–19; propagation of, 2–5, 14–15, 101–102, 115, 163, 176; public awareness of, 98, 109; reform of, 26, 42, 54–59, 154
Al-Islam (journal), 99, 128
Islamic Development Bank, 23, 113, 169
Islamic Endowment Fund for Kenya, 113
Islamic extremism, 7–9, 25, 103, 130, 166–171, 182; assessment of, 175–177; Christian fears of, 106–109; and education, 98; government response to, 122, 152–159, 170–171. *See also* Balala, Shaikh Khalid; Islamic Party of Kenya
Islamic Foundation, 26, 99, 128
Islamic Ittihad, 80, 175
Islamic Jihad Organizations, 159
Islamic law, 7, 22, 36, 42, 64, 103, 150; shari'a courts, 41, 89, 164; and Tabligh, 167
Islamic Party of Kenya (IPK), 7, 33,

102, 105–108, 120, 135–147, 174–175; antigovernment disturbances, 130–131; division in, 159–162; opposition activities of, 24–25, 155–159; support for, 58, 78, 130, 135, 145, 150–153, 157; and UMA, 66–67, 70–71, 164
Islamic Peoples Conference, 123
Islamic Propagation Centre, 113
Islamic Revolutionary Party of Uganda, 168
Islamic Salvation Front, 160
Islam in Africa, 116
Islam in East Africa, 5
Islam in Kenya, 5, 9
Ismaili sect (Sab'iya-the Seveners), 16–17, 163
Israel, 70, 82, 115, 127; aid from, 131; Muslim attitudes toward, 44, 65–66, 125, 165–166; relations with African countries, 38, 113, 132, 169
Ithna'ashriya sect (the Twelvers), 17, 118, 163
Al-Ittihad al-Islami, 80, 175

Jamal, ad-Din al-Afghani, 55
Jamal 'Abd al-Nasir, 111, 126
Jamia Mosque, 16, 24, 43, 49, 66, 113, 119, 128; Management Committee, 53–54, 66
Jeevanjee, A. M., 18
Jehazi, Mohamed, 21, 29, 65, 69, 71, 91, 126
Jewish community, 70
Jezan, Awadh, 27
jihad (holy war), 19, 39, 82, 106, 108, 135
Jilani, Habib, 32
jimbo. *See* majimboism
Jirongo, Cyrus, 38
John Paul, Pope, 105, 109–110
Joint Organization for Establishing Islamic Cultural Centres, 112
JPR (journal), 106, 109
Juma, Salim Ibrahim, 31, 118
Jumutia-til-Baladia, 27

Kadhi, Joe, 144
Kakuto, Shaikh Sulaiman, 171
Kalema, King of Buganda, 4

Kamera, Joseph, 91, 103
Kanu. *See* Kenya African National Union
Karanja, Joseph, 76
Kariuki, B. Njoroge, 74
Kariuki, G. G., 80
Kassam, Taj ad-Din, 128
Kassim, Hamid Mohammad, 59
Kassim, Shaikh Hammed, 41, 51
Kenya, 1–2, 4, 8, 9, 63; as Islamic center, 116; and Israel, 113, 125, 128–130, 133, 145, 169
Kenya African Nationalism, 77
Kenya African National Union (Kanu), 11, 23, 91, 120, 127, 166; elections in, 70; ethnic divisions in, 65–67, 69; leadership of, 17, 18, 21, 30, 31, 33–34; Muslim loyalty to, 24, 155; Muslim representation, 138–139, 140; and opposition parties, 37–38, 52, 73, 75–76, 120, 136, 151–152
Kenya-Arab Friendship Association, 113
Kenya Koran Teachers' Union, 158
Kenya Muslim Academy, 100
Kenyan government, 73, 81–82, 86, 166; control of Supkem, 23, 25–26, 41, 51, 77, 164; courting Muslim support, 34–35, 37, 40, 42, 77, 154; Muslim representation in, 29–32; selection of religious leaders, 41–42, 50, 51–52
Kenya Times, 120
Kenyatta, Jomo, 17, 68, 77, 125; Muslim ministers of, 29–30, 138, 170; and Muslim support, 33–36, 38–39, 48, 154
Kewasis, Stephan, 109
Khalif, Ahmad, 11, 85, 126–127, 158; and Supkem, 15, 24, 25, 29, 51, 52
khalif, proposal for, 51–52
Khamis, Shaikh Khalfan, 54
Khatami, Mohamed, 118
Khatib, Ahmad, 68
Khatni, Sayed Mohamed, 119
Khidmat Da'wat Islamiyya (Service for Islamic Propagation), 167
Khitami, Sharif, 59
Khitamy, Shaikh Abdul Rahman, 153
Khomeini, Ayatollah Ruhollah, 17,

68, 117
Khorasani, Ayatollah Waiz Zade, 52, 119
Kikwete, Jakaya, 171
Kindy, Hyder, 12, 62, 65, 127–128
Kinoti, Hannah, 102
Kiswahili language, 2, 12, 53, 67, 99, 118; use in public address, 33, 35–36; version of Qur'an, 18, 42
Korane, Ali, 131
Kuria, Archbishop Manasses, 75, 106, 109, 110
Kuria, Issa Hemed, 126
Kuwait, 50, 65, 113, 114

al-Lail, Habib Salih Jamal, 14, 95
Lamu, 38, 70, 109, 115, 131, 154, 157; Maulidi in, 43, 45; unrest in, 153, 157
land ownership, 58, 77, 142–143, 154
languages, 2, 8, 12, 14, 67, 99, 117–118; Arabic, 3, 35, 42, 67, 114, 117; and imams, 53. *See also* Kiswahili language
Larjani, Jawad, 116
Leakey, Richard, 53, 161
Lebanese Shiite Arabs, 17
legal system, 36, 37, 42, 61, 89–93. *See also* Islamic law
Levine, Daniel H., 5, 7
Libya, 22, 65, 129, 169; Islamic political activities, 70, 112–114, 122, 165, 167
Lord's Resistance Army (LRA), 168
Lugogo, J. A., 132
Luwemba, Shaikh Ibrahim Saad, 165

Maalim, Farah, 120
Mackinnon, William, 60
Madaka, Marsden, 87
Madhboti, Abu Baker Mohamed, 70
al-Mahdi, Sadiq, 116
Maitha, Emmanuel, 66–67, 71, 155, 156, 159
majimboism (federalism), 86–87, 110, 141, 173. *See also* separatism
Majlis al-'Ulamaa (Council of Religious Leaders), 50–51, 114
Makemba, Nyonga Wa, 159
Mapenzi Ya Mungu (*Love of God*), 18

marriage, 22, 55, 61, 93
Matano, Mohamed Hyder, 91
Mathai, Wangari M., 93
Matiba, Kenneth, 151, 162
Maulidi (Prophet's birthday), 33, 45, 163; cost of celebrations, 42, 55–57, 59; Matwari procession, 43, 81
Maulidi Jasho, 66
Mazrui, Ali, 143, 145–146, 171; opposition to Israel, 123, 130; support for IPK, 78, 106–107, 145, 151
"Mazrui: From Universalist to a Crusading Sectionalist: Ethnic and Islamic Particularism," 107
Mazrui family, 60
al-Mazrui Mosque, 126
Mbure, Jeff, 106
Mbwana, Mohamed, 57
Mecca, pilgrimage to (*hajj*), 24, 40, 43, 77, 149
media, 44, 45, 128, 129; bans on, 76, 112, 167; coverage of Muslim affairs, 32, 34, 39, 43, 122, 144; Iranian, 8, 117, 118; Islamic programming, 35–36, 59
Meir, Golda, 125
Mercy Relief International Agency, 84
Middle East conflict, 7, 65–66, 115, 125–133, 168–169
Minaret (journal), 26, 128
Mkapa, Benjamin, 170
Moayer, al-Haj Hamid, 52, 119
Mohamed, Ali, 30
Mohamed, Hussein Maalim, 15, 30–32, 56, 80, 136; as cabinet minister, 72, 139; protests to government, 32, 85, 138, 140, 141, 158; and schools, 100, 154
Mohamed, Jan, 29
Mohamed, Mahmud, 15, 30, 80, 139, 154
Moi, Daniel arap, 18, 23, 75, 80, 121; Balala criticism of, 7, 145, 149, 150, 159–160; ban on Muslim NGOs, 83, 84, 85; and Christianity, 9, 74–77, 102, 103, 109, 144; coup against, 30, 80, 139; courting Muslims, 34–35, 36,

37, 43, 92, 154; demonstration against, 156–157; and Israel, 133, 169; Muslims in government of, 30–31, 71–72, 138, 170; Muslim support for, 38–39, 158; Nyayo ideology, 30, 39, 69, 77; and opposition parties, 151, 161; and Sharif Nassir, 30, 34, 37, 39, 68–69, 70; on slave trading, 103, 152, 153
Mombasa, 33–34, 143, 160; disturbances in, 25, 151, 156–157, 173; Muslim groups in, 12–13, 17; politics in, 30–31, 68–71, 127, 129, 136; as port, 64, 127, 130–131, 152–153
"Mombasa—A Bosnia in the Making," 137
"More Caution over Booming Unrest," 157
Msallam, Shaikh Ahmad Muhammad, 50, 67
Muge, Alexander, 74–75
Muhammad, 44, 79. *See also* Maulidi
Muita, Paul, 151
Mukasa, Shaikh Ahmad, 165
Mukulu, Jamil, 171
Muli, Mathew, 112
multiparty system, 71, 74, 120, 136; demand for, 69, 102, 162, 166; effect on Muslims, 8–9, 33, 37–38, 52
Muluka, Barak O., 107
Mumias, 12, 14
Munawar, Shaikh M., 19
Munawarrah, Madrasatul, 96
Mungai, Njoroge, 16
Muntu, Munyisha, 165
Munyi, Kamwithi, 48
Museveni, Yoweri, 8, 164, 165, 166, 168, 169, 170
musical instruments, 54, 57
Muslim, Farouk, 22, 23, 98, 115
Muslim Academy of Kenya, 154
Muslim attire, 36–37, 57–58, 104, 117, 144, 150, 154
Muslim Consultative Council, 110
Muslim Education and Welfare Association (MEWA), 24, 27, 56, 58, 78, 97, 99
Muslim Missionary Movement, 101

"Muslim NGOs and Community Development: The Kenya Experience," 78
Muslim Parliamentary Group (MPG), 31
Muslims: Asian, 15–16, 18, 34, 44, 53, 71, 101, 163; Christian relations, 4, 9, 65, 81, 101–110, 112, 170; divisions, personal, 68–72, 81, 151–152, 165; divisions, political, 54–58, 85, 86; divisions, religious, 18–19, 47–54, 67–68, 165; divisions among, 47, 89–90, 92, 111, 146, 155–159, 171, 174; economic status, 7, 56, 105, 119, 142, 174, 175; government appeasement of, 153–155; government selection of religious leaders, 41–42, 50, 51–52; Indian, 15, 16, 18, 53; and Israel, 65–66, 125, 165–166; organizations, 21–27, 83–86, 174, 176 (*see also* Kenya African National Union; National Union of Kenya Muslims; Supreme Council of Kenya Muslims); Pakistani, 15, 18, 57; political status, comparisons, 163–171; political status of, 4, 8, 9, 33–40, 173–177; population distribution, 1, 2, 11, 138; religious leadership, 41–46; representation of, 29–32, 71–72, 138–139, 170–171; and the state, 38, 40, 43, 73–74, 77–87; unity among, 42–44, 57–58. *See also* African Muslims; Asian Muslims; discrimination; ethnicity
Muslim Students Association of the University of Nairobi, 26, 81, 122, 128
Muslim Women's Seminar, First, 117
Musumbuko, Omar, 155
Mutesa I, King of Buganda, 3, 4, 47
Mwakenya, 112
Mwakimako, Hassan, 11, 56, 58, 78, 99
Mwamazandi, Kassim B., 23, 29, 69, 91–92
Mwambao United Front, 63–65, 89. *See also* separatism
Mwangale, Elijah, 122

Mwaruwa, Ibrahim, 66
Mwavuno, Salim, 152
Mwidani, Ahmad, 71, 81, 131
Mwidau, Abdallah Ndovo, 34, 65, 69–70, 112, 127, 129, 130
Mwinyi, Ali Hassan, 167, 168, 169, 170
Mwinyi, Omar, 136, 155, 171
Mzee, Rashid, 66–67, 120, 131, 151, 152, 159, 161

al-Nahdi, Shaikh Nassor, 42, 49–51
Nairobi, 4, 12, 16, 82, 167, 168; Muslim distribution in, 15–16, 17
Nairobi Muslim Youth Organization, 52
Nakuru Muslim Association, 16
Nasr, Shaikh Abdullahi, 68, 91, 118
Nassir, Shaikh Abdillahi, 17, 89
Nassir, Sharif, 11, 44, 91–92, 100, 106, 154; attacks on, 81, 156, 159; and discrimination, 73, 139, 142; in government, 30–31, 54, 67; and Libyans, 65, 112, 129; and Moi, 30, 34, 37, 39, 68–69, 70; and Mwidau, 112, 129; and opposition parties, 136, 151, 158; opposition to, 67, 71, 152; support for government, 39, 77
National Association of African Muslims (NAAM), 26, 164
National Christian Council of Kenya (NCCK), 74–76, 78, 93, 106, 109, 144
National Convention Executive Council (NCEC), 75, 110
National Council of Women, 93
National Union of Kenya Muslims (Nukem), 21–22, 104, 108, 115, 128
neocolonialism, 8, 106
"New 'Ulamaa in Kenya, The," 58–59
Ngala, J. M., 29
Ngala, Roland, 21
Nganga, James, 83
Ngige, Maalim Hamise, 27
Ngumba, Andrew, 36, 38
Nigeria, 145, 177
Njonjo, Charles, 90, 103

nongovernmental organizations (NGOs), ban on, 27, 83–86, 174, 176
Noor, Mohamed Aden, 140
Norfolk Hotel explosion, 130
Northeastern Province, 25, 109; Muslim NGOs in, 84–85; neglect of, 32, 85, 139–141, 166; Somali Muslims in, 5, 14–15, 79–80, 90, 131
Northern Frontier District (NFD), 79
Nuhu Mbogo, Prince, 47
Nukem. *See* National Union of Kenya Muslims
Nuri, Ali Akbar Nataq, 116
Nurul-Islam (journal), 24, 45
Nyayo ideology, 30, 39, 69, 77, 103
Nyerere, Julius, 26, 170

OAU. *See* Organization of African Unity
Obote, Milton, 26, 164
Ochang, William, 107
Odeh, Mohammed Saddiq, 83
Odinga, Oginga, 150–151
Odinga, Raila, 159–160
Odipo, Dominic, 157
Odongo, Abubaker Jeje, 165
oil, 119, 121
Okello, Stephan, 105
Okullu, Henry, Bishop, 74, 75
Omani Arab Muslims, 13, 19
Omani rule, 2, 60, 79, 95, 138
Omar, Mazamil, 70
Omar, Sharif Hussein, 86
Omari, J., 81
Onzeki, Bishop Mwana, 75
opposition groups, 9, 74, 112
opposition parties, 42, 66, 75–76, 120, 136, 145, 158; and Muslims, 38, 52; Safina Party, 53, 161. *See also* Ford-Asili; Ford-Kenya; Islamic Party of Kenya
Orengo, James, 151
Organization of African Unity (OAU), 129, 132, 168–169
Oromo Liberation Front, 140, 141
Otunga, Maurice, 22, 107–108, 110, 152, 174

pan-Africanism, 118, 130
parliament, 17, 18, 31, 34, 58
Pemba, 2, 12, 60, 166
People (newspaper), 54
Philosophy of Revolution, 111
Pirbhai, Sir Eboo, 17
political parties, 73, 166; ban on religion-based, 7–8, 21, 73, 163. *See also* Islamic Party of Kenya; Kenya African National Union; multiparty system; opposition parties
prayers, dispute over, 13, 54, 165
Propagation of Islam (al-Da'wa al-Islamiya), 112
Protestant churches, 11, 73, 76, 106

Qadhafi, Muammar, 112, 169
Qadiriya order, 13, 14, 163, 164
qadis (religious teachers), 14, 61. *See also* chief qadi
al-Qumari, Muaalim Said bin Ahmad, 45
Quraishi, Mohamed, 98
Qur'an, 7, 19, 36, 81, 104, 155; on inheritance, 90–91; Kiswahili version of, 18, 42; study of, 55, 56, 58, 95. *See also* Islamic law

Rabin, Yitzhak, 132–133
Rabitat al-'Alam al-'Islami (World Islamic League), 84, 113, 114
Rafsanjani, Ali Akbar Hashemi, 116, 118, 119–120, 121
Rajab Sumba, 71
Ramadan fast, 13, 34, 36–38, 42, 152; timing of, 41, 48–52, 165
Ranger, Terence, 5
Rashid, Muhammad, 52
Al-Rasul al-Akram Islamic Centre, 117
refugees, 80, 123, 139
religion: freedom of, 39, 64, 73, 76, 91, 152, 159, 163; in politics, 5–10; separate worship, 63. *See also* holidays, religious; separation of church and state
Religion and Politics in East Africa, 5
religions, traditional, 11, 41
"Religious Movements and Politics in Sub-Saharan Africa," 5

Rida, Muhamad Abdul Rashid, 55
Rift Valley, 14, 27, 75, 90
riots, 82, 113, 157, 167
Riyadha Mosque College, 14, 96
Robertson, Sir James, 64, 89
Rubia, Charles, 70
Rushdie, Salman, 40, 44, 47, 155, 174

Saad, Yahya, 5–6, 27, 99
Sadat, Anwar, 129
Safina Party, 53, 161
Said, Khamis Ahmad, 45
Said, Omar, 27
saint worship, 42, 55, 59, 163
Sajad, Rashid, 17, 34, 71–72, 118, 131, 138, 156, 159
Sala, John, 154, 157
Salaam (journal), 117
Salem, Yousef, 128
Salim, Ahmad Idha, 31–32
Salim, Ali, 83
Samaye, Frederick, 167
Satanic Verses, The, 40, 44, 155, 174
Saudi Arabia, 53, 65; activities in Kenya, 26, 67, 114–115; ambassador to, 31, 71; contributions to Muslims, 22, 99–100, 165, 167, 175
secessionist movement. *See* separatism
Secretaries of the Episcopal Conference of Africa and Madagascar (SECAM), 107
secret ballot, 74–75, 77
security forces, 153, 158, 159; violence against Somali Muslims, 15, 80, 139, 140–141
Senegal, 145, 177
separation of church and state, 9, 73, 102, 155, 163, 177; Christian exception to, 144; in Islam, 7; Supkem on, 23
separatism, 8; in coastal strip (Sayyidieh), 63–65, 79, 89, 135, 153; in Coast Province, 63, 87, 173; majimboism (federalism), 86–87, 110, 141, 173; Somali Muslims and, 5, 15, 79–80, 132, 139, 141, 153, 174
sex education, 155

Shadiliya order, 13, 163
Shakombo, Suleiman, 71
shari'a. *See* Islamic law
Shariaat (journal), 167
Shee, Shaikh Ali Mohammed, 49–54, 66–67, 85, 93, 105, 119; on discrimination, 108, 142, 145; on family planning, 57, 110; opposition to Balala, 160–161; and Supkem, 24–25, 51, 86
Shi'a, 17, 18, 52, 53; propagation of, 68, 115, 118–119
Shiddiye, Mohamed Mukhtar, 140
Shiite Muslims, 8, 16–18, 24, 67–68, 71, 90, 163
Shweihidi, Taher, 112, 122
Slade, Humphrey, 90
slave trade, 2, 61, 103, 107, 145–146, 152–153
Soba, M. O., 92
Society (newspaper), 104, 158
Society for Closer Links between Muslim Sects, 119
Somalia, 5, 15, 79–80, 122, 125
Somali Muslims, 12–15, 49, 131, 136, 154; and elections, 38, 90; and government, 79–80, 125, 139–141; and secession, 5, 15, 79–80, 132, 139, 153, 174; Shifta, 15, 79, 125
Somen, Yitzhak "Izzi," 125
Stanbul, Deghow Ma'alim, 79
Standard (newspaper), 44, 122, 152, 157, 174
strikes, 38, 156, 157
students: expulsion for religious observations, 37, 152; organizations of, 26, 81, 122, 128
Sudan, 5, 83, 107; in Kenya, 114, 116–117, 122–123, 175; in Tanzania, 167, 168; in Uganda, 168
Sufi orders, 3, 13–14, 19, 163–164
suicide bombers, 159
Sultan of Zanzibar, 2, 60–61, 64, 89, 96
Sunnis, 8, 13, 18–19, 67–68, 90, 165; and Iran, 116; and Shiites, 52–53, 116–119, 121
Sunni-Shafi'i, 3, 12, 14, 15–16, 163
Supreme Council of Kenya Muslims (Supkem), 18, 22–26, 52, 69, 128; and Arab countries, 44, 50, 112, 114, 115, 122; on ban of NGOs, 85–86; and Christians, 104, 108, 110; criticism of, 24–26, 50, 58; Department of Women's Affairs, 23, 25, 98–99, 117; and discrimination, 119, 140; and education, 23–24, 98–100; government control of, 23, 25, 41, 51, 77, 164; on Islamic law, 56, 91–92; leaders of, 15, 29, 32; and political parties, 24–25, 52, 158; support for government, 39, 58; and women, 23, 25, 98–99
Supreme Council of Muslims in Tanzania (Bakwata), 26, 164, 171
Swahilis, 1–3, 11–14, 54, 58, 95, 163; Arab *vs.* African groups, 63–66, 69–70; divisions among, 57, 60, 62–63, 65
Swahili-Speaking People of Kenya's Coast, 32
Swalih, Ustath Harith, 50

Tabatabai, Hassani, 118
Tabligh movement, 57–58, 167, 168, 171
Taib, Taib Ali, 136
Tairara, Abdullah, 27
Tanganyika, 2, 4, 12, 163
Tanganyika African National Union (TANU), 163, 166
Tanzania, 8–9, 12–13, 26, 102, 107, 128; and Bakwata, 26, 164, 171; expulsion from, 104, 167, 168; Islam in, 2, 167, 171; and Maulidi, 45; Muslim political status in, 163–171, 176; and Ramadan, 48
"Terror Against Kenya: Islamic Fundamentalists to Take Over," 122, 152
"There Is Also Arab Neocolonialism," 107
al-Tourabi, Hassan, 123
trade, 1–3, 16, 17, 121
trade unions, 31, 56, 69, 70, 157–158, 158
Trimingham, J. Spencer, 5
Tsuma, Reuven, 67

Twaddle, Michael, 5
Twelve Tribes, 63, 64

Uganda, 13, 26, 47, 64; and Arab countries, 112–113, 169; Christians and Muslims in, 101–102, 122, 145; Islamic extremism in, 8, 9, 82, 167; Islam in, 36, 45, 48, 54, 58; and Kenya, 38–39; Muslim political status in, 163–171, 176; population in, 2, 3, 4
Uganda Muslim Supreme Council (UMSC), 26, 164, 165, 171
'ulamaa (religious teachers), 14, 55, 58–59, 164
unemployment, 7, 56, 105, 119, 142, 174
United Arab Emirates (UAE), 114
United Muslims of Africa (UMA), 25, 66, 70, 71, 137, 155–158, 164
United States: embassy bombings, 9, 27, 82–86, 123, 167–168, 173–175; and Iran, 119–120
"The Unity of Islam and the Enemies of Islamic Unity," 52, 119
universities, 112; Al-Azhar University, 104; Mikindani College, 154; plans for, 22, 120, 146; students' organizations, 26, 81, 122, 128; University of Moi, 146; University of Nairobi, Department of Religious Studies, 102

Velayeti, Ali Akbar, 119, 121
Voice of Kenya (bulletin), 112

"Wagalla Massacre," 137, 141, 174
Waiyaki, Munyua, 38
Wajir, 104, 126, 139
"Wajir Massacre," 25, 32, 141, 174
Wako, Amos, 93
Walji, Shirin, 99
Wandati, Abdulrahman, 136, 155, 171
Weekly Review (newspaper), 84, 86, 141, 143
West Africa (journal), 116
"What Ails the Muslims," 103
"What the Bible Says about Muhammad," 113
women, 57, 93; education for, 23, 55, 59, 100; Muslim attire for, 36, 37, 104, 117, 150; status of, 55, 59, 98–99, 160; Supkem, department for, 23, 25
World Bank, 31
World Islamic League (Rabitat al-'Alam al-'Islami), 84, 113, 114

YK92, 38
Young Muslims of East and Central Africa, 128
Youth for Kanu, 155
Yusuf, Mohamed, 22

Zanzibar, 2, 4, 19, 42, 164, 169; and Christians, 166, 170; Swahilis in, 12, 60, 63, 90

About the Book

Kenya's 5 million Muslims form an increasingly important minority group in a largely Christian country—though they are not always recognized as such. Arye Oded offers a balanced, accessible analysis of the role of Islam in contemporary Kenyan politics and society.

Against the backdrop of the developing Islamic expansion in Kenya and the evolving relations between Muslims and Christians, Oded examines the strengths and weaknesses of the Muslim community, its relations with the state, and the emergence of militant Islam in the 1990s. He also considers the influence of the Arab countries and Iran on the attitudes and political positions of Kenya's Muslims regarding both internal and international affairs. His thoughtful treatment of the complexities and controversies involved is a major contribution to the field of African studies.

Arye Oded is senior lecturer in the Institute of Asian and African Studies at the Hebrew University of Jerusalem. His numerous publications include *Africa and the Middle East Conflict, Religion and Politics in Uganda,* and *Islam in Uganda.* His service with Israel's Ministry of Foreign Affairs included positions throughout Africa, most recently (1992–1995) as ambassador to Kenya.